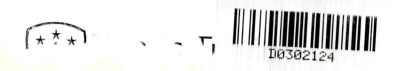

REVISIONING HISTORY

EDITORS

Sherry B. Ortner, Nicholas B. Dirks, Geoff Eley

A LIST OF TITLES

IN THIS SERIES APPEARS

AT THE BACK OF

THE BOOK

PRINCETON STUDIES IN

CULTURE / POWER / HISTORY

REVISIONING HISTORY

FILM AND THE CONSTRUCTION
OF A NEW PAST

Edited by Robert A. Rosenstone

PRINCETON UNIVERSITY PRESS
PRINCETON, NEW JERSEY

Copyright © 1995 by Princeton University Press
Published by Princeton University Press, 41 William Street,
Princeton, New Jersey 08540
In the United Kingdom: Princeton University Press,
Chichester, West Sussex
All Rights Reserved

Library of Congress Cataloging-in-Publication Data

Revisioning history : film and the construction of a new past /
edited by Robert A. Rosentone.
p.   cm. — (Princeton studies in culture/power/history)
Includes bibliographical references and index.
ISBN 0-691-08629-X — ISBN 0-691-02534-7 (pbk.)
1. Motion pictures and history.
I. Rosenstone, Robert A. II. Series.
PN1995.2.R48   1994
791.43′658—dc20   94-19563

This book has been composed in Sabon

Princeton University Press books are printed
on acid-free paper and meet the guidelines
for permanence and durability of the Committee
on Production Guidelines for Book Longevity
of the Council on Library Resources

Printed in the United States of America

10 9 8 7 6 5 4 3 2

Contents _____

Acknowledgments ⸻

THIS BOOK would not be in existence were it not for the help, inspiration, and support of a wide variety of friends and colleagues in the worlds of both academia and film. Beyond my obvious debt to the contributors, who literally made this volume possible, I wish to extend my deepest gratitude to the following individuals: David Ransel, editor of the *American Historical Review*, who was bold enough to take that distinguished journal into the visual age by starting a yearly section of film reviews, a section that provided space to try out some of the ideas elaborated in this volume; Allyn Roberts, assistant editor of the *AHR*, whose patience and editorial skills made my tasks as editor of that section much easier to perform; Joanna Hitchcock, who supported the heretical idea that one might have a book of essays without a prior conference; Nick Dirks, David James Fisher, Doug Flamming, Sumiko Higashi, Clayton Koppes, Pierre Sorlin, Bryant Simon, Moshe Sluhovsky, Margie Waller, Alice Wexler, and Robert Wohl, friends and colleagues who were willing to help me wrestle with questions of film and history; Howard Dratch and David Hamilton, who have taught and continue to teach me about the important choices made both before and after the camera is turned on; Sheryl Cobb, who easily handled the burden of so many details; Lauren Osborne and Lauren Oppenheim, fine editors who smoothed the process of publication; and Nahid, who helped me find the strength to get everything done.

REVISIONING HISTORY

Introduction _____

ROBERT A. ROSENSTONE

ANYONE INTERESTED in film and history will find this to be an unusual collection of essays. Although a number of prior volumes have been devoted to the topic, no work before this has ever taken the historical film on its own terms as a way of seriously thinking the past or considered the development and contribution of those kinds of motion pictures that constitute the New History film. Three elements in particular mark this volume as unique:

The premise: the visual media are a legitimate way of doing history—of representing, interpreting, thinking about, and making meaning from the traces of the past.

The approach: the historical film must be seen not in terms of how it compares to written history but as a way of recounting the past with its own rules of representation.

The films: traditional costume dramas and documentaries are less important as history than a new kind of film, made all over the world—one that seriously deals with the relationship of past to present.

Film on Its Own Terms

A century after the invention of motion pictures, the visual media have become arguably the chief carrier of historical messages in our culture. The major professional organizations have in recent years increasingly acknowledged this role of the media by devoting sessions at conventions and space in journals to film. Yet for all this scholarly activity, the history film has never been considered a way of constructing the past with a legitimacy of its own. In reviews, essays, and books, films that deal with historical topics are generally treated in two ways: either as reflections of the political and social concerns of the era in which they were made, which means that the historical content is not taken seriously; or as books that have been put onto the screen, which includes the unspoken assumption that a film should somehow convey the same data that would be delivered on a printed page.[1]

The aim of this collection is to revise these approaches by showing that history in the visual media can be a unique way of rendering and interpreting the past. The strategy is to have historians who are grounded in traditional history but sympathetic to the visual media explicate and analyze a single example of the New History film. Different as the resulting essays are, each contains an implicit acknowledgment that written word is but one way of doing history. That history, as we practice it today, is no more than a convention, or a series of conventions, by which we make meaning from the remains of the past.

This notion of history as constituted is hardly news. But it needs to be stressed here. Just as written history is not a solid and unproblematic object but a mode of thought, so is the historical film. This means that at the outset we must forget about comparing history on the screen to history on the page and focus instead on the larger realm of past and present in which both sorts of history are located and to which both refer. It is neither useful nor relevant to begin by asking, Does film convey facts or make arguments as well as written history? The important questions are, How does film construct a historical world? What are the rules, codes, and strategies by which it brings the past to life? What does that historical construction mean to us? Only when such questions have been answered may we wish to consider the following: What does film do to and for the past that the written word cannot? How does the historical world on the screen relate to the world on the page?

The New History Film

Anyone who follows cinema knows that the last quarter-century has seen an enormous change in the form and practice of the historical film—both dramatic and documentary. Filmmakers all over the world have, during this period, struggled to find new ways of coming to grips with the burden of the past. Their efforts have produced works that, in form and content, are far different from the Hollywood "historical," a costume drama that uses the past solely as a setting for romance and adventure, and far different, too, from the typical documentary, a mixture of old images and recent talking heads. If few of these films have been blockbusters, some have achieved national, regional, or international recognition or notoriety. Among such works covered in this collection are *Hitler: A Film from Germany*, *Hiroshima Mon Amour* (France), *Night of the Shooting Stars* (Italy), *Memories of Underdevelopment* (Cuba); *Repentance* (Soviet Union), *The Home and the World* (India), and *Eijanaika* (Japan).

The difference between such works and traditional historical films is a matter of intent, content, and form. Their aim is less to entertain an audience or make profits than to understand the legacy of the past. Certainly it is no coincidence that such works tend to grow out of communities that see themselves in desperate need of historical connections—postcolonial nations; long-established countries where political systems are in upheaval; societies recovering from totalitarian regimes or the horrors of war; ethnic, political, social, or sexual minorities involved in the search to recapture or create viable heritages. So intense may this quest be that filmmakers, finding the traditional forms of the historical film suffused with the values of prior social orders, have often created new forms for history, abandoning "realism" for other presentational modes, mixing genres, blurring the distinction between the documentary and the dramatic film.

Certain regions have been so active in producing historical films that it is possible to see them as movements that provide counterhistories to the usual nationalist narratives. In some cases, this visual historiography preceded parallel changes in written historiography. Latin America's political and cultural movements of the sixties produced films that told the story of colonialism from the native point of view. A decade later, African directors did the same. Both critiques of Western imperialism anticipated the debate over postcolonialism that has more recently spread from anthropology into such traditional fields as classics and medieval history. In Europe, German filmmakers of the seventies worked to create a viable past in numerous films that anticipated positions which academics would not stake out until the *Historikerstreit* of the eighties. The focus on daily life, the notion of the Germans as the first victims of Nazism, or of women as the victims of a patriarchal Nazi order—all these were depicted on the screen long before they were debated in the academy.[2]

The terms of the arguments over the Third Reich or colonialism were not, obviously, the same in the visual as in the written media. Movies do not provide a detailed factual portrait of the rise and fall of Hitler's regime. Nor can they detail the economic cost of colonialism to either colony or mother country. What they do resurrect are emotional contents of Nazism and colonialism in stories that show how the issues of those periods still lie like a dark shadow across contemporary consciousness. The past they create is not the same as the past provided by traditional history, but it certainly should be called history—if by that word we mean a serious encounter with the lingering meaning of past events.

Rules of the Game

Like any discipline, history is an agreed-upon game that creates its own rules, including rules for assessing what it is to contribute to the game. For over two centuries in the West, empiricism has been the heart of the enterprise. Since the rise of the academic discipline a century ago, the basic contribution has been the article or monograph, a work based upon well-researched data that is meant—in an image that surely nobody really believes any more—to become a building block for a huge historical edifice that will ultimately comprise all knowledge of the past. Other sorts of contributions can be made by finding new sources of data, or by creating methodologies for extracting data, or by rethinking and making new arguments with the data already used by others. Data has been, any way you look at it, the key to history.

And yet there has always been another kind of contribution to our understanding of the past, one that depends less upon data than upon what we might call vision, upon how we look at and think about and remember and make meaningful what remains of people and events. This is the vision that explains why historians like Edward Gibbon, Jules Michelet, and George Bancroft affect our sense of the past long after their data has been superseded.

The historical film is history as vision—a vision game that involves such an enormous perceptual and conceptual change from the academic sense of the past that to find its equal we would have to skip past the significant alterations in historical practices of the last three hundred years and return to that period over two thousand years ago when, in the Western world, the written word began to replace the oral tradition. Despite vast differences in the game, both historians and filmmakers approach the materials of the past with one major similarity. Both possess attitudes, assumptions, and beliefs—entire value systems—that color everything they express and underlie the interpretations by which they organize and give meaning to the traces of the past. Such interpretations may be seen as at once the most important and the most fictional part of history. They give a context of meaning to data but do so by abandoning the notion of data as a document (or mirror) of empirical reality and using it to create a notion of cause and effect that is fictive—that cannot itself be documented. As one theorist has put it, interpretation always involves an "imaginative leap" from "social relationships or events to mind or mentality, a leap that is rarely confirmed or, under current conditions, confirmable by evidence."[3]

For filmmakers, the leap may come early; for them, the kind of evidence or data so crucial to written history is never the major issue. (Filmmakers do routinely utilize, even create, new sorts of evidence that we might call "cinematic" data, visual and aural "facts" that the written word would find impossible to reproduce.) By academic standards, all historical films are, in fact, laced with fiction. Dramatic works depend upon invention to create incident, plot, and character (even documentable "historical" characters become fictional when re-created by an actor on the screen). The documentary may seem closer to fact, but fiction almost always enters it in generous amounts—the most obvious example being the use of generic, illustrative images from the past that are not specifically of the scenes they purport to depict. Such elements only underscore the idea that film must be taken on its own terms as a portrait of the past that has less to do with fact than with intensity and insight, perception and feeling, with showing how events affect individual lives, past and present. To express the meaning of the past, film creates proximate, appropriate characters, situations, images, and metaphors. Success in this endeavor has little to do with how the screen conveys data and everything to do with how well films create and interpret a meaningful and useful history, how adequately they embody its ongoing issues and insert themselves into the ideas and debates surrounding a historical topic.[4]

The Contribution of Visual History

This collection includes thirteen essays on works that fit into the category of the New History film—all are more serious about extracting meaning from the encounter with the past than with entertaining audiences or making a profit for investors. In form and country of origin, they are diverse. Several are standard dramas in which the screen is a window onto a "realistic" world. Others push beyond realism to more innovative and radical presentational modes. Of two documentaries, one stretches the boundaries of the form. The geographic spread is also wide. Four of the films were made in the United States, five in Europe, two in Asia, and two in Latin America (one by a British director).

The scope of films was the result of my desire to show that, like scholarship, the serious historical film is a global phenomenon. But the selection of films was made by the individual authors. That all opted for works that, in their seriousness or innovations, lie outside the boundaries of normal cinema suggests that the traditional drama and documentary are incapable of handling the densities and complexities of serious historical representation. One result of these choices of the New History film is that this is not a collection about how the popular media handle history but one about the possibilities of creating history on film. Its lessons have to do with testing the limits of the visual media, exploring the ways in which the past can be rendered into moving images. Because each essay charts its own approach, the book is also about how to understand the history created on film. Its specific studies thus have theoretical implications for both the practice and the reading of visual history.

With a volume this diverse and innovative, any attempt to impose order or to propose some common conventions of the historical film would do violence to the variety and complexity of both the films and the authors' arguments. Like film itself, the essays overflow with suggestions about the many ways in which the historical film can deal with the past. Yet within this diversity, certain ideas recur often enough to allow me to suggest that a major contribution of the historical film lies in the way it undertakes three tasks: contesting, visioning, and revisioning history. Although, as the essays show, any good historical film will to some extent do all three of these, I want to guide the reader by organizing the essays into categories that highlight the particular task that each film seems to undertake most fully.

Contesting History

History may claim to be the human science of the particular and the concrete, but it cannot make the past mean without creating abstractions. Revolution, progress, modernization, modernism, Stalinism, Manifest Destiny, the Resistance, the working class—so involved is written history with such concepts that we come to think of them as solid and unproblematic and are likely to make strenuous objections when some clever revisionist comes along and says, "There never was a French Revolution" or "a Renaissance" or a "First World War." The implication of such claims is not that the events we normally put under those labels did not occur but that the value-laden label itself privileges some things, hides others, and conceals as much at it reveals about the past.

Unlike the word, the filmic image cannot abstract and generalize. The screen must show specific images—not the changing status of women during periods of modernization but a particular Hindu woman, crossing the threshold from the women's quarters into the world of men; not Manifest Destiny but the antics of one band of American adventurers and their charismatic leader in Central America; not the working class but a specific British family grappling with the problems of depression, unemployment, war, and recovery; not the casualty statistics of nuclear holocaust but a pair of lovers in Hiroshima haunted by memories of wartime. In this large gap between the abstract idea and the specific instance, the historical film finds the space to *contest* history, to interrogate either the metanarratives that structure historical knowledge, or smaller historical truths, received notions, conventional images. Ideas contested on the screen may be narrow or broad, of importance to a minority group in a single country or to a large number of peoples or nations. They may involve a segment of a population or all of it, be part of the discourse of the scholarly establishment or belong to the common consciousness as reflected in the press and the visual media. They may even encompass the unspoken assumptions upon which rests an entire culture or civilization.

———————

Distant Voices, Still Lives undermines the sentimental notion, deeply inscribed in both academic history and British film, of the working class as the repository of all virtues—as composed solely of decent, honorable, homely people who overflow with feelings of class solidarity. In detailing the inner life of a single family, this autobiographical film suggests the working class family can be also be a cockpit of repression, violence, and unhappiness, devoid of the class solidarity that would in theory alleviate its misery.

The Home and the World contests India's metanarrative of modernization by showing the contradictions between optimistic political rhetoric and the private realms of experience. In its story of a rich Bengal landowner, the wife he liberates from the confining world of the women's quarters, and a revolutionary leader, all three characters learn that the most enlightened of political actions can lead to personal pain, disaster, and death—and not for the lower classes but for those privileged people who most benefit from the process of modernization.

Eijanaika takes on Japan's celebrated turn away from feudalism, the Meiji Restoration. By portraying its events from the margins of society, through the eyes of carnival entertainers, prostitutes, dancers, and freaks, the film undercuts notions of progress as conscious, designed, and purposeful. To Japan's two major modernization narratives—revolution from above by heroic samurai, and from below by a heroic people—it opposes a carnivalesque insistence that the real causes of historical change can never be determined.

Night of the Shooting Stars questions the comforting, traditional heroism of the Italian (and, by extension, European) resistance to fascism by telling its story from the viewpoint of a young girl. Rather than a conventional tale of unblemished bravery, the story becomes one of cowardice, political indifference, opportunism, cruelty, and random violence—not exactly the sort of heritage cherished by national narratives of liberation.

Visioning History

Rendering the past usually means telling stories—and the meaning of stories is shaped by the medium of the telling. The lengthy oral tradition created a poetic, metaphoric relationship to the past. The written word, over succeeding centuries, has tended to make history increasingly linear, analytic, scientific. Film may be history as vision, but it is not vision alone, for it provides a layered experience of moving images enhanced by language and sound. Consider its many techniques—the different kinds of shots, the movement of the camera, the ability to juxtapose divergent sorts of footage—black and white, color or tinted, sharp or grainy, documentary or staged. Consider the aural elements—music, dialogue, narration, and sound—and how they can underscore, question, contradict, intensify, or lead away from the image.

All these elements are used by the filmmaker to create stories that vision history in terms of how individual lives are altered by larger events or even abstract processes named by scholars—modernization, modernism, Stalinism, revolution, war, Manifest Destiny.

Hiroshima Mon Amour embraces the subject of nuclear holocaust not as a matter of statistics but in terms of lovers haunted by painful remembrances of war and devastation that are conveyed in hallucinatory, repeated, startling juxtapositions of image and sound. Like the horrors of Auschwitz, the atomic bomb inevitably raises the question of what good history is; but the answer of the film has nothing to do with honoring the dead or learning collectively from this event and everything to do with how the individual must come to grips with the traumas history inevitably inflicts.

Memories of Underdevelopment recounts the story of the Cuban revolution from an unusual and revealing angle, through the eyes of an alienated bourgeois who chooses to remain in Havana after Fidel Castro comes to power. To render the confusion and doubts created for such people by the change of regime, and to show the perspective of two kinds of consciousness, the film intercuts two kinds of film—documentary footage (objective) for the collective, revolutionary impulse; and dramatic reenactments (subjective) for the individualist, bourgeois mentality. This technique allows each consciousness to express its own, distinct identity.

The Moderns fleshes out the wholly abstract historical concept of modernism by focusing on the story of particular artists and hangers-on as they wrestle in daily life with the issues of creation, re-creation, appropriation, and duplicity in Paris in the 1920s. The artificiality of the historical category that the film explores is underlined by having the drama take place not in realistic settings but on what are clearly sets, created for the convenience of the filmmaker—much as modernism itself was created as a convenient shorthand for historians of culture.

Radio Bikini also highlights individuals (an American sailor and the native chief of the Bikini Islanders) who are caught in the Crossroads A-Bomb testing of 1946. These two contemporary figures are surrounded by other kinds of historical consciousnesses that appear in different sorts of footage—recent talking heads, government propaganda film, old newsreels, and Navy film exhumed from archives that, in its multiple takes, shows how in the guise of informing a free citizenry, the government manipulated islanders, service men, and the American public to construct the case that bomb testing was for the benefit of all humankind.

Revisioning History

For hundreds of years the only mode for historical representation has been what we call naive "realism," the attempt to make the world on the page seem as much as possible like the world we imagine we encounter each day—linear, regular, with a clear sense of cause and effect. History on film has generally adapted the same mode of presentation: the codes of representation that mark the classic Hollywood motion picture—camera position, continuity editing, lighting, acting, story—are all designed to make it seem as if the screen is a window through which we observe a world that replicates our own.

If the very medium ensures that film will create a unique sort of history, some films carry the process of revisioning further as they foreground their own construction and point to the arbitrary nature of knowledge, or move beyond "realism" to embrace innovative modes of representation such as surrealism, collage, expressionism, mythic rumination, and postmodernism. Such a push beyond the confines of realistic representation also serves to probe the limits of rationalist discourse—the heart of the historical enterprise since the eighteenth century.

Repentance utilizes a surrealist mode to depict the Stalinist Terror of the thirties. Implicit in the film is the claim that some historical experiences are so horrific that any attempt to represent them in a realistic way would do violence to their meaning by normalizing that which was not normal. Because the purges and the surrounding Terror were, literally, instances of political and social surrealism, only that mode of presentation can do justice to the historical flavor and meaning of those events.

Hitler: A Film from Germany underscores the notion that some periods of history are so extreme that they can only be represented with extreme aesthetic modes. The film suggests that Nazism cannot be shown at all—except in the most artificial way, with puppets and actors delivering long monologues on overtly theatrical sets on what is obviously a sound stage. Virtually no authentic historical imagery is used in this quasi-documentary, and no rational explanation mars its cosmic rumination. A major implication is that no rational account of Nazism can ever be satisfactory. Here is explanation that refuses to explain, that says sometimes history cannot tell us why but can only point in the direction of what happened.

Walker proves that the revisioning of history on the screen need not be lugubrious. This postmodern telling of a small but bloody American imperialist venture into Nicaragua in the nineteenth century gives us history as black farce. Filled with absurdist humor, slapstick, and violence, the film indulges in anachronism (Marlboro cigarettes, computer terminals, and *Time* magazines in the nineteenth century) to portray the deadly continuities of history, to show that the doctrine of Manifest Destiny, which has led to repeated American incursions into Nicaragua, remains alive.

From the Pole to the Equator represents a more extreme attempt to transcend traditional film practice. No sound disturbs the images of this film, a compendium from the works of an early Italian filmmaker who traversed the globe, capturing the antics of Europeans in what was yet to be named the Third World. Portraying Westerners in a world of natives and big game, the film refuses all words—either sound or intertitle—as it creates a wordless tale of empire, one that points toward the possibility of a history in images unmediated by language—history as pure vision.

Speaking for the Past

The New History film poses difficult questions for the study of history, questions about who speaks for the past, and in what medium, by what rules, and for what audience—the latter issue being raised in the penultimate essay on *Walker* and *Mississippi Burning*. The New History film also provides a series of challenges to written history—it tests the boundaries of what we can say about the past and how we can say it, points to the limitations of conventional historical form, suggests new ways to envision the past, and alters our sense of what it is. That has certainly been the case for the contributors to this volume. All are academic historians; all produced works of written history before becoming interested in film. If they diverge in their notions of how to approach the historical film, that is only to be expected. For as there are many ways to write history, there are many ways to film history—and many ways to read history on the page or on the screen. Anyone who cares about the study of the past will be interested in the way their articles strive to carve out a space in which the historical film can exist on its own. Anyone who cares about the past has a stake in their quest to understand history in the visual media, this past that is somehow different both from fiction and from academic history, this past that does not depend entirely upon data for the way it asserts truths or engages the ongoing discourse of history.

Part One

CONTESTING HISTORY

1

Distant Voices, Still Lives

THE FAMILY IS A DANGEROUS PLACE: MEMORY, GENDER, AND THE IMAGE OF THE WORKING CLASS

GEOFF ELEY

IN BRITAIN, a certain kind of working class peoples the imaginary landscape of the 1950s.[1] Its dominant qualities, the elements of a social mythology, are ordered around a deeply conservative if populist sentimentality. Its faces stare at us from a thousand photographs and films. In popular representations the virtues are familiar: decency and common sense; homeliness and family strength; a reserved but good-natured neighborliness; community and a sense of everyone pulling together, everyone "doing their bit"; deference to one's betters and sympathy for the underdog; stoicism and resilience under duress; gruff fatalism and a philosophy of modest but legitimate expectations. In the more politicized versions, quite rare in the mainstream of cultural expression, solidarity, collectivism, and a belief in social justice compose a more combative but no less reassuring rendition of this attributed culture. In any case, in the course of the 1950s the working class in Britain comes to embody a powerful representation of the national essence, a particular kind of typicality, an allegory of national wholeness and unity after the wounding and divisions of the war and depression. This was, of course, a working class defined as a "whole way of life" by popular culture, not the working class of production and exploitation defined by Marx. As commentators sought to make sense of the postwar changes, they were drawn increasingly toward this ground of culture. Indeed, through a discourse of nostalgia in the making, the idea of the working class has been continually repositioned somewhere beyond political economy, where culture seems or aspires to be a "safe" place, whether for left or for right. This essay explores the continuing effects and recent instabilities of this imagery of the working class, both in relation to collective memory and as the ground of possible futures.

I

The imagery has many sources, which conjoin in a powerful narrative of the years between the 1930s and the end of the 1950s, between depression and affluence, between bleak memories of deprivation and "never having it so good." The pioneering photojournalism of *Picture Post*, the rise of the *Daily Mirror*, the films of George Formby and Gracie Fields, the postwar corpus of Ealing comedy ("the Studio with the Team Spirit," as the slogan put it), the writings of George Orwell, the endless commentary of J. B. Priestley—and, of course, the political discourse of the Labour party—would all be part of this story. The Second World War—whose meanings were condensed into a rhetoric of shared adversity, the Dunkirk spirit, the Blitz, and backs against the wall, of plucky resourcefulness and British indomitability, of the bulldog breed and the refusal to give in—was crucial. For three decades the welfare state and the affirmation of common dignity, of benefits for all, was the monument to this common story, in rhetoric and tangible social goods.[2]

But at the same time, the working class is seldom center stage itself. Its supporting role is usually literally the case, as in the Ealing comedies, where the working class appears as a series of archetypes and secondary characters. When imagined as a collective force, most famously in Orwell's *Animal Farm* (1945) and *Nineteen Eighty-Four* (1949), it can certainly be heroic, but it is defined essentially by its masculine physicality—elemental, strong, stoical, and dependable but without the full-fledged agency of indigenous and independent thought. More often the working class as such simply dissolves into the sign of a more general celebration of the common culture and its values—"tradition, loyalty, community, and social responsibility," or "love of family, sympathy for others, and decency"—which resided in a populist argument for belief in ordinary people and the "common man" rather than any analysis of interests in struggle, social inequalities of power, and political agencies of class.[3] Of course, this last set of terms evokes a much more fundamental area of political and theoretical definition that lies beyond the representational repertoire altogether, concerning how class is thought to be constituted in the first place.

Right at the end of the 1950s, things changed. The fifties have perhaps become best known as the "angry decade," after John Osborne's memorable *Look Back in Anger* (first produced at London's Royal Court Theatre in May 1956), with its indiscriminate rage against archaism, conformism, and conventional morality. But equally notably, 1959–63 saw the arrival of the so-called British New Wave cinema, whose desire to make a more realistic connection between film and ordinary people took it to a very different setting from the metropolitan environment usually dominating depictions of urban life—namely, to the "other" England of the industrial north, which in these films was marked by landscape, language, and general sensibility as radically different from the setting of Englishness otherwise entrenched in the British cinema.[4] These new treatments, invariably adapted from books, stories, and plays, followed each other in quick succession: *Room at the Top* (Jack Clayton, 1959); *Saturday Night and Sunday Morning* (Karel Reisz, 1960); *The Kitchen* (James Hill, 1961); *A Taste of Honey* (Tony Richardson, 1961); *A Kind of Loving* (John Schlesinger, 1962); *The Loneliness of the Long Distance Runner* (Tony Richardson, 1962); *This Sporting Life* (Lindsay Anderson, 1963); and *Billy Liar* (John Schlesinger, 1963) are the core. This body of filmmaking—northern realism, or working-class realism—brought the working class to the screen in a quite new way. Doing so involved a deliberate act of political and imaginative sympathy, which separated this moment of production from the "social problem" films of the preceding decade—with their obsessive circlings around the issues of juvenile delinquency, prostitution, and "deviant" sexuality—which *The Blue Lamp* had helped begin. But these new representations of the working class were equally specific—equally laden, that is, with the complex meanings of their own historical moment—and instead of idealizing the departure, it is important to be clear about what those meanings were.[5]

First, while breaking with a set of cinematic conventions, extending dramatically the range of legitimate experience represented on the screen, and proposing a very different film aesthetic, working-class "realism" gave far from unmediated access to the "realities" of working-class life. As one critic wrote in response to *Room at the Top*, "For years and years we have known that the British film picture of ourselves was phony. Everyone in the country knew it, it was one of the big national lies that everyone concurred in."[6] But despite their greater closeness to the descriptive context of much northern working-class experience, which *was* genuinely impressive, it would be a mistake to think that Reisz, Anderson, Richardson, Schlesinger, and the others were presenting anything other than an artfully constructed image of the working class of their own. Moreover, this was a view formed in the dissenting cultural politics of the late 1940s and grounded in a larger and in many ways dominant cultural critique of what had been happening to British society since the war. Anxieties about "Americanization," about the commercialization of leisure and the superficiality and tawdriness of mass-produced popular culture, about the gullibility of the masses, about the crass materialism of emerging values, and about the decline of traditional values of working-class community, were the ground from which the new filmmakers spoke. By the time Arthur Seaton, the film's appealing but nihilistic, live-now-pay-later, working-class protagonist, looks down on Nottingham's alienating industrial grayness at the end of *Saturday Night and Sunday Morning*, we know that the consumer affluence proclaimed in the Conservative budget and election campaign of 1958–59 is not exactly the answer. As Reisz said of this film, which was perhaps the most careful, sympathetic, and rounded of these class statements, "The film began to ask the question whether material improvements in people's lives weren't going to be accompanied by a spiritual crisis."[7]

escape

Second, while importantly validating working-class life—as something that deserved to be represented "accurately" on the screen and yet still as the repository of value in British society—these were films primarily of *escape*. By the 1950s working-class culture, with the vitality of its traditional institutions eroded and increasingly infected by the new consumer materialism and its superficial pleasures (as the new filmmakers saw them), is seen to be restricted and confining. In this situation, the antiheroic individualists of the films find various forms of flight—whether through the cynical and opportunistic upward mobility of Joe Lampton in *Room at the Top*, via the various combinations of casual crime, hedonism, and illicit sexuality, or just through dreams, as in *Billy Liar*. Schlesinger called Billy Fisher's society "a society of conformity. . . . There is captivity and lack of communication in his relationships with his family, and the dullness of the routine of his work. . . . He hates it all but ultimately he doesn't have the courage to break away from it. . . . The problem is universal."[8]

crisis mapped on to gender

Third, the crisis in working-class culture—in particular, the tensions between traditional ideals and the consumer society and its values—is mapped by these films onto differences of gender. As John Hill says, here the films participate in a time-honored tradition of cultural critique, going back to the late nineteenth century and especially the 1920s, in which the feminine is identified with the dangerous modern: "Whereas the traditional working class . . . had generally been characterized in terms of a pronounced masculinity (male pride in tough and demanding work, militant trade unionism), the identification of the modern era is in terms of its opposite, the 'triumph' of female consumerism."[9] Without displaying quite the unabashed misogyny of *Look Back in Anger*, the new films manage to present women in a variety of negative lights, as the agents of a confining domesticity (but conversely the necessary and dependent providers of children and domestic labor), the embodiment of unregulated and threatening sexuality (but the proper objects of heterosexual desire), and the source of the frivolous and corrupting urge to consume. For films so dependent on an aggressive construction of active masculinity, the feminine was bound to acquire this predominantly negative and subordinate meaning, and in the meantime, of course, the terms of this binarism have been subject to devastating feminist critique, which by the 1980s had begun to affect the ground from which the working class as such could be imagined.[10]

In these ways, it becomes clear that the northern realist films were produced from within a particular kind of transition, as the circumstances that structured a particular kind of social sensibility—the bases on which one powerful story of class differences could resonate, a paternalist but social democratic story of suffering and reform—began to disappear. Writing the history of filmic representations of the working class since that time would extend beyond the limits of this essay, and would require extensive grounding not only in the remarkable transformations of British television in the 1960s and early 1970s but also in the complex place of working-class life in British sociology, social history, and what became the new field of cultural studies in the same period, quite apart from the intervening political experiences and the histories they entailed. From the "affluent worker" study, through the engagement of the New Left with the changing coordinates of class in the "components of the national culture," to cultural studies' pioneering focus on the "rituals and rebellion" of youth, new generations of intellectuals began working through the significance of the postwar changes that the northern realist films had tended simply to decry or regret. However, the stable referent of this new engagement remained in common, a definite cultural nostalgia, a romance of the working class that was. Although the present was faced, and the experience of change historicized, the working class was scarcely freed from sentimental address. The new narratives pinned it in the sentimental position, even as they loosened the continuities of the present. Richard Hoggart provided one point of orientation for this, as did the more sophisticated and radical contribution of Raymond Williams. The vast social history effort stimulated by, among other things, Edward Thompson's *The Making of the English Working Class* was both a commentary on and a realization of this powerful construction of the working-class past.[11]

In fact, "traditional working-class culture" (the world that was disappearing, from the vantage point of the 1960s) was a historically specific formation of the period between the 1880s and the 1940s, linked to a set of distinct urban-industrial environments and accompanying social structures, and to a certain structure of local and central government relations, all of which helped sustain a separate working-class identity. As Eric Hobsbawm classically put it, this was "the working class of cup finals, fish-and-chip shops, palais-de-danse, and Labour with a capital *L*," recognizable "by the physical environment in which they lived, by a style of life and leisure, by a certain class consciousness increasingly expressed in a secular tendency to join unions and to identify with a class party of

Labour."[12] Formed between the 1880s and 1920s, the political effectivity of this tradition transcended the circumstances of its rise, carrying through to the Labour party's famous victory in 1945. But since the 1950s, manufacturing decline, labor force recomposition, suburbanization and inner-city decay, changes in the public sphere, and the commercialization of leisure have damaged its purchase, producing in the process that familiar discourse of nostalgia for which *Uses of Literacy* was an early marker.

In the meantime, some fundamental changes have steadily undermined the surviving bases of that traditional working-class culture: the drastic dismantlement of the remaining infrastructure of Britain's historic manufacturing and extractive industry, for which the defensive militancy of shipbuilders, dockers, and miners between the early 1970s and the terrible climax of 1984–85 were the main markers; the unraveling and willful destruction of the postwar Keynesian welfare-state consensus, which had been organized around strong public-sector policies, corporative economic management, and strong ideals of trade-union recognition and social citizenship; and the general transition to a nonmanufacturing, service-oriented, post-Fordist economy. These developments have left Britain's social landscape profoundly different from the one still visible in the early 1960s.[13]

A principal aspect, of course, is the massive recomposition of the salaried and wage-dependent work force, and it is interesting how the working class has now been reimagined in some of the more successful British films of the 1980s. For instance, I remarked earlier that at the end of the 1950s "realism" had located itself geopolitically at a distance from the given sites of national fantasy, that is, in the industrial North as opposed to metropolitan London, with important consequences for the norms of national culture that the 1960s were about to refigure. Now, however, working-classness was returned to the capital city, in a restoration of the previous landscape, a deportation from the provinces, a reemplacement in the hegemonic national spaces.[14] Moreover, to a great extent, after the modest centering of working-class experience bequeathed by northern realism to the cinema of the 1960s and 1970s, workers receded again to the supporting roles and incidental settings, which (however evocative, like the carefully drawn references to printers' working culture in a film like David Drury's 1985 *Defence of the Realm*) are familiar from the 1950s. Such incidental treatments have become very much a part of the general texture of filmmaking in Britain, given the strong traditions of naturalism and social realism established by television drama; but representations of working-class life of any kind even more rarely compose the main story.

The surprise success of the early 1980s, *Chariots of Fire* (Hugh Hudson, 1981), a story of track heroics at the 1924 Paris Olympics, was an interesting symptom of this change. While subtly class-conscious in its way (as in an early juxtaposition of privileged students and the unemployed war-disabled), this was quickly harnessed to a main story line that in its various genres became paradigmatic for the critical cinema of the Thatcher years—namely, the effeteness, privilege, and corruption of an old-style Establishment (in this case the heads of Cambridge colleges) versus the meritocracy, ambition, virility, and achievement-driven individualism of the film's twin protagonists, Harold Abrahams (the Jew of Lithuanian parents) and Eric Liddell (the Scottish missionary), whose identities and desire to win disobeyed the conventions of gentlemanly sportsmanship. The film was actually an interesting play on the questions of belonging, outsiderliness, and national identity (the mastermind of Abrahams's victory in Paris was another outsider, the hired Italian-Arab coach, Sam Massabini). But the main narrative of class exclusion was one of middle-class entitlement, and amid the patriotic excess of the Falklands-Malvinas war, the film's critique became tantamount to a Thatcherist parable.[15]

Narratives of power and corruption, combinations of aristocratic decadence and middle-class greed, supplied a dominant motif of the 1980s cinema in Britain, and in one strand of the latter the working class reappears figuratively as the repository of the superseded traditional values. There are various ways of elaborating this point, but I am thinking especially of a certain kind of violent urban drama—the "underworld thrillers like *The Long Good Friday* [John MacKenzie, 1980] and *Mona Lisa* [Neil Jordan, 1986], where the 'old' London . . . confronts a new ruthlessness in a world where secrecy is a visual climate of neon-lit alleys, gloomy railway arches, and smoke-filled nightclubs," in a metaphorical "battle between old-fashioned working-class bandits and new yuppy brutality," or the " 'new-style' poncy pimp-dealer" and the "old, solid, beer drinking working-class gangster."[16] The lead character in both these films was played by Bob Hoskins, whose unglamorous screen persona—his essential "man-in-the-street" (and white) ordinariness—perfectly embodied the claims involved. As George, the old-style, working-class villain in *Mona Lisa*, likable and moralistic, who emerges from prison to find that the world has changed, he is counterposed uncomprehendingly to the new Thatcherist sleaze of Mortwell, the gangland boss who services the demands of an amorally pleasure-seeking society. By contrast with some of the more radically experimental critiques of the new London, such as *Sid and Nancy* (Alex Cox, 1986) or above all *Sammy and Rosie Get Laid* (Stephen Frears, 1989), where the urban environment and its traditional class certainties are shown completely disordered, however, *Mona Lisa* is ultimately redeemed by precisely the old virtues—the loyalty, the stoicism, the rough-edged but comforting ironies, the resilience—of the lovable, working-class Londoner George, who despite everything the New

World can throw at him is still left standing, secure on the ground of ordinary (male) friendship, within a relatively resistant everyday life.

In other words, the filmic images of working-classness in the 1980s stand in a fascinating continuity with those of the early 1960s, with their foreboding of the "spiritual" consequences of materialistic individualism and modernizing social change. In this sense, the businessman-mobster Mortwell's London—all glitz and glitter, a sordid supermarket of arcades, strip joints, gambling clubs, and sex for sale—becomes the monstrous apotheosis of the consumerist anxieties spoken by the cinema of northern realism twenty-five years before. Likewise, femininity continues to perform its warning functions—more independent, more enigmatic, more aggressively self-sufficient, and more complex and indeterminate by far, but nonetheless endangering and destabilizing, the embodiment of the city's risks and attractions, now refigured into an urgently self-conscious postmodern, as opposed to modern, condition. A greater explicit possibility of agency, pleasure, dignity, and resistance may now be allowed, but the function of the female characters is often to "serve" the social problem plot much as before, and the repetition of the earlier structure is thereby secured. In *Mona Lisa* the high-class call girl Simone (by her blackness doubly "other"), whom George is to chauffeur and protect, is a genuinely impressive character, whose subjectivity of cool, self-protective independence owes everything to the possibilities that, as a result of the postsixties feminism, filmmakers are now allowed. But at the same time, she remains caught in the most obviously exploitative of cinematic male-female relationships (pimp and prostitute), stands for sexual ambiguity and disturbance (by managing the "power" of heterosexual desire, and by her own desire for the missing friend Cathy), and is the agent of George's personal journey into darkness. Ultimately, female desire (the desire of and for women) is here once again the source of danger, which offends decency and betrays romance.[17]

The foregoing is not meant to serve as any kind of complete survey of film in the 1980s. But it can suggest the difficulties of imagining forms of self-confident and attractive working-class agency appropriate to the emerging social relations of the end of the twentieth century, where the old industrial Britain has become so completely a landscape of ruin and decay. The bases of the labor-movement politics that might have supported representations of working-class dignity have now fundamentally changed, and this process of social recomposition is simultaneously Thatcherism's deliberate cultural work, a brutally effective political dialectic, driving the social changes in order to shape them. In this new situation, the available image of any counter to the rampant entrepreneurialism and individualizing acquisitiveness of the Thatcherist project seems heavily dependent on the conservative representations of the old-style working-class decency/female indecency polarity that *Mona Lisa* tends to display. At the same time, the Thatcherist emphasis on "family values" and "individuals" over class or other mass-based politics has reconfirmed the "working class" as a phenomenon of culture as opposed to politics, and one implication of this intervention into the ethicopolitical is the disruption of the relationship between the idea of the working class and "the nation" itself. A film like *Mona Lisa*, so acute in its allegorical rendition of life in the eighties, recurs too easily to a kind of nostalgia, for the time when "Britishness" meant even a simulacrum of working-class virtue. Moreover, if the character of George is a slightly bewildered refugee from an earlier time (or as one reviewer facetiously puts it, from "WLNM, the Way of Life that Is No More"),[18] it is perhaps not surprising at this moment to find British filmmakers revisiting the period between the Second World War and the sixties directly, treating it as a rich source of material.

The resulting products range from self-conscious political allegory (David Hare's *Plenty*, adapted for the cinema by Fred Schepsi, 1985) to commentary on social-sexual mores (David Leland's comic but disturbing *Wish You Were Here*, 1987) and a variety of period pieces focused on the hypocrisies of British justice and upper-class sexual profligacy (Mike Newell's *Dance with a Stranger*, 1985; Michael Radford's *White Mischief*, 1987; Michael Caton-Jones's *Scandal*, 1989). Peter Medak's two films, *The Krays* (1990) and *Let Him Have It* (1992), are unashamedly trips down memory lane, engaging the working-class world we have lost via the device of well-known criminal histories, the one a biography of the notorious East End gang between the Second World War and the mid-1960s, the other a study of Derek Bentley, who was hanged in 1952 in a flagrant miscarriage of justice. Perhaps the most successful of this growing genre of historical reassessment have been autobiographical accounts of working-class childhood: John Boorman's commercially successful *Hope and Glory* (1987), set in London during the Second World War; but above all the critically acclaimed but seldom seen trilogy by the late Bill Douglas, *My Childhood* (1972), *My Ain Folk* (1973), and *My Way Home* (1978), which moves from excruciating poverty in a Scottish mining village during the war to the conclusion of the protagonist's national service in Egypt in the early 1950s.

It is within this doubled context, working-class autobiography in a pose of critical nostalgia, that Terence Davies's *Distant Voices, Still Lives* (1988) must be set. Actually two films hinged together, this is a finely constructed study of working-class family life, set in Liverpool (as the screenplay tells us) between 1940 and 1959. Although other characters are important—friends, extended family—the film's primary meanings are composed from the interior of the nuclear family itself: the father, mother, and three offspring, Eileen, Maisie, and Tony. Each of the two parts is framed by the primary rituals of family life, marriage, birth, and death—*Distant Voices* by the funeral of the father, which in the narrative montage of the film's beginning is merged into the wedding of the first child, Eileen; *Still Lives* by the birth and christening of Maisie's baby and the wedding of the third child, Tony. In the film as a whole there is no dramatic action in the conventional linear, plot-related sense, or even specific happenings beyond the life-course events mentioned above, around which the film is arranged. The central feature of the film—the violent patriarchy of the working-class father—is clear enough, but the character development and explanatory scaffolding we expect from the realist cinema (through extended dialogue, flashbacks, the significant scene, and other plotting devices) is completely missing. Instead, the film is a deliberately stylized composition of vignettes and images, held together by visual statements and song rather than dialogue, a "mosaic of memory," as Davies himself puts it, or "a pattern of timeless moments."[19]

For anyone used to the naturalistic conventions of the commercial cinema, this formalism is the most striking thing about the film, apart from the general bleakness of its vision of working-class family life. This is achieved in a number of ways—by particular techniques of cutting, by the extensive use of voice-over, singing, and the sound track in general to connect scenes together, by the jumping around in time, and by the general montage effect of the film's construction. The stylized, static, photographlike quality of many of the shots (frequently the main characters are posed in a tableau, as if for a photograph, including twice at the start of the film, for the funeral and for Eileen's wedding) is also part of this formalism. So are the dominant visual tones, for though it is shot in color the film leaves an enduring impression of black and white. Individual scenes are very formally and precisely composed, with the camera rather than the people supplying the movement, and shots are often held a fraction "too" long—that is, long enough to break the naturalistic moment.

This is best illustrated by an extended example. The film opens with a shot of a terraced house, seen through the rain and a background of thunder. As the BBC announcer intones the shipping forecast, the mother opens the door to collect the milk. Inside, we see the empty hallway and stairs before the mother reenters the frame and calls her adult children down. She exits, and over the empty hall and stairs her singing ("I Get the Blues When It's Raining") joins the radio, which by now has switched to "Lift Up Your Hearts." The footsteps and morning greetings of the mother and three siblings are heard disembodied above the still-empty hallway and stairs. As the mother continues singing, the camera repositions itself by 180 degrees, so that the front door and hallway are now seen from the stairs. The front door dissolves open, and through the sunlight a hearse draws slowly into the frame. On the sound track Jessye Norman sings "There's a Man Goin' Round Takin' Names."

In this brief sequence several things are established. First, a certain mood of sadness, of somber regret, has been instated. Second, the house itself has been marked as the key setting of the film, as the space of painful remembering, a physical metaphor for an intense interiority that we expect to be oppressive. Third, there is the emplacement of song as an important site of meaning , which through this opening repertoire of forms—blues, hymns, and gospel, as media of consolation, redemption, and regret but also of utopian projection, a desire that things be other— enframes the significance for the film of the mother's memory, as a tacit source of counterknowledge to the patriarchy we are about to see.[20] Fourth, the time has subtly shifted. From a number of cues (the mother asks Eileen if she is nervous, the father is absent, the weather changes) and from the hindsight of the rest of the film (and the screenplay), we know that the film begins in the mid-1950s after the father's recent death, probably on the morning of Eileen's wedding. But while life continues, and in a sense is to rebegin through generational reproduction, the dead father's presence nonetheless exerts its continuing effects.

He is introduced during the first tableau, immediately after the hearse sequence mentioned earlier, in the form of a photograph on the wall behind the four surviving family members as they pose. The photograph is brought slowly into close-up, thereby fixing the father's centrality for what is to come. After a further funeral sequence, a second tableau forms against the same wall, this time on Eileen's wedding day, the father's symbolic presence still in place. It is from this second pose, held again for an unnaturally long time, that the memories of Maisie, Tony, and Eileen are successively projected, assembled (as Davies's screenplay puts it) from "years of hurt."[21] In the rest of *Distant Voices*, Eileen's wedding and the associated celebrations provide the recurring point around which the mosaic of memory is arranged, a metaphor that beautifully registers the film's central and discomforting ambivalence. For memory exceeds the promise of a consoling and managerial nostalgia. On the one hand, it can be organized around a putative center, like the rituals of reproduction, which manage the transitions from one generation to another and which the film also uses. But on the other hand, these very moments (weddings, christenings, funerals) also unsettle the regimes of familial intelligibility, which need to be refigured on the other side of the events, reorganized for the purposes of remembering. Memory thus becomes as much a site of defamiliarization and unsettling as one of intelligibility. It is about the release of meaning as much as its accumulation.

The first part of the film is dominated by the father—by his physical brutality, by the emotional coldness of his rule, by his illness and death, and by his general power within the family. This is not an unrelieved picture. In one scene the father's dignity is secretly observed by his young children, who watch from the hayloft as he grooms a horse. But this, no less than the other scene of this kind—the Christmas memory, in which the father places the Christmas stockings and lovingly observes his sleeping children—is defined by secrecy and distance, where the emotions are one-sided and contained, without mutuality, openness, or exchange. The auratic fragility of such family affection and respect is re-created in the moment of its shattering: the Christmas sequence ends with a jarring act of violence as the father rises from silence to hurl the Christmas dinner to the floor, furiously commanding the mother to clean it up. The violence in the film is genuinely shocking (in this respect Davies employs a naturalism that is powerful and stark), from the beating of Maisie as teenager, which as the film's first explicit recollection abruptly establishes its general tone, to the battering of the mother roughly halfway through *Distant Voices*. These scenes of violence are actually rather specific and a relatively small portion of the film's content. But they are so grim and dominant that they carry over to the second part, regulating our perception of the whole work.

By contrast, *Still Lives* constructs a different kind of memory, one more familiar and more akin to the positive and good-natured exercise of cinematic nostalgia, although the spareness of Davies's exposition is still maintained. It concentrates on the years 1955–59, moving sequentially from the birth and christening of Maisie's baby to Tony's marriage, rather than cutting backward and forward quite as freely in time, with most of the material devoted to the celebration of the christening. In this second part the defining presence becomes the mother (whose more positive memories also close *Distant Voices*) and her late-in-life serenity. If the first part of the film is framed immanently by the mother's memory (especially by her singing, which draws us into the maternal habitus), the second is situated within the mother's agency. The new calm of everyday life contrasts with the oppressiveness of the earlier atmospherics. In Davies's gloss: "As in painting, the drama lies not so much in the bowl of fruit or the vases of flowers but the ways in which these objects are perceived—in effect, stasis as drama." As he says, "All the family history is packed into *Distant Voices*, while in *Still Lives* life has reached an even keel and ticks silently away."[22]

II

At one explicit level, *Distant Voices, Still Lives* is a film about memory—about the director's own memories, about how the period has been mainly remembered, about how that remembering has been changing, and (less openly) about how the period's memory *should* be defined. Descriptively and contextually, of course, the film is a reconstruction. As such, its focus on "ordinary things happening to ordinary people" is consistent with the turning away from the political history of big events and toward the microhistories of everyday life that have been so key for the social history of the last twenty years; and we know that Davies and his designers give close attention to re-creating the period settings in this sense, to "getting it right," from the clothing and the artifacts, through the period-defining counterpoint of the radio programs and popular songs, to the visual feel of the pub and the street.[23]

But this verisimilitude is also an illusion. The film is frankly autobiographical, taking its place with the earlier trilogy of *Children* (1976), *Madonna and Child* (1980), and *Death and Transfiguration* (1983), and the more recent *The Long Day Closes* (1992) in a career-long personal cycle.[24] Yet Terence Davies himself was born only in 1945, after the early childhood scenes depicted in the film had taken place, so that he was also too young to have experienced the character of Tony directly himself. In fact, the specific memories fashioned into the film are those of his mother and two eldest sisters and brother (he was the youngest of ten children), from whom he acquired them secondhand: "They talked about my father and the way he had treated them, and their telling of it was so vivid to me that their memories became mine." And "most of the things filmed happened, but not necessarily in that order. I employ a great deal of elision and indeed poetic license. Whole periods of time are elided into a few seconds of screen time while other moments, insignificant in themselves, are expanded into whole sequences. There is no hard and fast rule."[25]

This is an important reminder, which reestablishes the difference between telling a story, on film or on the page, and history as we would usually regard it. As Christopher Hobbs, Davies's production designer on *The Long Day Closes*, puts it, the object was not "a re-creation of fifties Liverpool" but "a re-creation of Terence's memory," a "memory realism" rather than a "real realism," which in reproducing this visual and emotional relationship to a personal past set out to realize an affective truth.[26]

But the film has been read as "memory realism" of a more public and collective kind as well. Its circumstantial detail and the background texture of daily life (what John Caughie describes as "the calling to memory of the voices and sounds which those of us in Davies's generation barely knew we remembered"),[27] manage to be fairly faithful to how childhoods are actually recalled. Moreover, the assembling of the memory fragments is the very opposite of arbitrary or whimsical but forms a powerful causal configuration. It tells us: this is how the father was experienced in his power and mystique; and: this is where the hatred was produced, the fury engendered. Moreover, we carry our childhoods with us for the rest of our lives, the film insists, not as some cliché of the "inner child," as a

subjective panacea of innocence and enjoyment simply waiting for volun-
taristic and self-therapeutic activation, but as a complex history of pain
and hurt, which we work on from time to time and which is shaped or
misshaped into the stories we tell ourselves about who we are. *Distant
Voices* casts a bleak shadow across the mellower recollection of *Still Lives*
in this respect, establishing an emotional baseline for the film as a whole
and subverting the sentimentalism of the nostalgia into which the second
part threatens to slide.

Memory depends on conscious and unconscious capacities, resources,
and interventions—an apparatus of remembering, a field of discursive
possibility, a complex of media and sites (film, television, photographs,
advertisements, songs, museums, tourist spots, fiction, ceremonies, history, political speeches, and more), a collective common sense, a repertoire of cultural scripts that are given to us, become memorized, and
allow coherence to be secured. In the 1980s this collective common
sense—or popular memory—became subject to extreme political dispute.
During the Thatcher years Britain's national past became worked upon to
reconstitute its relationship to the present—sometimes dramatically, as in
the "Churchillian" rendering of the Falklands-Malvinas War (or very differently in the relationship of the 1984–85 miners' strike to 1926), or
more insidiously in a general refiguring of poverty and its meanings in the
recent past. In both ways, the 1930s and 1940s have been the particular
focus of these attentions.

In popular memory the poverty of the 1930s has always been a sign for
the difference and desirability of the present. From the vantage point of
the 1950s, the thirties signified a massive failure of the system—the
"wasted years," the "devil's decade," the "low, dishonest decade" in
some of the familiar phrases for the time. The imagery of dismal hard-
ships, mass unemployment, and hunger marches defined an unacceptable
past that could not be repeated, a misery that required collective action
and public responsibility. The Second World War, accordingly, was a
good war, not just because of its antifascist character (another settling of
accounts with the thirties, in this case with the foreign policy of appease-
ment), but because the egalitarianism and social solidarities required for
victory also made an irrefutable case for equitable social policies in the
peace to come. The breadth of the postwar consensus for the welfare state
rested rhetorically on this suturing of the depression and the war, of patriotism and social need, national interest and common good. In popular
memory this rendition of the 1930s and 1940s became a particularly effective and resonant story of how the present came to be.

Since the late 1970s, however, this logical linkage has been severed, the
story retold. On the one hand, the poverty of the 1930s is successfully
banished from the present, in a contrast that does not so much use it as a

constructive challenge as deny its relevance. For a politics aimed at dismantling the welfare state, Roger Bromley has argued, such a reimagining
of the past is a crucial concomitant. Poverty is placed in a time that is
gone, an unfortunate side effect of progress, whose dilemmas have since
been resolved; and if (to use an arresting trope of the 1980s) the past is
"another country," where things were done differently, poverty is subtly
displaced from the present, and with it the politics—class politics—whose
relevance was derived from the same ground. In other words, "*once* times
were hard and poverty was real, and there was *then* a case for 'welfarism'
but not now." By these means, "the past is domesticated, made part of
memory lane, an album of snapshots in an archive."[28] Yet earlier nota-
tions of poverty cannot simply be reclaimed, to be reinstated in a yet-to-
be-attained anti-Thatcherist discourse of the present. The contemporary
meanings of poverty, after all, those at the end of the twentieth century,
require a different political language.

On the other hand, this political project of displacement or forgetting
has also encouraged (and sometimes directly inspired) corresponding
forms of cultural production, in autobiography, fiction, television, and
film, as well as all manner of public imagery (including, most obviously,
the tourism-directed national heritage industry)—"a particular *genre* of
remembering . . . whose effect is to dehistoricize and depoliticize the poverty and deprivation of the 1930s, aestheticizing them in the stylized sentimentality of 'sepia-tinted victims'." Filmically (and in Britain television
and cinema are continuous in this respect), this has sustained a distinct set
of thematic, iconographic, and stylistic codes, so that history (*this* history) is now signaled by "a repertoire of lighting techniques, camera angles, stock shots, costume, and physiological 'typing'" and by "a carefully selected range of highly visual imagery relating to housing, sleeping
accommodation, pawnbrokers, clothing, hairstyles, faces, all framed in
sepia-tinted stills." While outwardly addressing the past, this body of
work actually aims "to take the 'history' out of the interwar period,"
substituting "a series of images which *stand in* for history and which
condense, conflate, and profess to sum up the period." Such images compose a process of "cultural mediation," through which they "collectively
'editorialize' the process of memory making." Arguably, the reworking of
popular memory, cultural representation, and the politics of Thatcherism
have combined finely together: "To maintain power at a symbolic level is
to attempt to 'colonize' people's memory of the past, to obliterate dreams
and ambitions other than those which correspond with a particular set of
ideological definitions. Thatcherism has created an empty space in people's lives, filled it with public images of a privileged national past *and* of
people building their own lives in their own way, while actually taking
the past away from them in some respects."[29]

How should we place *Distant Voices, Still Lives* in this regard? For one thing, the film makes no explicit connection to the political context of its time, either the film's own time (1940–59) or the Thatcherist present. While instantly recognizable for those of us who grew up during the same period, the setting is placed exclusively through entertainment (radio shows, popular song, cinema) rather than politics and public events, with the exceptions of the air raid sequence (1940) and Tony's national service (early 1950s). Moreover, for the most part the film refuses the historicized narrative codes described earlier, whether in Bromley's general argument about the "Thatcherizing" of the thirties and forties or in my own earlier comments on the sentimentalized working class of the anti-Thatcher critique. Here again, Davies's carefully deployed formalism is important. The direction engages with the visual codes of authenticity— what Caughie calls "the familiar habitat of working-class nostalgia: a rain-drenched urban landscape transcended by community."[30] And one of the film's strongest features—the dignity, endurance, emotional strength, and blamelessness of the mother—is also one of the most powerful and problematic conventions of the working-class representational repertoire, as I shall argue further. But on the whole, the film's formalist strategy (including its "aestheticization of drabness"), which, as Caughie says, "struggles to keep its distance from sentimental nostalgia even while it is celebrating sentimentality," works successfully against such conventional identification.[31]

What does the absence of public/political referents mean? As a general treatment of working-class life, after all, the film is extremely incomplete, even if we allow that in this partialness its composition deliberately replicates the typical architecture of remembered childhood (that is, the directly experienced or consciously recounted parts of the latter, as opposed to the wider contexts in which childhoods occur). There is no description of the neighborhood or the other inhabitants of the street, no wider context of adult friendship or network of childhood friends. The world of wage labor (aside from the horse-grooming scene and one from 1940 in which the family is shown silently bundling wood, presumably for sale) is also missing, and any work-centered activity in this sense, from trade unionism to friendships and organized sociability, is left out. The church is introduced for the christening and weddings, but not in its organized social and cultural presence. Schooling is absent. So is national politics, the political parties, and (most tellingly for the time) the newly expanded welfare state. These larger social worlds are glimpsed only via the rent collector and the insurance man. The settings include (briefly) the army, the air-raid shelter, the seaside hotel, the church, the hospital, the cinema. But otherwise the action moves exclusively between the home and the pub. Even the public scenes are shot within dark, enclosed, closely framed, claustrophobic interiors.

This historical editing differs from Terence Davies's other films and is explicable in terms of his immediate purpose, to present a personal emotional history. But one result of excluding the "external" contexts of the public sphere—both the public world of politics and the organized activity of the working class, its arenas of collective identity—is to magnify the characters' passivity and to make them the ciphers of everyday circumstances in an apparently never-ending way, to reduce their subjectivity in fact, to show them excessively fixed in their ways, removing their significant agency or relationship to change.[32] The northern realist cinema of the early sixties handled this problem of change via individual metaphors of escape, by making its protagonists restless individualists of one kind or another—those who were not "ground down" by their lot, as *Saturday Night and Sunday Morning* put it. In *Distant Voices* there is no escape, only brief, nonidealized respites (national service, summer waitressing) from which Tony and Eileen are in any case rudely recalled by the illness and death of the father; in *Still Lives* marriage (and attained adulthood) is no escape at all. It is not that change cannot occur (Terence Davies himself made the break, achieved the distance, conceived this film), just that the film shows us no immanent possibility. And yet, another aspect of memory (one not addressed in this film) is precisely its ability to keep open such a sense of opportunity—to protect, or produce, the desire for something else, the belief that it could all have happened in another way, the secret and regretful cultivation of unrequited hope that Alessandro Portelli calls "the narrative shape of a dream of a different personal life and a different collective history."[33] This reworking of memories, the psychic transformation of past experiences into partially buried projections of a different future, is missing from the film. Instead, the work of fantasy—in the space of desire—is performed exclusively by the popular culture of entertainment, which is itself a site of nostalgia's mobility. Longings are expressed through popular song, or projected toward the end of the film (in anticipation of the successor work, *The Long Day Closes*) in Technicolor on the cinema screen.

In another sense, this image of a different future is built into the structure of the film and is defined simply by the father's absence. If we ask: what is the present from which the film speaks; then the death of the father, not the advent of Thatcher, provides the answer. This is the point around which the painful rememberings of *Distant Voices* are ordered and from which the future, the *Still Lives* of the second part, a tranquil repetition of established ways after the father has gone, then unfolds. For this is the ultimate purpose of the deliberate timelessness of the film's construction—that is, the removal of externally defining public histories, the pared-down character of the provided contexts, and the formalism of the direction, from the slightly stilted, slowed-down, family-album quality of the action to the tableaux through which the family is frequently presented to us, and the artfully blackened frames through which its members take their leave of us at the very end. The film is not formally about the public meanings of its subjects' poverty or working-classness at all but is about the violent interiority of the family, and it is here that our strongest attention is meant to reside. It is the brutality of the father that dominates our perceptions of what has happened, the depictions of his violence that militate most strongly against the aesthetic of nostalgia that seeps into the dominant sensibility of the film's less disquieting second part.

III

The emphasis on interiors is the key aspect of the setting in this respect. Much of the film is constructed around interiors, sometimes viewed from the outside, through open doorways or windows (though without a known, explicitly visualized vantage point—or point of view—from which the audience is told it is looking), sometimes providing the vantage point themselves, from which the outside is glimpsed. From the beautiful opening sequence, when the hearse glides slowly into the front-door frame, the terraced home of the family is consistently used in this way, as the emotional prison from which an exterior world may be desired, even imagined, but not achieved, as a physical metaphor for psychic constraint, the threshold of unarticulated, desperately longed-for, and ultimately unattained (or perhaps unattainable) possibility. The family is the subject here, and Davies's films are among several recent such efforts (e.g., those of Bill Douglas and Mike Leigh) to use family life to explore how working-class subjectivities are made. At the same time, the particularity of Davies's storytelling (and that of Douglas)—this is autobiography set in the distant past rather than a contemporary fiction set in the present—makes it in one dimension less discomforting and subversive than, say, the cinema of Leigh, precisely because Davies's medium seems to be memory ("then") rather than the current time ("now")—the way we *were* rather than the way we *are*.

　　How, then, does *Distant Voices, Still Lives* differ exactly from the representational world of northern realism? Carolyn Steedman has developed a stinging critique of the prevailing mythologies of the "old working class" to which the northern realist films partly belong (i.e., the working class deemed to be disappearing by the 1960s because of affluence and consumerism), which she also attributes to several cohorts of "scholar-

ship boys" between Richard Hoggart and more recent writers on working-class childhood, such as Jeremy Seabrook, whose personal journeys
out of the working class (they feel) allow them to speak with authority
and nostalgia about the decencies of traditional working-class culture
that have since been betrayed. As Steedman says, several decades after
The Uses of Literacy, the affluent worker study, and the films of the early
1960s, such writing is still agonizing over the effects of postwar materialism, establishing the loss of an old-style childhood (marked by austerity
and discipline, along with the security of stable values, decency, and simple pleasures, as against the tawdry hedonism and cultural drift ascribed
to present-day youth) as a "metaphor for all that has gone wrong with the
old politics of class and the stance of the labor movement towards the
desires that capitalism inculcated in those who are seen as the passive
poor."[34] In the minds of those like Seabrook, "The old defensive culture
of poverty gave working-class children . . . a sense of security which is
denied the present generation. . . . Instead of the children of the working
class being subjected to rigorous self-denial for a lifetime in mill or mine,
they have been offered . . . the promise of easy and immediate gratifica-
tion which, in the end, can sabotage human development and achievement just as effectively as the poverty of the past."[35]

Terence Davies's film will have no truck with most of this romance. It
knows that many working-class childhoods were bleakness and pain and
that such histories of hurt deserve a telling that Seabrook's dignifying of
suffering in the past will not allow. In attacking the latter—which proceeds from the power of material circumstances and the "sameness" they
impose on working-class experience, to which psychological richness and
complex subjectivity or individuality are thereby denied—Carolyn Steedman sets out herself "to open the door of one the terraced houses" so that
the nostalgia of Seabrook's "profoundly a-historical landscape," his
"map of an upright and decent country," can be deconstructed, the gener-
alities particularized, the assumptions turned into a problem.[36] *Distant
Voices, Still Lives* begins with just such an open door, and the physical
interior of the terraced house becomes the framing for the wounded childhood that Davies presents in the first part of the film and for the psychic
and emotional interiors depicted in the part that follows.

The distance marked from northern realism by Davies's film has several aspects. The antinaturalism has already been discussed. The film also
breaks with the pessimistic disdain for mass culture, the popular culture
of commercial entertainment. Commercial television, jukeboxes, rock
music, and so on (the particular banes of the northern realist filmmakers)
were still in the future. But the sources of pleasure shown in the film—of
collective enjoyment and personal introspection—come from popular
song and the cinema; there is no "traditional" working-class culture

(brass bands and pigeon fancying) here. Likewise, the women are no longer the harbingers of corruption and decline by way of their mindless devotion to popular entertainment and its moronic pleasures (as the northern realist directors saw them); instead, the enjoyments of dancing are simply presented, and in Davies's film the women's knowledge of song and the movies make them far more the keepers of fantasy in a positive sense. Of course, in itself this ascription is completely conventional, but the valorizing of mass culture makes it nonetheless a significant statement. It is, however, the graphic depiction of emotional (as opposed to material or cultural) poverty and domestic violence that really measures the distance between 1960 and 1990, with jarring effects on the representations of the working-class family to which we have otherwise been accustomed. The family, *Distant Voices, Still Lives* seems to say, is a dangerous and destructive place, constituted by the power of men over women and by a terrible inwardness that marginalizes other social attachments.

This point is made quietly and insistently in *Still Lives*, from which the physical brutality itself has been removed. When Eileen and her old friends Monica (Micky) and Jingles are reunited at Maisie's christening celebration in the late 1950s, it dominates the conversation. Jingles is being abused by her husband Les: as the three friends burst into the "special song," she breaks down ("No—I'm all right—honest. It's just Les—you know what he's like when he turns . . ."), and an angry set of exchanges about the behavior of men ensues ("They're all the same—when they're not using the big stick, they're farting—aren't men horrible?"), finally mediated by the mother's call for another song. Monica and her husband Red relate exclusively through a good-natured but ceaselessly antagonistic banter. Eileen herself is kept isolated from her friends ("Oh, you'd better not, Micky, he's funny about having visitors . . ."). Although marriage represents the escape to acknowledged adulthood, for the women of the film the terms of this passage are fresh confinement rather than independence. As Eileen's husband Dave puts it (after several years of marriage, also at the end of the 1950s): "You're married now—I'm your husband—your duty's to me, frig everyone else. Monica, Jingles, that's all ancient history now."[37] In *Distant Voices* we have watched the exercise of this male power—in the father's methodical beating of Maisie in the cellar with the yard brush, in his enraged destruction of the Christmas dinner, in his smacking of Eileen across the face in the air-raid shelter, in his relentless battering of the mother. But this catalog leaves an interesting question: for if the family is a place where men (fathers or husbands) do violence to women (daughters or wives), where does this leave the position of sons?

Tony is the one family member whom the father does not directly as-

If the family is a place where men (fathers or husbands) do violence to women (daughters or wives), where does that leave the sons? Copyright © Avenue Entertainment, Inc. Used with permission

sault. Instead, it is Tony as a young man who challenges the father, smashing the parlor windows from the outside with his bare fists, demanding that his father "Come out and *fight*!" But *this* violence is no demonstration of power: it is drunken, frustrated, incoherent, self-damaging, and also ineffectual.[38] Moreover, while each surviving family member is explicitly given "equal dramatic weight," the film subtly identifies with Tony.[39] This is no doubt partly because of the director's own gender. But it also comes from two of the film's most enduring images (which likewise supply the most commonly used stills), both of which position Tony ambiguously in relation to the home—which itself bears contradictory meanings, as security and confinement, the empowering and imprisoning space of male authority. In the first—Tony as little boy—we see him from the back, facing the front door, from which (for reasons we are not told) he is shut out; the door opens revealing the father, the embodiment of physical menace ("Why can't I come in, Dad? . . ." "There's no place for you here—frig off!"); the door slams. In the second—Tony as young man—he stands in the doorway, looking out, on the evening of his own wedding party, and weeps. It is hard to render the truth of this moment, which is all to do with recognition and regret, with relinquishing one kind of indeterminacy, between the past we have been watching and the future of being a man: "The young man cries because he knows that *it will go on like this*, that nothing will change; that the endless streets, the marriages made like his parents', the begetting of sons and daughters, all will stretch on forever: no end in sight."[40]

The symbolics of these two images are very powerful. In the one, Tony is looking in—excluded, expelled, refused admittance; in the other, he is momentarily suspended, looking out from the place that his own marriage has finally secured—"the door frame itself showing that he is neither inside nor outside; betwixt and between."[41]

IV

This returns us to the film's organizing metaphorical opposition inside/outside and shows us the terms of the predicament the film is trying to explore—that of being "inside the law," the law of the father, of patriarchy, of men. How far Davies the author has intentionally engaged with pyschoanalytically informed feminist theory is less important here than the congruity of the film's stance. Violent fathers have been depicted before but seldom with this bleakness and precise political resonance, and the film conspires with its audience to this end, because its meanings require a knowledge (of contemporary values, attitudes, sensibilities) that the film does not itself supply. It speaks a script of masculinity, one its characters seem compelled to enact, that is written elsewhere. It is a film for whose central imagery—of the power and violence of men—twenty years of feminism have prepared us, and it importantly transcends some of the standard gender oppositions. Thus, as the film positions them, the characters of the brother and two sisters are largely elided; within the terms of the film, Tony does not repeat the pattern of patriarchal violence; and the almost-final, "feminized" image of Tony crying on the doorstep is an eloquent counterpart to the father's brutalities earlier in the story. This contrasts with the gender texts of most of the cinema of the 1980s mentioned earlier, where constructions of masculinity are rather simplistically mapped across images of hard, aggressive criminality on the one hand and ineffectuality on the other, and where "feminine" qualities of passivity and respectability have their familiar negative coding.[42]

Yet, in another way, this is where the film is most beholden to the sentimentalizing syndrome attacked by Steedman—that is, to the given representational conventions surrounding the British working class, especially those of working-class sons remembering working-class mothers: every construction of masculinity entails its feminine counterpart, and in Davies's film the repressiveness and violence of the father is matched by the nurturing and serenity of the mother. It is in this central aspect of the transition from *Distant Voices* to *Still Lives*, as the film recenters itself around the emotional stereotype of "our mam" (Davies refers to "the all-pervasive, all-enduring power of the love of and for my mother") that it comes closest to a conservative sentimentality, to what Caughie calls "the quality tradition of English period nostalgia," which in the American market, through "Masterpiece Theater," David Lean, Richard Attenborough, and Merchant-Ivory films, has built a niche all of its own.[43] Likewise, the film obliquely affirms old mythologies of women and work, for while the patriarchy of visual representations of wage labor is not incorporated directly into the film, its converse of the working-class housewife certainly is, and the chosen imagery (scrubbing floors, cleaning windows, making dinner) works very much with the grain of an older history that feminists and social historians have compelled us to doubt. It is not that working-class mothers could *not* be pillars of emotional security or that domestic labor was *not* performed, obviously. It is more a matter of how the film's choice of representations works with or against certain dominant forms of now-questionable understanding. This brings us back to the question posed at the start of this essay: how is the working class represented?[44]

Distant Voices, Still Lives may not be intentionally and explicitly *about* the changing terms of being working-class in the second half of the twentieth century. But in terms of what the film *does*, this becomes a highly pertinent question. To this extent, the film's meaning derives from a discourse of the decline of class—or at least of the insufficiency, even obsolescence, of class as an explanatory device—that lies beyond its overt narrative frame. What it has to say about patriarchy would be much harder to imagine, for instance, if we had not come to see class in a particular skeptical way. I shall let Carolyn Steedman make the argument here: "All the stories that follow, told as this book tells them, aren't stories in their own right: they exist in tension with other more central ones . . . Accounts of working-class life are told by tension and ambiguity, out on the borderlands. The story . . . cannot be absorbed into the central one: it is both its disruption and its essential counterpoint."[45] In other words, the strength of this particular story, the story Terence Davies tells, which is deliberately removed from any explicitly indicated contexts of large-scale historical argument, derives in no small part from the larger histories (or tropes of historical understanding) to which it also connects.

Earlier in this essay I remarked on the difficulties of fashioning sympathetic portrayals of working-classness that are simultaneously capable of mobilizing the political imagination now that industrial decline and political reaction have rendered older models of class-political action so apparently dead on their feet. Neither the social democratic narrative of suffering, social need, and collective good nor its radical socialist rival of class-conscious masses in struggle, with their attendant mythologies and

iconographies, both of which can be historicized as the achievements of
a particular period between the 1880s and 1950s, enjoy widespread pop-
ular-democratic credibility any longer. Both had allowed positive constructions of dignified, heroic, working-class masculinity, and it is these
workable myths that the decimation of manufacturing and heavy-indus-
trial employment, demonizing of trade unions, and—in specific ways—
feminist critiques have now dismantled. Thatcherism has emptied out the
older categories of class identity and affiliation, assaulting them unforgiv-
ingly with its rampant individualism, leaving behind a wasteland of ruined solidarities and dead metaphors, which disconnected groups of the
marginalized, joined by the multiplying inequalities of gender, race, access, and ownership, and the incommensurable radicalisms of identity,
are now seeking vainly to refill. Amid the detritus of once-valued but
now-receding public goods, a credible future of class-collective aspiration
has yet to be reimagined, and this is not part of Terence Davies's project.
Distant Voices, Still Lives may be read as a bleak and depressing break
from the tradition of historical retrieval that the sixties so passionately
began, in which the past was valued for its examples of sacrifice, achievement, and struggle. But perhaps this is precisely the point. History—as
memory work—may be worked upon therapeutically. Analytically and
rhetorically, history will also always be in play—as a site of difference, a
context of deconstruction, where our present's specificities may be pinned
down, and the naturalizing of hegemonies upset. But as a source of models for the future, maybe it should be let go. This is also what Davies's film
seems to say. *This* past is not usable. It cannot help.

It is worth thinking further about this question of hegemonies, about
which of the latter exactly are dislodged by the film and which are not, for
although it denies us the security of one well-tried stereotypicality, the
iconic decency of the British working man, other safe places are left for us
to find, such as the one I have already mentioned, the no less iconic
strength and dignity of the long-suffering working-class mother; and we
need to ask what else the film protects or ignores, what other fugitive
knowledges demand to be applied. In this essay I have considered *Distant
Voices, Still Lives* from a particular point of view, as one site of an important cultural revision, concerning the place of the working class in the
national fantasy of postwar Britain, and the palpable decay of old-estab-
lished class-centered political understandings. The film is a compelling
symptom of contemporary changes in this respect, and I have tried to tell
its complex class story by mobilizing larger cinematic and political histories and by thinking about how the politics surrounding class have now
become muted, both in our Thatcherized present and in the historicized
moment of the film's depiction. To tell this story of change fully, however,
other muted contexts would have to be brought in, which lie beyond the

film's explicit representations but which are also crucial to the present's emergent democratic potentials and to the utopian counterstory they might allow us to tell.

One such context would be the field of religious affiliation; for although Catholicism is key to the biographical framing of Davies's earlier trilogy, it is notably understated in *Distant Voices, Still Lives*, and yet the negative coding of Irishness and Catholicism remains no less vital to the national fantasy of the present than to the discursive working class of history. A second important but underexplicated instance would be the heteronormative context of power in the film, which Davies's own gayness and earlier thematics again call into view but which in any case describes powerful modes of fantasy and domination in its own right. Another essay will have to address the question of how these other contexts for power and identity would change the class-centered reading I have produced. But for now, the film's story of masculinity can certainly be mentioned, and the inevitabilities of its characters' inscription in the conventions of the patriarchy that it otherwise discredits can now be resisted from the standpoint of a recently emerging queer theory as well as by the feminism I have mainly deployed. By this means, the conventional gender binarism would be further upset, and in some ways the most arresting image of the film, Tony's weeping for his marriage, thereby appears in a still more poignant light, as the space of a different kind of loss, where the reproduction of heterosexual family life, in its unbending working-class normativities, has already foreclosed the possibilities of other sexualities and modes of recognition, the gayness that fails here to speak its name. But the challenge of queerness also goes much further, problematizing the conventional assumptions of citizenship in the national culture, the resilient hegemonies of family and community, on their most hallowed and securely embedded ground.[46] While *Distant Voices, Still Lives* unsettles the spaces of patriarchy and heterosexual family futures, in other words, clearing the familiar (but not the familial) ground and providing incitements for alternatives to be imagined, there are bounds to its positive vision.

In conclusion, then, I want to use my reflections on the film's gendering of memory (in the transition from the masculine qualities of the working-class dignity bleakly desentimentalized in *Distant Voices* to the feminine or postpatriarchal countermemory of *Still Lives*) to return to the grand thematics of class and nation raised at the very start of this essay.[47] For if at one level the film is an act of disposal, discarding some tried but limiting and directly harmful and oppressive images of heroic working-class masculinity, we still need to ask what it puts in their place. If the pastness of working-class culture and its seductive authenticities (which in any case were always suspect) is now to be acknowledged, and the present tense of the film is postpatriarchal, then where is its "poetry of the future"? If we are asked to give up what we know of the working class in the nation—its centrality to the postwar consensus of the welfare state, its place in the national allegory—so that "national culture" loses its propriety in the received imagery of the working class, then how might a popular politics be reimagined?

Here the dissonance between what Davies's film is saying and what I have called the working-class representational repertoire of the British cinema (figured most recently through the eloquent character of George in *Mona Lisa*) is key. As I have argued, *Distant Voices* painfully deconstructs the received imagery of British working-classness, and while its own counterargumentation remains oblique (the public arenas of working-class collective identity are omitted), it leaves little of the postwar era's foundational mythology—the heroic reliability, dignity, and decency of the British working man—intact. In that sense, the film is a document of our Thatcherist times, recording the exhaustion of a certain national icon, that of the white patriarchal working class as a figure of Britain. By contrast with a film like *Mona Lisa*, which ends with George, his sardonic friend, and his teenage daughter walking indomitably into the sunset, *Distant Voices, Still Lives* provides no sense of positive futurity, beyond the privatized everydayness implied by the metaphor of the "still life" that is left simply "ticking silently away." But this transformation in the representational norms of what counts as the meanings of working-class life, its complex incitements to collective memory, nonetheless provides devices for thinking about how the dialectic of class and nation might now be posed. And here the film's formalism becomes important, because the self-conscious abandonment of established narrative convention, through disruptions and estrangements of form articulated precisely in the most familiar of moments (weddings and so on), encourages us to imagine *different* ways in which the future might occur: through tradition, lineage, ruptural conjunctures, mere repetition, disparate fields of possibility—the list could go on.

These possibilities are manifest in *Distant Voices, Still Lives* only as a series of ambivalent gestures. On the one hand, there is the shedding of what might wishfully be called archaic forms (the authoritarian patriarchal family) through the desolate exposure of family life in the film's first part, and through Tony's "feminized" recognition at the film's end, of patriarchy's wrongness and the terrible sadness of its repetition. But on the other hand, there is the consent still to be reinstalled in the conventional *events*, by the reinduction of, in particular, the film's women into the form of the patriarchal culture via the ritual days of weddings, christenings, and funerals, and by Tony's understanding that it will, after all, go on as before. But the space of this ambivalence might nonetheless be used for thinking about the larger arguments beyond the film. This could generate not only the energy for imagining the horizon of the present, which I have elliptically called "Thatcherism" here, but also the courage to "unlearn" old political habits, the compulsion to go on reproducing dead models for the future, those of "the working class" and "the nation" in the traditional sense. Perhaps the nonrepetition of patriarchy, in other words, can work as the sign of the possibility that other nonrepetitions might occur.

This returns us to the question of popular culture.[48] It appears in the introduction to this essay as a site for the postwar consensual deployment of "working-class Britishness" on the part of a conservative and normalizing cultural nationalism; it figures in the discussion of the "northern realist" films of the late fifties and early sixties as a contested term of cultural critique, as the negative to the positivity of vanishing working-class traditions; and it returns in the discussion of song and other popular forms in *Distant Voices, Still Lives*, to be marked as something important, positive, and pleasurable, and not as the corrupt successor to a working-class authenticity that has now been lost. The stress on dancing, on going to the "pictures," on popular radio variety shows, and on popular song interpellates the working-class persons of Davies's film in relation to the commodity culture of the marketplace and no longer in relation to the superior virtue of those old and valued "traditions." This is an important move, for (as I argued earlier) it finally breaks with the familiar dismissiveness toward mass culture that has been such a salient feature of British cinema since the war. But it also adumbrates a new positivity, a space of possibility that exceeds the functions of mere escapism and consolation that most reviewers tended to see in the film's constant recurring to popular song. It describes the production of popular collective identities not in the entailments of patriarchy (the past that the film remembers) but in the modalities of transition to a new terrain of popular culture, which is postpatriarchal in the sense that a new boundary is being drawn, waiting to be filled. *This* is the future tense of *Distant Voices, Still Lives*— a tense of the possible—in which a new mode of memory, of interiority, of intimacy, of repetition might begin to be imagined.

2

The Home and the World

THE INVENTION OF MODERNITY IN COLONIAL INDIA

NICHOLAS B. DIRKS

> My story, my fictional country exist, like my-
> self, at a slight angle to reality. I have found this
> off-centering to be necessary; but its value is,
> of course, open to debate.
> —*Salman Rushdie,* Shame

The Home and the World (in the original Bengali, *Ghare Baire*) was one of the last (1984) in a long line of extraordinary films by the Bengali director Satyajit Ray, who died in April 1992. The film recapitulates many of the central themes in Ray's cinematic worldview as well as in that of the work of Rabindranath Tagore, Ray's frequent source of stories and inspiration. *The Home and the World* contains many echoes from Ray's earlier *Charulata*; both films are based on stories by Tagore.

The film begins with a fire, which when the camera pulls back is revealed as that of a funeral pyre. The camera pans from the fire to the face of a dazed and grief-torn woman whose tears and immobile features signify mourning. A voice-over glosses the image: "I have passed through fire. What was impure in me has been burnt to ashes." The beginning is the end, and thus the tension becomes not how the story will unfold but why. The foreknowledge of tragedy frames in advance the notions of destiny and inevitability, of free will and determination, and ultimately of the immense risk and danger inherent in the collision of tradition and moder-

I am grateful to Robert A. Rosenstone, who initially suggested I write about Satyajit Ray after we taught a course together on Indian film at Caltech in 1985, for his support and suggestions. I would also like to acknowledge the critical assistance of Lauren Berlant, Partha Chatterjee, Marjorie Levinson, Gyan Prakash, Lucien Taylor, and the students in David Ludden's graduate seminar at the University of Pennsylvania in the autumn of 1992.

nity. The voice, and the story of the film, belong to the mourning woman, Bimala; the tragedy is simultaneously that of her marriage and that of her motherland, the nation.

The film is set in rural Bengal in the traumatic year 1905. Lord Curzon has just divided Bengal presidency into eastern and western halves, in what was simultaneously a classic act of divide-and-rule and a clear assault on the administrative fortunes of the politically all too conscious Hindu elite (or *bhadralok*) of Calcutta (not to mention the administrative basis for the creation first of East Pakistan and now Bangladesh). The partition precipitated the swadeshi movement, in which foreign commodities, particularly cloth, became the symbols of colonial domination and the cry *swadeshi*—meaning "of our own country"—became the principal focus of nationalist politics. Political symbolism followed from economic analysis, in particular the contention that India's raw materials and markets had been used to service the English industrial revolution with the direct result of impoverishing and further enslaving India.

The image of fire occurs not only at the scene of the funeral pyre but also to depict two critical features of the swadeshi campaign: the burning of foreign cloth in what was the central political ritual of the swadeshi movement, and the chaotic destruction and frenzy of a communal riot. The movement began with rallies held throughout Bengal where political leaders encouraged citizens and merchants to dump all foreign cloth into a large fire, a fire that both consumed the cloth and symbolized the death of colonial domination. But within a year of the euphoria of political action that was part of the early days of protest, Bengal was the scene of serious communal riots that led figures such as Tagore to reconsider the movement and prefigured the tragic association of nationalist politics in India with social ruptures between Hindus and Muslims.

At one level the conventionalized story of a lovers' triangle, the film is almost allegorical in its clear reference to a set of homologized antinomies: home/world; woman/man; private/public; love/politics; tradition/modernity—all put within the larger classical frame of the struggle between free will and determinism. Although the story in its original textual form could perhaps be read without the rich texture of implied significations, the film—with its insistent images from that of fire to the much-photographed corridor between zenana and drawing room—ineluctably impregnates the story with multiple meanings. Ray's use of cinematographic images allegorizes what is otherwise a simple story set in a highly specific historical and social landscape.

After the opening scene of final conflagration, the story begins with Nikhil, a young and progressive landlord (zamindar), reading an English poem to his beautiful wife while boating on the river. It is a scene that could have taken place in the lake country and certainly evokes the colonizer's culture of romantic love. Only the scene is set in India, and the young woman understands not a word of this language of love. Nikhil chooses this moment to ask if his wife would like to learn English. She protests, as the voice-over says, in vain; for—in a demonstration of his own traditional authority—he prevails and hires an English governess. The governess teaches Bimala not only English but also piano, English singing, even how to pour tea. The young pupil makes splendid progress until the English governess suddenly must leave town, the victim of rocks thrown by a group of politically excited and inspired students.

Politics enters even more graphically with the arrival in town of Nikhil's oldest and dearest friend, Sandip, who has now become a leading swadeshi activist. He delivers an impassioned (and, for a feature film, a remarkably long and detailed) speech about swadeshi. The historical setting is thus given specificity and political content, and the rally ends with the song by the Bengali poet Bankim Chandra Chatterjee, *Bande Mataram* (later rejected as the national anthem of India because of its strong Hindu associations). With Nikhil's approval, the rally takes place in the courtyard of the landlord's house. From the safety of the zenana, Bimala listens, and is deeply moved.

Later that evening Nikhil tells his wife that he would like her to meet Sandip; over the years he has told Sandip all about her, but since her marriage she has remained within the confines of the zenana and spoken with no man other than her husband. Meeting Sandip thus also means coming out of the women's quarters, entering into a male world of public intercourse. That her coming out should engage both the "male" and the "political" in the person of Sandip is, of course, no accident. But Nikhil's impulse to bring his wife out appears somewhat mysterious from the start; he tells her about Sandip's many affairs (even with "nonswadeshi" women), and he makes it clear that he disapproves of Sandip's politics.

It is evident that Nikhil wishes to do more than simply show off his beautiful and accomplished wife. He incites her interest in Sandip and politics in equal measure. When Bimala tells Sandip that she believes in the cause of swadeshi, Nikhil says, "Now you are a free agent." Nikhil believes he can bring his wife not only out of the zenana but out of the traditional world, which, through the arrangement of their marriage, dictated both her exclusion from his public world and her love for him. At the same time, Nikhil makes clear his sense that Sandip is not as much of an idealist, nor swadeshi politics as ideologically sound, as they might seem on the surface. He further says that the emotional appeal of "Bande Mataram" is best suited for women: "I can't think like that." And he wryly observes that the more one gets to know Sandip, the less one likes him. The "Home" and the "World" seem equally problematic; and Nikhil wants his wife to learn about both so that she can choose, as he has done, a kind of middle ground. But, perhaps even more than this, in tones that subvert the promise of freedom he holds out for her, he wishes his wife to choose him.

As the story unfolds, Nikhil's altruism and deep faith in rationalism appear increasingly admirable—not only does he argue against swadeshi measures because they hurt the poor Muslim merchants far more than the British (or the rural landlands and urban bourgeoisie) but it emerges that he had, by trying to manufacture soap and other commercial goods locally, been a swadeshi before his time. He is by all accounts a very good man. But something is not quite right. Sandip, with whom Bimala does develop a passionate if short-lived love, may be a crass opportunist, but Nikhil is ironically most imperious when he compels his wife to choose him and his ways out of her own free will. Nikhil's commitment to rationalism seems overzealous, ill-conceived, hopelessly romantic. The conceit of freedom is played out against the backdrop of predestined tragedy and overwhelming fatalism. By the time Bimala returns to her senses, realizing that her husband is a genuine treasure—far more the political hero than his rival in love—the die has been cast. Communalist riots, set off by swadeshi agitation, engulf the estate in flames. And Nikhil, compelled by his own sense of nobility and responsibility, no sooner knows that his wife has returned to him than he rides off to quell the riot that engulfs him, too. Bimala's last words, "I knew I would be punished," leave little doubt that her freedom has not only underscored the determinations in her life but also made her the most unhappy of traditional Hindu women: a widow in the prime of life, just like her spiteful and unattractive sister-in-law, who spends most of her time glowering at Bimala from the moral purity of her bitter fate.

In the penultimate scene of the film, Nikhil's body is solemnly marched down the path leading back from the estate to the landlord's house. The image recalls the earlier scene of the corridor between the zenana and the drawing room; both are powerful sites of passage and transgression. Each oppositional world is metonymized in Ray's obsessively choreographed cinema. Even the beautiful textiles that play such an important role in creating the visual fabric of the film become signs of the relations between home and world. When Bimala is in her bedroom she spends her time incessantly folding and admiring exquisite cloth, saris as well as the blouses she designed to blend European and Bengali fashion. These textiles, though based on Indian colors and designs, are sensuous symbols that mark the infiltration of the traditional zenana by the West, for the cloth was all loomed, as Nikhil reminds her, in English factories. The swadeshi fire that burns foreign cloth never reaches Bimala's wardrobe but instead becomes the fire that consumes her husband, consigning her to a world of plain white cotton.

The costs of transgression seem now to be signified in this ultimate scene of sadness, the funereal procession and the widow's grief. The final scene, juxtaposing an image of flame from the communal riot and the woman—transformed before our eyes from a bride to a widow shorn and in white—evokes the memory of sati, the ceremony in which the widow mounted the funeral pyre and followed her husband to the next world. A century before, sati had become the symbol of oppressive tradition in Bengal, where the great reformer Rammohan Roy had argued for the abolition of the rite and the British had asserted their civilizing mission through the condemnation of this horrible cruelty to women. But like so many other episodes in colonial history, the controversy over sati raised the contradictions of colonial rule to a new level and revealed that women's bodies could be used for a variety of purposes that in the end, like Nikhil's fatal gesture, accorded neither freedom nor agency to women.

Modernity, less in the form of colonial denunciations of Indian tradition than in enlightened Indian efforts to reform a society in which women often bore the brunt of caste and custom, is perhaps the more critical focus of Ray's cinematic scrutiny than the nationalist politics he seems so readily to dismiss. For if Ray worried that the development of nationalism subjected women to modernity's most virulent contradictions, he was neither an avid traditionalist nor a modernist retreating altogether from the harsh and horrific politics of the contemporary world. *The Home and the World* seems at one level a self-conscious aesthetic reflection on the antinomies I listed earlier. These concerns are not new to Ray, for they were clearly depicted in *Charulata*, made twenty years before. But whereas *Charulata* ended with the possibility of hope, with public and private, politics and poetry, male and female, united in the final—if still provisional—reconciliation and collaboration of a political newspaperman and his poetic wife, this film ends with death and widowhood. No doubt this shift could be construed as the difference between the India of Nehru and that of postemergency politics, with its resurgent communalism and corruption. But whatever Ray's specific intention, history has taken on epic proportions. Destiny, inscribed in character, plot, and image, seems like fire to be engulfing the history of unilinear development and liberal optimism. Modernism—with all its assumptions about history, politics, and society—is subjected to radical doubt. This film is about history in more than one sense. Although critics have justifiably complained that Ray's politics, perhaps even more than

Tagore's before him, seem dangerously reactionary, the film ends, as it begins, by calling into question the very categories we use to think about politics, and its relations to both art and life.

If Ray frequently took his narrative and aesthetic inspiration from Tagore, it is not without importance that the two figures lived in very different historical moments and contexts. Tagore's literary career (born in 1861, he lived until 1941) spanned much of the modern period; and both his prose and his more literary works reflected his changing though always complex relationship to the political whirl around him. He always emphasized the importance of education, and the need to use the mother tongue not only to cultivate an autonomous domain for the arts but also to bridge the chasm between the elite and the masses; he also was consistently concerned with forms of extremism that either neglected the costs of obsessional politics or abandoned the distinctive strengths of Indian civilization. But in the first two decades of the twentieth century his concerns underwent a series of changes in large part because of his involvement in and reactions to the swadeshi movement and its aftermath. In the years between 1901 and 1906 Tagore emphasized the "essential distinctness of oriental civilisation and its superiority over the European."[1] In so doing he began providing a very different reading of Indian social customs than he had earlier enunciated. For example, he wrote poetically about the Hindu past, he discovered virtues in the functional differentiation of caste and traditional village social life, and he even articulated justifications for child marriage, restrictions on widows, and accorded sati a certain kind of past honor.[2] This new poetics of the past was also accompanied by a critique of elite politics, which he saw as cringing in the deracinated shadows of colonial intrusion. Above all, Tagore stressed self-help, or "atmasakti," and thus was tapped into the collective resolve that built into the swadeshi movement of 1905. As Sumit Sarkar has noted, "In retrospect, it is Rabindranath Tagore rather than the professional politicians who stands out as the most vivid and remarkable personality of those stirring 1905 days—participating in the rough-and-tumble of politics as never before and after, suggesting far-reaching schemes of autonomous rural development. . . , bestowing with the vision of a poet a rare beauty and imaginative appeal to the whole movement . . . , and composing at the same time a magnificent series of patriotic songs."[3]

The Hindu Muslim riots of 1906–7 not only marred the enthusiasm of many avid supporters of swadeshi but also brought home the contradictions of mass politics and the socioeconomic conditions of colonial India. Although the riots reflected the tensions between a landed Hindu elite and largely landless Muslim peasants, they also revealed the extent to which nationalist reliance on indigenous production was ironically a luxury for the rich; local merchants and traders, many of them Muslim, were committed to selling foreign cloth and goods because they were more readily available, better produced, and far cheaper than swadeshi brands. A swadeshi economy would have to await the massive investment of independent India's five-year plans in order to become even partially viable. And during the heady days of swadeshi agitation, even though moderates made sincere efforts to achieve communal amity, considerable numbers of extremists, often viewing Muslim rioters as mercenary agents of the British, exacerbated communal feelings and threatened to turn any form of mass nationalist politics against itself.

Tagore's initial response to the extreme turns of swadeshi politics was silence, but by late 1907 he was writing important essays that indicated decisive shifts from his earlier positions. First, he attacked the prejudice of Hindus against Muslims, arguing that the problem was one not of political manipulation so much as of the fact that religious difference could be used at all as the basis for social conflict: he wrote, "Satan cannot enter till he finds a flaw."[4] Tagore further suggested that prejudice was predicated on unacceptable social and economic disparities; he wrote that the boycott had not taken into account the economic position of the masses— indeed, that it had been imposed on them through methods of social ostracism that were clearly part of the problem rather than the solution. To remedy these structural impediments to any genuine national movement, Tagore, anticipating Gandhi's constructive program, emphasized social reform and village work. More generally, Tagore no longer advocated a return to the glorious traditions of Hinduism but argued instead for the upending of caste divisions, religious intolerance, and social snobbery. Having witnessed what he took to be the dangers of reinvoking traditional religious values in swadeshi agitation—the symbols, songs, and rituals of the movement—he began to call for the modernizing of India.

It could be argued that Gandhi's emphasis on social reform and the constructive movement some years later was tolerated only because he also established for himself a remarkably astute command over the political organization of the Congress party and the reputation as the only leader who could genuinely mobilize mass political action. In any case, Tagore's disillusionment with politics led him to disavow any involvement in formal political action, and his call for constructive rural work ended up, devoid as it was of any complementary political platform, sounding tame and irrelevant. By the time he wrote *Home and the World*,[5] he was aware of his growing marginalization from the mainstream politics of nationalism. And so Nikhil became a symbol of Tagore's own predicament; though he was a progressive zamindar who had attempted to introduce self-reliance and home manufactures long before it had become fashionable to do so, he was seen as politically naive and hopelessly idealist by the political figures of the time, most dramatically through the contempt and ridicule of the figure of Sandip.

Ray's film is remarkably faithful to Tagore's novel, though it inevitably fails to capture the discursive reflectivity that Tagore achieved by telling his story through the consecutive and overlapping first-person stories of the three characters of the triangle. Perhaps the greatest cost of the translation from novel to film is the loss of the power and autonomy of Bimala's voice, her self-conscious sense of the tortured passage to the outer world of politics and passion. Bimala seems fully aware that she is being pulled toward something both dangerous and deceptive, that Sandip's power over her makes her misrecognize the goodness of her husband and the manipulativeness of Sandip's attention. And Tagore demonstrates how Bimala's voice struggles against momentous odds to speak itself; one of the most powerful lines of the novel comes when Sandip's speech is repeated by Bimala. The tropes of nation, deity, and woman fold together, collapsing the dangers of religious rhetoric and the power of Sandip's sexual attraction, when Bimala reports Sandip as saying, "Have I not told you that, in you, I visualize the Shakti of our country? The geography of a country is not the whole truth. No one can give up his life for a map! When I see you before me, then only do I realise how lovely my country is."[6] Some pages later Bimala confesses, "When, in Sandip's appeals, his worship of the country gets to be subtly interwoven with his worship of me, then does my blood dance, indeed, and the barriers of my hesitation totter. . . . I felt that my resplendent womanhood made me indeed a goddess . . . Why does not my voice find a word, some audible cry, which would be like a sacred spell to my country for its fire initiation?"[7] And so the real transgression Tagore decries is revealed; the slippery movement between desire, devotion, and demagoguery is the result of the precipitant passage down the corridor leading from the home to a world that has been shaped without any of the moral protections of the home.

Tagore's despair about the direction of nationalist politics is expressed clearly even in Sandip's reflections about his own political strategy: "With our nature and our traditions we are unable to realise our country as she is, but we can easily bring ourselves to believe in her image. Those who want to do real work must not ignore this fact."[8] Tagore's own sense of the costs of this strategy, as also its fundamentally European origins, emerges most poignantly in Nikhil's conversation with the master, the local schoolteacher who defends Nikhil and yet cautions him against his own self-destructive faith in Bimala: "I tell you, Nikhil, man's history has to be built by the united effort of all the races in the world, and therefore this selling of conscience for political reasons,—this making a fetish of one's country, won't do. I know that Europe does not at heart admit this, but there she has not the right to pose as our teacher. . . . What a terrible epidemic of sin has been brought into our country from foreign lands."[9] The easy linkage of Nikhil's vision of the modern and its apparent genealogical connection to Europe is thus dramatically disrupted; it is Sandip who is most fully, most corruptly, Westernized—not Nikhil. And it is in the very fetishization of the figure of the nation through religion and sexual desire that nationalism too betrays a foreign pedigree; thus the horrible confusion of mother India and erotic lover spills the sin of lustful adultery onto the canvas of modern politics in India. Religion and sentiment bear the burden of Sandip's tragic misrecognition. India's glory—and its nationalist apotheosis—is now rendered inaccessible and unknowable.

And so the passage from the social constraints of a determinate traditional world to enlightened reason, framed in the rational terms of freedom and self-discovery, is hijacked by shortsighted and self-absorbed forms of venality and exclusion that grow out of reason itself. Tagore's novel is in part a critical reflection on the European Enlightenment's relationship to nationalism and colonialism, which both curtailed the possibilities of the new universalism and justified forms of oppression and exploitation that made a mockery of Europe's modernity. Closer to home, the passage provides a powerful allegory of the shift from the Enlightenment terms of the Bengal Renaissance to the political opportunism of terrorism, extremism, and communalism. Nevertheless, Tagore's biography suggests his final sense of the futility of either returning to a traditional Indian world or assuming that the Bengal Enlightenment's enthusiasm for things Western was still acceptable. Instead, Tagore seems to suggest the need to negotiate new relationships between tradition and modernity, between women and men, between the home and the world, formulated in Indian terms. But he does so in the context of his nuanced delineation of the pathos of Nikhil's ambition: not only was his attempt to manufacture soap and cloth ill-conceived; his assurance that freedom and love could be the instant product of enlightenment becomes the tragic precipitant of his own downfall.

Nikhil's faith in the emancipatory project of modernity is reflected early on in the novel; he says, "Up till now Bimala was my home-made Bimala, the product of the confined space and the daily routine of small duties. Did the love which I received from her, I asked myself, come from the deep spring of her heart, or was it merely like the daily provision of pipe water pumped up by the municipal steam-engine of society?"[10] But soon he finds the "the passage from the narrow to the larger world is stormy." When he discovers the effects of freedom on Bimala, he blames her, expostulating that her "infatuation for tyranny" was not socially

produced but "deep down in her nature."[11] As time goes on, he discovers
that the situation is more complicated; although he never loses faith in his
ideal vision, he enigmatically laments, "My house, I now see, was built to
remain empty, because its doors cannot open."[12] But he can never understand the paradoxical character of Bimala's ultimate revelation; at the
very moment she has completed her passage, she knows that she is lost:
"But women live on the trust of their surroundings,—this is their whole
world. If once it is out that this trust has been secretly betrayed, their
place in their world is lost."[13]

So much for the world to which Nikhil had tried to entreat her; even he
is not sure at the end of the story whether the devastating misunderstand-
ings between him and Bimala might ever be made good.[14] The evacuation
of the home has led to the hollowing out of her world, and at the moment
she falls back at the feet of her husband as her god he disappears forever;
modernist narrative turns into epic in the overdetermined moral tragedy
of the conclusion.

Tagore's use of desire to drive the tension and action of the novel ironically works to conceal Nikhil's own relentless and imperious desire to
shape Bimala in the image of his own modern god, both to fulfill himself
(assuring him that she loves him genuinely) and to liberate her in his own
terms (he compels her to submit to this plan). The displacement of male
desire onto women, even when women's interests are most eloquently at
stake, becomes, whether Tagore, or for that matter Ray, is fully aware of
it, a paradoxical recapitulation of the limits of tradition so excoriated by
Bengali modernizers at the same time that it reminds us of the contradictory position of women in the projects of social reform and cultural modernity in India since the nineteenth century.

Although Ray's film is not an intervention in contemporary political debates in the same direct sense as Tagore's novel so clearly was, the film
raises many of the same questions about the relationship of women—and
by extension the nature of the home, understandings of marriage, the
predicament of love, the meanings of caste, and the reinventions of tradition—to the project of modernity and the history of nationalist politics.
Significantly, in the ten years that have passed since Ray released the film,
these issues have become even more pressing, and the threats of communalism, as well as the related risks of mass political mobilization, lend
further urgency to the historical problematic of both novel and film. And,
with renewed debates over sati, secularism, and Muslim personal law, the
role of women has achieved critical currency in the cultural politics of
South Asia once again.

Ray's allusion to sati was meant to symbolize the pathos of Bimala's position; despite her excursion outside the home she must return with a vengeance, to the lot of the traditional widow. But if sati is now used to establish the terms of tradition in cultural debates in India, it is important to stress the extent to which tradition itself is a category that could come into existence only with modernity. This is not to argue that nothing changes in history, or that a variety of "traditional" practices did not take place, or even that "modernity" has only a phantomlike existence either in India or in Europe, but rather to note that the idea of a static traditional world as antonym to the dynamic modern world could emerge only with the modern world, at the precise moment it began to present itself as new, progressive, universal, and—perhaps both most important and most contradictory—Western. This is so both in a general categorical sense and in a wide variety of substantive historical cases. I have elsewhere argued that caste—as a traditional, essentially Indian, foundationally religious, atavistically hierarchical, social and ritual institution—was a colonial construction; which is to say that it was produced out of the entwined discursive projects and historical effects of colonial rule.[15]

The very terms used to define tradition have themselves been changed dramatically by colonial history. Religion, for example, often taken to be the key sign of difference between old and new, tradition and modernity, East and West, became only an autonomous domain and specifically privileged category under the weight of colonial efforts to contain difference and control what were seen as the most disruptive consequences of colonial rule. Lata Mani has convincingly argued that religion became mobilized both as an explanation for sati and as the domain in which any effort to suppress it had to seek official sanction.[16] When the British sought to prohibit sati to assuage their own horror at the rite and send a clear message about the civilizing mission of colonialism, they established a scripturalist method for assessing the question of religious justification, exposing myriad contradictions in the social and cultural performance of sati at the same time that it gave unprecedented and ostensibly unified authority to certain texts and their interpreters for advising government about a range of extremely important issues.

If sati is no longer a transparent trope for the traditional subjection of women, and its abolition no more the story of the modern march of progress, an examination of Bimala's predecessors in the walk out of the home into the world can further deepen our sense of the contradictions of colonialism's impact on women in India. Although a major source of difficulty in the Indian context is the mutually embedded character of Westernization and modernization, we must not forget that feminist historiography has made the liberation of women in relation to the emergence of bourgeois social forms in the West a similar tale of contradiction.

Modernity was not a problem in India merely because it was linked to colonial rule.

Nevertheless, when eminent Bengali intellectuals and activists advocated social reform in areas related to women, they necessarily echoed colonial denunciations of Indian society. Given the colonial linkage of a modernizing, universalizing, reformist discourse with British condemnation of Indian society in cases such as sati, no Indian reformer could fail to feel a kind of civilizational ambivalence when arguing for progress in women's issues. If women were used as a measure of civility, they also became the fundamental symbol of tradition. The colonial collision of tradition and modernity took place in a succession of contests over women's bodies.

After sati, the two major issues confronting social reformers in nineteenth-century India concerned prohibitions on the remarriage of widows, and the problem of child marriage, contested principally through attempts to legislate the raising of the age of consent. Directed to the opposite ends of women's lives, the issues were related in the sense that many women were widowed at an early age, some even before they cohabited with their husbands. Both these issues provided platforms for a variety of concerns about women, freeing them from the worst abuses of traditional institutions that ironically seemed to grow stronger in the early years of colonial rule, both because of reaction to the West and because the escalating character of social mobility led increasing numbers of groups to emulate upper-caste mores, the very ones most restrictive to women. At the edges of these debates came calls for changing the character of marriage itself, making the wife a loving and supportive companion to her husband rather than a servile subordinate in an extended family network of relations whose principal status accrued from motherhood. Thus Nikhil was rehearsing a critical trope of modernity in his own passionate efforts to force Bimala to love him freely as well as to share his life and his agency. But the obstacles to companionate marriage throughout the nineteenth century and well into the twentieth were multiple, ranging from the inscription of male anxiety onto virtually every status position accorded to women in the household to significant age differentials, the lack of emphasis on female education, and the very solidity of the gendered boundaries between the private and the public.

In the early nineteenth century, attempts by missionary groups to provide opportunities for women to gain some education only deepened concerns that education would lead to conversion and the loss of traditional values. Partha Chatterjee has noted how salient, in much of the literature on women in the nineteenth century, were concerns about the "threatened Westernization of Bengali women."[17] In particular, there was a great deal of ridicule about the idea of a Bengali woman trying to imitate the ways of a memsaheb, wearing Western clothes, cosmetics, and jewelry, reading novels and romances, riding in open carriages. But as time went on, it became clear that education could be controlled and adapted to indigenous needs. Education could be used to train women to become better mothers and homemakers, fulfilling the domestic and reproductive projects of bourgeois Bengali society. Women could leave the home, but only to make the home a far better place than it was before.[18]

This resolution differed markedly in details, and was never fully satisfactory. But it is striking how a bourgeois cult of domesticity worked to displace the centrality of women's issues to nationalist politics. Whereas the nineteenth century had put such issues as widow remarriage and the age of consent at the forefront of public debate, women emerged in the twentieth century as Gandhi's self-sacrificing helpers in a movement dedicated now to political emancipation on the one hand and the abolition of such institutions as untouchability on the other. Partha Chatterjee has argued that the explanation for this phenomenon is that nationalist politics consigned women, and women's issues, to a new kind of inner sphere to be kept closed off from the colonial gaze. The new nationalist patriarchy justified itself by using refigured oppositions of home/world, inner/outer, spiritual/material, and so on, to contain the threat that women's issues, and women's emancipation, posed to nationalist politics.[19] Civilizational ambivalence not only undermined the career of social reform but also helped to reinvent traditional India by making women guardians of the transformed home, with the responsibility to protect the integrity of the men who trafficked in the deracinated discourses of the nationalist world.

But if the nationalist imaginary freed modernity from its nineteenth-century commitments to social reform and the cultural politics of private spheres, Tagore refused to follow suit. For Tagore, the linkage of modernity with both Nikhil and Sandip—with imperious and misplaced idealism in the first figure and cynical, manipulative, explosive materialism in the second—suggests precisely the failure of colonial nationalism; the narrative closure of death and widowhood in *The Home and the World* marks out the inevitable limits of the career of modernity in India, the likelihood that misreadings and rereadings of tradition will swallow up the promise of modernity through the relentless narratives of fatal appropriation and misrecognition. For artists such as Tagore and Ray, working in extremely different historical milieus and political contexts, the only discernible bottom line to this predicament seems to rest in the compelling project of artistic production itself, the sense that art must contest politics and complicate the categories used to think about contemporary India. When read literally, this position has affiliated Tagore and Ray to reputations of political conservatism; but it now seems possible to discern a disturbing critical vision in their work. For when art is opposed to politics in the same way that terms such as *tradition* and *modernity, women* and *men, home* and *the world* are set against each other, we can recognize that the categories themselves are under interrogation. It is time to return both to Ray's film and to the contemporary discussion about the character of modernity in India that necessarily frames our viewing of this film today.

In this, our postmodern, age it is fashionable to critique the modern. With all the pieties that are mouthed about the slippery surfaces, depthless interiors, nostalgic pasts, referential simulacra, and fragmentary particles of the postmodern world, and their connection to the critical assessment of modernist totalizations, master narratives, liberal mystifications, universalist rhetoric, scientific hubris, and so on, it is useful to remember that the critique of the modern began in the colonial world. The terms in which this critique was developed often parodied Western characterizations of India; the spirituality of India was turned from an indictment to a claim for affiliation with higher powers and values—the economic success of the West, the triumph of colonialism itself, was attributed to the baneful influence of materialism and self-interest. But the point is that the Indian encounter with the West led to sustained criticism of the West itself and culminated in the colonial period with the well-known assertions by Gandhi that India should not blindly mimic the colonizers, that India had much to offer the West in its inevitable crises and moral bankruptcies.

Criticisms of the modern West, from Vivekenanda to Tagore to Gandhi, are today being echoed, even as they are deployed in a new contemporary theoretical idiom, by social critics such as Ashis Nandy.[20] Nandy, who turns his aim both at the legacies of colonialism and at the postcolonial conceits of modernism, has written that "it has become more and more apparent that genocides, ecodisasters and ethnocides are but the underside of corrupt sciences and psychopathic technologies wedded to new secular hierarchies. . . . The ancient forces of human greed and violence, one recognizes, have merely found a new legitimacy in anthropocentric doctrines of secular salvation, in the ideologies of progress, normality and hyper-masculinity, and in theories of cumulative growth."[21] Nandy uses as one of his examples Iswar Chandra Vidyasagar (1820–91), who though profoundly influenced by Western rationalism committed himself to the formulation of dissenting positions in indigenous terms— although Mohandas Gandhi is the figure who usually makes the ultimate point. Nandy seeks to follow these examples by formulating an "unheroic but critical traditionalism: . . . the tradition of reinterpretation of traditions to create new traditions."[22]

Nandy's position provides an important critical sense of the limits of

Nehruvian socialism in postcolonial India; much of his argument tren-
chantly identifies the uses made of science, technology, and ideologies of
progress by state power that too rarely interrogates its own continuities with colonialism, its inevitable partialities and excesses. Nandy is
also particularly good when he insists that much of the ethnic and religious conflict in contemporary India is not the result of the resurgence of
precolonial traditions but the specific outcome of postcolonial processes
of state formation and political mobilization, interestingly echoing Tagore's critical sense of swadeshi politics. But Nandy treads on extremely
dangerous ground when he goes on to link secularism, as an ideology
mandating state exclusion of religion from politics and civil respect for all
religious faiths, with the worst excesses of postcolonial modernism in
India. He proposes that secularism was "introduced into Indian public
life in a big way in the early decades of the century by a clutch of Westernized Indians—seduced or brainwashed by the ethnocidal, colonial theories of history—to subvert and discredit the traditional concepts of inter-
religious tolerance that had allowed the thousands of communities living
in the subcontinent to co-survive in neighborliness."[23] In an article in
which he declares himself not to be secularist, he makes the charge that
"to accept the ideology of secularism is to accept the ideologies of progress and modernity as the new justifications of domination, and the use of
violence to sustain these ideologies as the new opiates of the masses."[24]
This seems to be not simply provocative but irresponsible, given the fact
that it is the critics of secularism, in contexts such as the dispute over the
mosque in Ayodhya, who have advocated violence in the name of religion. Although he engages the Enlightenment project with the combined
theoretical firepower of Mahatma Gandhi and Michel Foucault, Nandy's
concerns about modernity make him in the end disturbingly uncritical of
tradition and naively unaware of the impossibility of recuperating old
traditions of religious tolerance in the postcolonial context that is India
today.

   Thus perhaps we can appreciate all the more in retrospect the degree to
which the residual idealism of Tagore and Ray, as well as their clear sense
of the inevitable loss associated with any nostalgia for the past, maintains
the necessary edge for their extraordinarily critical vision of modernity.
Neither Tagore nor Ray would share the conviction of those unnamed
villains of Nandy's polemic who might continue to feel, whether sincerely
or not, that rigorous adherence to secularist values will provide sufficient
grounds for the avoidance of communalist conflict.

   But they also know that tradition can no longer be recuperated without
coming to terms with the myriad effects of modernity. Nikhil fails because of his overzealous and fanatical faith in freedom, not because of his
secularism and his clear distrust of the uses made of religion by political

leaders. And Sandip makes it clear that the dangerous politics of uncondi-
tional nationalism depend not upon allegiance to secularism, contra
Nandy, as much as on complicity in the proliferation of devotion, deifica-
tion, and displaced desire that requires a modern nationalist language of
religion. And so it is art rather than tradition that can hold modern reality
at an angle to itself, that can provide the grounds of critical distance without abdicating the responsibility of staking out these grounds in the first
place.

Tagore's art was celebrated even as it frequently played an important
role in discussions and debates within India, and particularly within Bengal, about the way to define what was most distinctive about India, as
well as how to chart out a course in the struggles against the forces of
poverty, exploitation, colonialism, and modern change. Once Tagore
began to opt out of direct political struggle, roughly at the same time that
Bengal became less visible than other newly important regions in defining
Indian strategies for nationalist politics, his work continued to be heralded as a symbol of Indian artistic glory and as textual solace for the
daily traumas of the colonial predicament. Tagore continues to this day
to be seen as the major cultural figure of India's nationalist struggle,
though he has been strangely ignored in most recent writings on nationalist intellectual history.[25] And yet few Bengali intellectuals and artists
could conceive of their own cultural practices without paying elaborate
tribute to the influence of Tagore in their life and art.

Satyajit Ray's relationship to his times, to contemporary politics, as
well as to the issues of tradition, modernity, art, and nationalism, is far
more difficult to characterize than in the case of Tagore. Although Ray
was born into the same Bengali elite background, that of the bhadralok,
he came of age in the final years of the Raj, and always stayed away from
politics. Tagore was clearly a towering presence in his life, and he studied
at Tagore's rural University in Santiniketan for several years before join-
ing a British advertising firm in Calcutta in 1943. Working as a commercial artist, Ray honed his drawing and design skills and supported himself
in the difficult years of the war. Although he clearly had great talent in
graphic art, his great passion was music, a passion later reflected in his
meticulous attention to the musical scores of his films. Soon after India's
independence, Ray organized a film society in Calcutta and began for the
first time to imagine putting art and music together. As early as 1948, Ray
had begun a project for a film by writing a script for *The Home and the
World*, a plan that fell apart because Ray was concerned that his col-
laborators were too influenced by Hollywood. In 1949 Ray met Renoir,
who was in Calcutta to make the film *The River*, and he hung around the
set and gave advice to Renoir on the script. By 1950, Ray had committed
himself to the project of filming *Pather Panchali*, though it took five years

of heroic effort and extraordinary adversity to make what most observers still believe is his most haunting and beautiful film.[26]

The first showing of *Pather Panchali* was in New York, at the Museum of Modern Art. Ray's success in film, and indeed his reputation in India, was due largely to the enthusiastic acclaim his films received in the West, though Ray resolutely remained in Calcutta and conceived of himself as an Indian filmmaker. And Ray continued to work through the extraordinary influence of Tagore on him and his cultural milieu through filming *Charulata, Three Daughters, The Goddess,* and finally *Home and the World.* Bengalis have often claimed that Tagore's influence was always limited by the difficulty of translation; and interestingly, only Ray has fully succeeded in transcribing Tagore's genius in another language, the language of film.

It is difficult to emphasize the beauty, and choreographical exquisiteness, of Ray's films, the way narrative is inscribed in architectural interiors, lighting angles and physiognomic close-ups, musical scores and the lyrical pace of cinematic story. Drawing upon diverse influences, Ray made films that were very much his own, formulating his own version of Indian modernist cinema. Ray has always worked against formidable odds—small budgets, inadequate technology, limited audiences, and an unaccommodating film industry—but has used these odds to maintain maximum control over the making of his films and the development of his projects. He has frequently written the script, sketched the scenes, held the camera, and composed the music for films that bear his personal imprint in ways that seem virtually unthinkable in the present age of Hollywood.

Although Ray quickly became recognized as a postcolonial artist of world renown, he stayed at home and worked most comfortably, and powerfully, out of his home. Writings about Ray depict him either behind the camera on the studied and scripted sets for his films or in the cluttered comfort of his central Calcutta flat. Unlike other postcolonial figures such as Naipaul and Rushdie, Ray's postcolonial predicament has never been lodged in his homelessness. Whereas Naipaul's modernist lament has always seemed aimed at his own postcolonial inability to claim an authentic genealogy for his own civilizational ambivalence, and Rushdie's postmodernist critique directed at the inchoate displacements of both the traditional and the modern in the contemporary diaspora of South Asia, Ray has looked comfortably inward, and backward, with the help and inspiration of Tagore. But in this era of the transnational dislodgement of identities, when postcoloniality seems to stand for everything except the quiet desperation of those who have never left their homes for the world, it is perhaps high time to revision the world through Ray's cinematic sensibility. For it is still the case that for many in places like Calcutta the world continues to be that contested terrain where the promises of the

New World are soured by the contradictions of modernity, mired in impersonal markets, perpetual poverty, alienating anonymity, the disparities of class, and the tragic constraints of free choice. For many the postcolonial world lives out its off-centered excesses within the very homes that Ray has so powerfully explored in his films.

Ray's modernist realism may seem old fashioned in an age of magical realism, but films such as *The Home and the World* continue to possess extraordinary power at the same time that they remind us that the agonistic relationship between tradition and modernity is as troubling today as it was in earlier eras. Ray's cosmopolitan perspective makes it clear that the old worlds of zamindars and court artists are not used to measure the depravity of the new in order to argue for the old. On the contrary, these worlds make it especially clear that there is no going back, even as it is never clear where one should now set one's sights. Ray may have been criticized for his apparently unprogressive and anti-utopian tendency to emphasize what was being lost in the old and sacrificed in the new, and he may be increasingly ignored for his dated perspectives, but he raised concerns that are now at issue in the most contemporary of postcolonial critiques.

At a time when critical studies of colonialism insist that we attend to the ambivalent status of any colonial subject, situating the colonial predicament in a moral narrative of European responsibility, I should perhaps put more emphasis on reading the complex play of power and domination in the figuration of modernity as a kind of impossible object—a utopia idealized through exclusion rather than failure—for characters such as Nikhil and Sandip. At the same time, Ray seems to argue, obsessive attention to colonialism as a monolithic and overdetermining presence tends also to obscure the linkages between colonial and postcolonial predicaments, ironically allowing the idealization of modernity while diverting critical attention away from it.[27] Tagore anticipated this concern by worrying that political nationalism too readily lost sight of more wide-ranging critiques of the colonizers, their teeming though complacent cultural inheritance and their alluring though contradictory political institutions. And Ray's reading of Tagore leaves out the political not only because he rarely took on explicitly political subjects but also because he cared more passionately about the ambivalence of his position as a modern subject, a subjectivity not unrelated to his growing up in late-colonial Calcutta but also part of his love of Beethoven, John Ford, and Eisenstein. Neither Tagore nor Ray disavowed the pervasive reality of colonialism—it is the distant thunder behind much of the pathos they surveyed—but their own sense of ambivalent alterities engaged colonialism in ways that critical colonial studies have only dimly prepared us for.[28]

Pleasure and politics, intimacy and commitment, tradition and
modernity—all are reflected in the mirror of Bimala's gaze.

Ray's film asks powerful questions about the character of India's nationalist past—about the costs of revolutionary politics, the nuances of
dispassionate reflection, the nostalgia for lost pasts, and the contradictions of modernity in India today. The film also evokes the problematic
relationship of the political to those private realms of experience and action that until recently were kept outside the focus of discussions about
nationalism and postcoloniality. By cinematically depicting how the
world infiltrates the very fabric of the home—both the furnishings of the
innermost zenana and the intimate scenes and dramas around domesticity, familial relations, love, and sexuality—Ray not only allegorizes but
also disturbs the boundaries and constituent categories of the modern.
Bimala's body—her shorn head, her sari-draped figure, the fervent devo-
tionalism of her feelings for the nation and the clumsiness and ultimate
disavowal of her passion for Sandip—becomes the victimized bearer of
the great betrayal of modern nationalism. Bimila's devastated face in the
final shot of the film, when she turns into the sad reflection of her widowed sister-in-law, expresses personal tragedy at the same time that it
reveals the unbearable cost of neglecting the irreduceable banality of
India's contemporary disaffection.

When Nikhil entreated Bimala to come out of the home and enter the
world, he was confident he could contain the danger of her passage. His
failure to transcend his own self-absorbed ambition, and his ultimate in-

ability to control the apotheosis of her enlightenment, recapitulates the failure of modernism itself. Instead of release we see new forms of confinement, expressed both by the specter of communal violence and the reiteration of traditional enslavement. Instead of enlightenment, we encounter the reactive dialectic of modernity's double, tradition gone bad. We lose both the promise of the new and the solace of the old. In this allegorical tale told by Tagore and Ray, we run aground against the limits of national modernity and the excesses of fundamentalist ideology.

At the end of the story, Bimala loses her voice for the last time. Her pleasure in playing out the mimetic drama of modernity, shown so vividly when she was singing with her English governess a sweet song about the impossible fantasy of recovering lost love after years of wandering, is disrupted first by Nikhil's own intrusiveness in her life—his narcissistic relationship to both love and the home—and much later by Nikhil's peculiar heroism—his final but selfish sacrifice. Pleasure and politics, commitment and courage—the home and the world—become the ultimate victims of what in the end is a very old story. Bimala's body carries the burden of this story, and she is punished despite Nikhil's well-meaning assurance that she had done nothing wrong. And so the early images of Bimila's ornamentation and experimentation fade away, and the opening image of fire flashes up over and over after the lights come back on. The film, at times painfully slow and sternly theatrical, leaves us in crisis over the dilemmas of modernity, gender, politics, love, and narrative—dilemmas that we academics would no doubt rather control with the dispassionate apparatus of our professional trade. But as we do so, perhaps we do nothing more than control the extent to which our own art, such as it is, can engage—at a slight angle—the fractured realities of the postcolonial world shown to us so brilliantly by Ray.

3

Eijanaika

JAPANESE MODERNIZATION AND
THE CARNIVAL OF TIME

THOMAS KEIRSTEAD AND DEIDRE LYNCH

> The new historian, the genealogist, will know
> what to make of this masquerade. He will not
> be too serious to enjoy it; on the contrary, he
> will push the masquerade to its limit and pre-
> pare the great carnival of time where masks are
> constantly reappearing.
> —*Michel Foucault, "Nietzsche, Genealogy,*
> *History"*[1]

THE MEIJI RESTORATION provides a reference point for almost all histories of Japan. Conventionally heralded as the founding moment of the
modern Japanese state, the Restoration has been declared a bona fide
event, a signifier of change toward which histories lead or from which
they depart. Yet this is a curious event on which to found a nation. The
"restoration of imperial rule" that was proclaimed on 3 January 1868 in
the name of the sixteen-year-old monarch signaled precisely nothing. It
marked neither the end of the Tokugawa Shogunate (the last Tokugawa
Shogun had resigned two months earlier) nor the beginning of a new era
(literally, since the restored reign would not acquire the name Meiji until
late in the year); it did not sweep aside organs of government or realign
class structures (though this would follow). Instead, the Meiji Restoration "restored" to the nation a line of monarchs that, it was averred, had
never been broken; it brought back something that had never been absent. The very name by which the event is known captures some of this
ambiguity. *Meiji ishin*, the designation adopted by imperial decree in
1870, negotiates delicately between alternative constructions prominent
in contemporary discourses: *ishin*, a Confucian term connoting something like "to promote the new," was sufficiently flexible to accommodate definitions of restoration as both an innovation and a return, as a

change inaugurating Japan's progress toward modernity and a mere return to things as they were.[2]

Set on the eve of the Restoration, Imamura Shōhei's *Eijanaika* alludes repeatedly to issues that have an established place in the historiography of the era: the schemes of samurai from Satsuma and Chōshū to overthrow the Shogunate, the effects of foreign contact, the baleful economic condition of the country (beset by inflation and political uncertainty). The film uses these materials to reroute the master narratives of Restoration and modernization. Instead of the Meiji Restoration, Imamura presents us with a pastiche of historical possibilities, as in a scene near the beginning of the film that juxtaposes two pieces of history. Passing through his shop, Kinzō, boss of the pleasure quarter in which most of the action takes place, picks up two broadsheets his men have prepared: one remarks on the fourfold increase in rice prices; the other announces the arrival of an elephant. Moments later the film reenacts the entry of this elephant—one of the first ever seen in Japan—into the district.[3] This, the only historical event faithfully reproduced in the film, is of course a nonevent, an insignificant episode in Japan's cultural history. Although the rising price of rice supplies motive for a narrative that moves from economic distress to political unrest and thus to the Restoration, nothing happened as a consequence of the elephant's arrival. By placing the two on the same plane *Eijanaika* destabilizes the conventional narrative line. The film engages what many regard as a revolutionary moment in Japanese history—the birth of the modern nation—but its allusions to the historical do not confirm the audience in its possession of the historical capital, the "cultural heritage of . . . dates, events and characters" that "allows [it] to find its bearings."[4]

Instead *Eijanaika* frustrates expectations. Everything seems out of place. Characters who ought to be nameable cannot be named; events that should be recognizable are not. The film hints repeatedly at events and characters that every Japanese person knows lead to modern Japan, only to refuse to engage them. This is only fitting, since the film is inspired by one of the most enigmatic episodes in the history of the Restoration era. From the fall of 1867 through early spring of the following year, commoners throughout Japan took to the streets in frenzied celebrations. Most of Japan's major cities, from Hiroshima in the west to Edo (present-day Tokyo) in the east, were visited by these dancing crowds, whose songs were punctuated by the refrain *eijanaika*, "Why not? What the hell!" Compared to the major events in Restoration historiography—from the arrival of Commodore Perry's Black Ships and the opening of the country in 1853 to the Shogunate's last-ditch efforts in 1866 and 1867 to work out a compromise with the rebellious domains—these outbursts have little narrative potential. The people danced, authorities by and large paid them no heed, things returned to normal. Mainstream histories thus tend to dismiss the riots as a popular sideshow to the political drama acted out by the samurai elite. If the riots occasion comment at all it is merely because their outbreak coincides with the crucial period immediately preceding the Meiji Restoration.[5]

The *eijanaika* disorders are, moreover, hard to classify. Though the dancers sometimes chanted political slogans, the outbursts cannot really be considered in the tradition of popular unrest, since the crowds neither demanded tax relief nor remonstrated against corrupt officials. The dancing, feasting, drinking, and cross-dressing, the mood of anarchic release captured in the chant "Why not? What the hell!" identify *eijanaika* with village festivals. This, however, slights an important element: a pervasive demand for "world renewal" (*yonaoshi*), expressive of a kind of millennial consciousness, distinguishes *eijanaika* from ordinary festivals. Since the dancing was sparked by charms—usually pieces of paper printed with the name of a deity—falling from the sky, some histories have aligned it with the mass pilgrimages to Ise Shrine that erupted periodically during the Tokugawa period. Again, though, *eijanaika* seems to lack the direction of these pilgrimages: it had no clear objective like the Grand Shrine.

"What the hell!" is too ambiguous a refrain. It suggests a purposelessness that history written in a linear mode cannot easily accommodate. Only by borrowing some of the historical capital invested in the Restoration, "the model event in Japanese history,"[6] can historical narrative give meaning to these crowds and read the rioting as sign of the raw energy of the people unleashed in a time of political uncertainty.

Eijanaika carnivalizes this standard narrative. Imamura's version of the era emphasizes the margins, bodily pleasure, the "festive laughter" of the crowd swept up in the antilogic of "What the hell!"[7] Yet *Eijanaika*'s is not simply a view from below. Imamura draws on the carnivalesque to unsettle identities and suspend hierarchies, in particular those hierarchies that anchor the orthodox history of the nation. The proper rank and order of events are thrown into question by a narrative that treats the arrival of an elephant as a historical event on par with the arrival of the nation. This parodic equation of the unquestioned founding event and an unknown incident refuses history its accustomed role, in which it transforms "life into destiny, a memory into a useful act, duration into an orientated and meaningful time."[8]

Eijanaika's critique of the practice of history echoes—with certain decisive differences—concerns raised by a strain of Japanese historiography known as "people's history" (*minshūshi*).[9] Championing the people (*minshū*) against the elite and the "authentic" traditions of the village against the invented traditions of the state, people's history has sparked interest in precisely the kinds of subjects that concern *Eijanaika*. Peasant beliefs, popular entertainments, the *eijanaika* outbursts themselves—all are topics made respectable by people's history.

If, in a sense, people's history made Imamura's film possible, it nonetheless supplies the material for Imamura's critique of historical reasoning. For, its anti-elite and anti-state attitude notwithstanding, people's history positions an abstract and essentialized "people" as the agents of history. Although people's historians tend toward an expansive definition of the people—variously described as consisting of "the lower classes" or simply "the ruled"—it is evident that certain individuals do not qualify for membership.[10] The people belong to the village, to an agricultural "folk world" presided over by "conventional morality" (*tsū-zoku dōtoku*), where harmony, industry, and self-discipline prevail; urban dwellers, tainted it seems by proximity to the political and economic centers where Japan's modernization was carried out, are seen as vagrants, "forced out, evicted from the village . . . exiled from the only society that matters."[11] Purified of such misfits, the people can also be presented as a collective. Thus Irokawa Daikichi, perhaps the most influential of the people's historians, writes with equanimity about "the people" or "the Japanese masses" as if they constituted a single, undifferentiated body, an "it" rather than a "they." Even when his subjects are clearly uncommon, he reclaims them for the people by portraying them as "spokesmen," as articulators of an otherwise inarticulate popular consciousness.[12] Intended as a progressive counterweight to the top-heavy and homogenized past proffered by the state, people's history predicates its vision of the past on a similarly homogenized folk. Therefore, while "the people" may not, as in other kinds of history, coincide with that political abstraction known as the state, it nonetheless has an essence that can be described; it has what all authentic Japanese must have seemingly as a condition of their being—a *furusato*, a hometown, a rural place of origin.

In this respect, the trajectory of people's history intersects with that of an argument (equally prevalent in Japan and the West) that insists on the "uniqueness" and homogeneity of Japanese society. Active in a stunning variety of discourses, this argument furthers what Masao Miyoshi calls the myth of "we Japanese": " 'We are harmonious in Japan,' 'rice is our soul. . . ,' 'we work harder in Japan,' 'we Japanese are moral,' . . . Such innocuous-sounding statements are gathered together to construct an exclusivist myth of Japanese culture, changeless and pure."[13] People's history, Imamura seems to suggest, offers a disturbingly similar vision of the Japanese people as a unitary collectivity among whom *Eijanaika*'s shift-

less entertainers, thieves, beggars, con men, and conniving entrepreneurs
have no place. And surely Imamura had in mind as well his protagonists'
current counterparts: Koreans, immigrant workers, Ryukyuans, Japanese
who have lived abroad, and others whom the Japanese state and media
cast as outsiders or "homeless" people.

To make "the people" an abstraction is a more difficult task when the
historian's medium is film rather than the written word. Film assembles
its narrative order from sounds and images—physical elements that not
only contribute to the narrative but also, invariably, exceed it, occasion-
ing a surplus of meaning.[14] The first eight shots of *Eijanaika* offer an
allegory about what it means to *watch* people make history: Imamura pits
perceptual pleasure against secure historical knowledge, knowledge of a
kind guaranteed when history has a monolithic central subject, one unifying the atomistic elements of the past.[15]

In this prologue the camera tracks through the pleasure quarter of
Ryōgoku without indicating whose path it is that we should follow
through the crowded streets, where innumerable figures seem to move in
innumerable directions. We miss the editing that would organize our
point of view. Refusing the technique that is a staple of Hollywood historical film, Imamura does not mobilize our identification with a singular yet
typical character whose very individuality will be derived "from the historical peculiarity of [his] age" and whose look will relay the film's own
attitude to the historical.[16] Instead of matching audience and character
perspectives and thereby anchoring historiographic authority, Imamura's
camera makes us spectators to the lurid spectacles provided by the show
people who populate the Ryōgoku tent shows—among them, a lady
sumo wrestler, a monster-woman with a serpentine neck that can telescope out of her shoulders, a monster-man with eyes that can pop out of
his head. Catching sight of the latter two, the film audience is itself caught
looking. In the case of the long-necked woman, the audience is caught
looking at someone who enjoys precisely that viewpoint, above the
crowd, that the spectator has been denied.

Even before its titles scroll across the screen, *Eijanaika* complicates the
spectacle of a people's history. It decenters the perceptual field (not allowing us to see, yet also confronting us with our libidinal investment in
visual pleasure), and it dislocates the action of history, displacing it to the
impure margins of the polity.[17] The protagonists of *Eijanaika* put a face
on the historian's abstraction of the "minshū," but with their split alle-
giances, their homelessness, they also exceed this function. They call into
question the presumptive unity of history's central subject, much as the
Ryōgoku freak shows surveyed in the film's prologue bank on the spec-
tacular *dis*unity of "the human." *Eijanaika* points to the heterogeneity

and internal antagonisms distinguishing "the people"—to the gender divisions that sustain a patriarchal economy, the exclusions that are operated by Japan's internal colonialism, and the diverse temporalities that are lived by the people's individual representatives.[18]

Thus, Genji, the first character in the film to be named, is first heard speaking English rather than Japanese and is seen in Western-style trousers rather than kimono. Six years before the film's opening, we learn, an American ship saved him from the shipwreck of a coastal freighter. In 1866 Genji returns to Japan as a naturalized American citizen, having spent his time abroad acquiring the desires of a modernizing, self-improving, upwardly mobile citizen, including the desire to be his own master and own his own land (preferably "in America"). Genji is, to cite the terms with which postcolonial theorist Homi Bhabha describes the mixed results of imperialists' civilizing missions, a "reformed colonial subject," "a subject of a difference that is almost the same, but not quite." He is "not white/not quite." A mimic representation of Abraham Lincoln (his ego ideal), Genji confronts the West (an American film audience, or within the film the Anglo-American merchants and diplomats who are drawn into the ongoing political machinations) with a "flawed colonial mimesis." He represents Western norms only partially, and somehow inappropriately, and so can be seen, again following Bhabha, as a "parodist of history . . . [who] inscribe[s] the colonial text [and the narrative of modernization] erratically, eccentrically."[19]

Itoman, whom Genji meets when the shogun's constabulary responds to the return of this native by throwing him into jail, is another character who affronts concepts of national purity and whose interests cannot be assimilated to those of the collective. A native of the Ryukyu islands, Itoman has a history shaped by the violence inflicted on the people of the islands by Satsuma—the daimyo domain that throughout the 1860s also conspires against the Shogunate. The homogenizing version of the Japanese nation that emerged in the aftermath of the Restoration and the Satsuma victory was to make the racial and economic oppression of Itoman's ethnic group a national and nationalist priority.[20]

There is a certain inevitability in the way that these exotics—strangers who are not quite foreigners, and victims, one witting and the other unwitting, of Japanese and Western imperialisms—find their way to the carnival of Ryōgoku. There, Genji rejoins his wife, Iné. Both he and Itoman find work with Kinzō, who is the chief of the tent shows and the carnival's presiding pimp. Genji fits nowhere else but Ryōgoku. In the course of the film he does come to own land in his native village: the villagers, however, expel him from the community. They insist to Genji that he is really an American and that they "don't want Americans working our land." (The

In the shows of the carnival, perceptual pleasure vies with knowledge as history
moves to the margins of the polity.

scene epitomizes Imamura's wry view of the collective spirit—*kyōdōtai*—
and folk morality—*tsūzoku dōtoku*—that earn the unequivocal praise of
the people's historians.) Genji's efforts to return to America are also
foiled: through his own bad timing, through Iné's reluctance to leave
Ryōgoku, and through the bad faith of the American Legation in
Yokohama, which, upon hearing of Genji's altercation with his village
headman, strips him of his citizenship. Genji's repeatedly futile trips to
the port of Yokohama underscore his placelessness. His double exile,
from America and from village Japan, underscores the distance that sepa-
rates him from narrative patterns that might tell his story—narratives
about Westernization and modernization, or, alternately, about a re-
demptive return to indigenous tradition.

Such narratives often depend structurally on the heterosexual couple.
Cinematic convention dictates that the married woman (the woman who
waits up for her wayfaring man, who makes the coffee for the stakeout)
should provide the still point in the turning world of the action film.
Western as well as Japanese myths of history sort out the relations between past and present, placement and mobility, through a gendered division of labor in which women stand for the ahistorical, either for the

point of departure that grounds the adventure of modernity or, indifferently, for truths that have been left behind and that must be rediscovered. Commentary on Imamura's films works with this same binary opposition between men's and women's relation to historicity when it links women's prominent place in these films to Imamura's interest in the survival in modern Japan of the premodern and shamanistic.[21] To be sure, the films as a group define women as survivors and so associate them with the timeless rather than timely;[22] but it is worth noting how *Eijanaika*'s portrayal of Iné complicates this association, thereby raising questions about how thoroughly any of the films endorse the notion of womanhood as a vehicle for tradition.

Genji's reunion with the wife (and the past) he left behind is complicated because Iné too has moved, from country to city; it is complicated because, in Iné's eyes, Genji has stayed the same for six years, while she has not. In Genji's absence, a time of bad harvests in village Japan, Iné was sold into prostitution by her father and brother. (This fate is common to all the women of *Eijanaika*, whether they belong to the peasant or to the samurai classes.) When Genji finds her in Ryōgoku, Iné is starring in a tent show of her own devising that offers the audience the chance to "Tickle the Goddess." Her show is an occasion for her clitoral pleasure, communal hilarity, and manifestations of a divine femininity—at the same that it is an occasion for her commodification, an occasion when Kinzō, Iné's owner, capitalizes on the desires of what the *eijanaika* singers will call "all the impotent men in Edo."[23]

Iné has come to inhabit a simultaneously archaic and modern body. Throughout the film her body functions as a testing ground for relations between tradition and change. Genji scolds her, for instance, when she cites her conviction that she is the reincarnation of a bear ("Granny Bear") as a motive for not emigrating to America. When Iné points to the marks on her body that prove that she is a bear, Genji speaks as a modern man of reason and dismisses the marks as moles. By contrast, when the couple make love, they do so in terms that Iné determines and that she defines as modern, as she demands to know the "American" words for the parts of her body that she wants Genji to attend to.

Iné's tent show calls up the archaic energies of Shinto primitivism, but it also partakes of the temporality of capitalist modernity, in which fashion is the measure of time. The show's novelty-value and Iné's worth within the Ryōgoku economy are threatened when a similar act opens up in the pleasure district across the river. Throughout the film, Iné announces her boredom: she wants change. Where Genji desires America and tries to no avail to set forth on the Western empires' much-traveled modernizing path, where Itoman works for revenge against the Satsuma clan and uses his present to right wrongs committed in the past, Iné desires emancipation from what is given. Perhaps Iné desires a history in a mode not yet written.

> I wonder who scattered these charms first—the gods or the people? It doesn't matter . . .
> —*Iné,* Eijanaika

> We helped it, but I'm not sure who started it.
> —*Comment by a Satsuma samurai during the* eijanaika *dancing,* Eijanaika

> We want to know what *they did*; but between such terms as "they" and "did," subject and action, historical being and historical becoming, opens a slight misfit. This misfit is the mystery of predication, the core puzzle of any historicism.
> —*Alan Liu, "The Power of Formalism: The New Historicism"*[24]

In a film set at the historical moment that is supposed to bring forth the Japanese polity, a new experience of collective identity within the nation-state, Imamura's protagonists decenter the image of the people. The oppressions they experience and the complexity of their relations to the time point up Imamura's sense of the displacements, differences, and political contests that are devalued by models of national wholeness and narratives of national development. For this reason, even in the concluding minutes of the film, when we witness hundreds of *eijanaika* dancers seemingly moving as one, apparently actuated by the same utopian desire, the identity with which Imamura endows the people has to be understood as conjunctural rather than essential.

Furthermore, to even begin to attend to Iné's desire for history in a different mode, we have to acknowledge as well that *Eijanaika* addresses not just *who* makes history but also the nature of that making. That is, *Eijanaika* does not raise just the questions about origins that Iné and the Satsuma samurai pose, as they try to assimilate experience to an orderly history of the *eijanaika* dancing. It also raises questions about what it might mean to *originate* an *action*. National history has, in a classic formulation, been called "a novel of which the people are the author."[25] The historiography of the nation-state and its destiny relies not just on a notion of a unitary and conscious subject of history but also on a notion of an unmediated relation between this consciousness and its expressive means, a relation that allows the subject to make sense. By contrast, one might quote Mikhail Bakhtin on how meaning does "a cartwheel" in the carnival setting to describe how the script of history is inscribed in *Eijanaika*[26]—how it is inscribed, that is, through parodic repetition, equivocation, and chance slips of the tongue. For instance, the myriad written texts embedded in the visuals of the film—banners, broadsheets, and, most important, the paper charms (*ofuda*) that set the crowds dancing—are all messages of indeterminate authoring. Imamura takes pains to remind us, too, that throughout the events of the 1860s rumor, equally authorless, was as often as not the sole basis for the various factions' formulations of political strategy. In the brilliantly edited sequence that exemplifies the indeterminacy of historical causality in the era, a dog with a sun-goddess charm about its neck suddenly appears on the screen just after we have witnessed a political assassination in Kyoto, an action bearing a simultaneously crucial and tangential relation to Restoration-era power shifts. The dog moves forward toward us, only to veer offscreen when it is already in close-up. It instantly reappears, moving laterally, in Edo, where it gambols past the military training grounds where the Shogunate is training its recruits in the use of Civil War surplus rifles. It gambols past the prison where Genji is being flogged for his altercation with his village headman. Finally, the dog is stopped by a poor man in the street who discovers the charm, spreads the word, and thereby spreads the so-called epidemic of popular dissidence from Kyoto to Edo. The motor of history is shown at this moment to inhere not in divine intervention, or in the machinations of elites, or in the people realizing its historical mission, but in chance and in a dog having fun.

Eijanaika suggests the necessity of thinking of historical agency not so much as a fixed point but as a process of circulation, something passing erratically between both elites and commoners, sometimes eluding human jurisdiction altogether. Thus, throughout the film, the Satsuma samurai are confident that Kinzō, as boss of Ryōgoku, is doing their bidding and directing his henchmen to subvert the Shogunate's political authority, whereas Kinzō, to the bewilderment of those who receive his contradictory instructions, is also doing the Shogunate's work, protecting silk merchants from the peasant rioters who aim to smash their establishments as well as stirring up the peasants to do just that. Kinzō, for his part, believes in his own historical agency. He views the inhabitants of Ryōgoku as means through which he will achieve his ends (ambitions realized when the Shogunate grants him a license for a Western-food restaurant). However, Genji, Itoman, and the others eventually tell Kinzō that, having started thieving, "for equality's sake" and with Kinzō's encouragement, they are now having too much fun to stop, even though he wants to rein in their enterprise. Their collective hilarity has a momentum of its own. When, in the film's conclusion, Kinzō relays the will of the shogunal forces and orders the dancers to stop at the river's edge, the crowd ignores him: it dances on, taking possession of the boats that cross the river and of the bridge that leads out of the pleasure district. *Eijanai-ka*'s historiography is constructed out of unintended effects, out of the gaps distancing intentions from their execution.[27]

> From the very first, as though of right, human figures enter film, spilling out of the train, leaving the factory or the photographic congress, *moving*—this is the movies, these are moving pictures.
> —Stephen Heath, "Narrative Space"[28]

As Imamura shows, rumor in the disorders of 1867 represented a peculiar conjunction of too much meaning—a surplus of messages—and of meaninglessness—uncertainty about authorship, intention, and import. Similarly, the production of a forward-moving history is in this depiction of popular movements frustrated by too much action (so that one feels as if history amounts merely to "one damn thing after another," to contingencies that escape narrative ordering) and also frustrated by too little action (by a dearth of actions that can be construed unequivocally as making a change). Moving us from the summer of 1866 to the summer of 1867, the film offers not advance toward the new but repetition instead. We get two virtually identical scenes depicting the nighttime burglaries perpetrated by Kinzō's men and two scenes depicting Genji's fruitless interviews with the American consul.[29] Genji tries to play Abraham Lincoln and emancipate the slaves of Ryōgoku: he buys a prostitute's freedom from her madam, but his action merely enables the woman's father to sell his daughter into prostitution for a second time, commending her for being "doubly filial." When the Ryōgoku tent show opens its 1867 season and features, as its latest novelty, a goddess come to renew the world, the goddess turns out to be the female sumo wrestler in an altered costume. The encounter with the millenarian—with what might be a divine intervention that would bring present time to a halt—fails to impress one audience member, who comments, "Humph, seen her before . . ."

Imamura's effort to rework the hegemonic histories of the Restoration and to reconceive this history in nonlinear terms, as something other than a progress from tradition to modernity, entails a parody of the visual style of samurai movies.[30] It entails, that is, a reworking of the logical premise of these action films—the premise, namely, that a "situation can give rise to an action capable of modifying it."[31] Imamura makes heterodox use of the moving camera. Repeated sequences in *Eijanaika* sacrifice depth in the composition to feature lateral movement that passes from left to right or right to left across the film frame—as in the shots showing us the dog running past the shogunal training grounds; showing Genji and Itoman and other Ryōgoku men moving in single file on their way to commit a burglary or rowing upstream as they escape afterward; or showing rioting peasants rushing one after the other alongside a wall environing a usurious silk merchant's warehouse. In these sequences the relations between camera movement and object movement are conceptualized not in terms of smooth continuity, as in Hollywood cinema, but in terms of contradiction and reversal. Thus, in the protracted tracking shots with which Imamura films these lateral movements, the camera repeatedly gets ahead of the figures it films, thereby undercutting whatever straightforward allegory of advance might be conveyed by the sight of a procession of peasants, hoes and bamboo lances in hand, striding toward their class enemy. When Genji and Itoman run along the riverbank, across the film frame from right to left, the film audience is torn between following them and tracking a file of rifle-bearing shogunal recruits marching in the opposite direction. The composition of the segment seems actuated by the same spirit of contradiction that informs the political strategy Kinzō transmits to his dependents ("But, Boss, that's contradictory!").

While alluding in these ways to the movies' bases in motion, *Eijanaika* features a people's movement that does not go anywhere. From a point of view that the film does much to question, that movement fails, yet the film asks us finally to think about the ways in which a historiography based on a single narrative line, and on a notion of the fateful day when the time had come, obscures modes of political struggle less suited to hegemonic modes of historicizing. In an essay that is partly an account of the aftermath of the British miners' strike in 1984, Laura Mulvey explains why she avoided using the phrase "the end of an era" when the strike failed and resisted the sense of historical closure that Britain's Conservative government was only too eager to inculcate: "Just as feminist avant-garde aesthetics has argued that representations must make their formal structures visible . . . so perhaps should the transparency of history and abstract ideas be questioned to reveal their material underpinnings. Then, it could be easier to decipher the constraints that lead to entropy and endings, to build from one historical context to another without the endless loss inherent in the tradition of the new."[32]

In *Eijanaika* Genji never reaches America. No new world is ushered in. Japan's revolution in 1867 is also a Restoration: change upholds things as they really always were.[33] Incited by Iné's newest show, a "world renewal can-can from across the seas," the people of Ryōgoku dance and sing their way across the river. Doing so, they momentarily disrupt the geography of the film, in which the river has always featured as something the characters move up, down, or alongside, and as a limit to the spectator's vision. But this opening toward transgression and advance is closed off again when the group comes face to face with the shogunal forces, who are armed with the rifles that Kinzō sold them and that before that "Lincoln used to defeat the South." At the urging of the women, who lift their kimono, moon the soldiers, and urinate at their feet, the crowd defies the shogunal ultimatum as it has already defied Kinzō's. But the group does, moments later, turn back to the bridge, apparently having no particular investment in being on the other side of the river in the first place. They heed Kinzō not so much out of obedience but because "this is no fun." It is then that the shogunal forces open fire.

Robert Stam makes a telling slip in his account of the moments before this massacre, as he recounts how "the dancing crowds[,] . . . convinced that everything is possible, take increasingly greater risks, eventually deciding to take over the palace."[34] Imamura's way of telling "what they did" is traduced if one ascribes a destination to this people's movement, with the result that one may then class the movement as a failure because it never arrived. The utopia glimpsed in these concluding moments must be acknowledged as having everything to do with the spirit of nonsense and little, finally, to do with the shogun's palace (which is never mentioned in the dialogue anyhow).

Play has been transported across the river. Play has no destination. In George Wilson's rendering, *eijanaika* translates as "a phrase [that] denotes both closure and transition. About what has already happened, 'Wasn't that great?' rhetorically asks the refrain. 'Right on! Go for it!' follows the rhetorical implication."[35] The refrain suspends narrative. Similarly, carnival (hostile, as Bakhtin said, "to all that was immortalized and complete") reconfigures the tradition/modernity opposition that organizes the narrating of the Meiji Restoration. *Eijanaika*'s carnival reveals a past that is incomplete and unimmortalized. It relocates historical subjects of impure, questionable identities in a political space and a narrative form that have excluded them.

4

The Night of the Shooting Stars

FASCISM, RESISTANCE, AND THE
LIBERATION OF ITALY

PIERRE SORLIN

ONCE UPON a time, there was an enslaved and persecuted people whose members knew that, one day, they would be massacred. One man stood up and said: "Come with me; I shall lead you to a better country." They followed him, and after a painful journey they reached a land of peace and love. This—the myth of Exodus—is one of the oldest tales, told not only in the Bible but by many other religious traditions.

Still, things can be taken in another way. In July 1944, one of the retreating Germans was killed by partisans near the village of San Miniato in Tuscany; the villagers were ordered to gather into the church, and all those who obeyed were killed. Two young boys from San Miniato, the Taviani brothers, were deeply affected by the tragedy and, once they had acquired enough skill and money, made it the theme of their first documentary, *San Miniato, July 1944* (1954). The two went on to achieve worldwide fame and, in 1982, turned the episode into a feature film, *The Night of the Shooting Stars*.

Fiction rather than documentary, this picture emphasizes the fact that it is a story. After the opening credits, spectators observe a limpid summer sky crossed by shooting stars. A woman, in a tender, sweet voice, tells someone whom we do not see—someone meant to belong to the universe of the film, a lover perhaps—that she is to speak of another summer night: "I don't know whether events went exactly like that; I was only six then. Yet it is a true story." The adult voice continues, but there, on the screen, appears the six-year-old girl. She looks inquisitively at the world, and for the most part we see what she sees; she guides us through the story. It is wartime; people are being killed, and yet she never seems frightened: what could happen to her so long as she is sheltered by her mother? The weather is gorgeous; the air is filled with strange, exciting sounds; she smells the sweat of men, the powder of guns, the smoke of burnt timbers; she meets brave warriors, as valiant as the ones her grandfather showed to her in ancient books. To her, it is a pleasant journey; and for the woman, recounting the episode to her dearest more than forty years later is a pleasure as well.

Chronicle of a Civil War

The Night of the Shooting Stars is not a "history film" in the ordinary sense of the phrase: it does not contain archival footage; all its characters are fictional; it disregards Americans, who are presented as mere phantoms, illusions contrived by imaginative girls; and the few Germans that it portrays conform to stereotypes by killing innocents and singing Wagner arias while retreating. Moreover, the movie wavers between the repetition of a myth and the recollection of an actual, dramatic event; its story is conveyed through the biased view of a child and the unreliable memory of a loving woman. Yet it is not a pure fantasy. The past is not used as a pretense for making elegant, artistic pictures, as with Kubrick's *Barry Lyndon*; instead, the filmmakers start with a slaughter that darkened their childhood, and they deal with a moment in history, the year 1944, which is of capital importance for all Italians born before the middle of this century.

If *The Night of the Shooting Stars* had been a "real" history film, what would have it been about? Many Italian movies have described the German occupation and illustrated aspects of the Resistance. In the Tavianis' film, the blowing up of the village takes place very quickly. As for the partisans who enter the story shortly before the end, they are armed countrymen who express no political commitment; they are there, ready to fight fascism, but they play only a peripheral part in the plot. A handful of people do not comply with the occupiers' orders and run away: such is the main thread of the film—and, after all, this might be an unwitting, nonpolitical sort of resistance. Such an assumption involves a shift away from the belief, current in Italy after 1945, that, because the Germans and fascists had led a merciless struggle against the partisans, *resistance* meant exclusively militaristic action (derailments, bombings, arson, etc.) against the enemy.

Is it possible to understand the word differently? Let us examine the second sequence of the film. While the camera takes us to the village, bits of conversation, caught at random, tell us that the Germans, who want to destroy the houses in retaliation for their dead comrade, have instructed the inhabitants to take shelter inside the cathedral, which will be spared. Churches have always been places of safety; and the bishop, who will protect his flock, is there. Rich and poor, youthful and elderly—everybody obeys. But after a while, an old man, Galvano, has his doubts. He

There they were, tense and silent, waiting for one of them to get up and say, "I'll take you to Liberty."

does not try to justify his fears; he simply states he will leave the cathedral at night and that the others may join him. This is surely something that happened quite often during the war, but nobody noticed it at the time; it was seen as pure cautiousness—perhaps even as cowardice. Here the Tavianis emphasize a notion that emerged in Europe after 1968, similar to Thoreau's contention that men, if they want to be real men, must "serve the state with their consciences, and so necessarily resist it for the most part." Resistance is not a military enterprise here but a decision to act rather than passively wait for God to work a miracle or for the Americans to come.

Galvano is a poor man, the domestic of a lawyer. But it would be misleading to presume that the more affluent people stay where their belongings are while the less well off run away; in fact, whole families split up, and in some cases the oldest or richest depart while the youngest and poorest remain. The film does not attempt to explain individual attitudes; it merely shows us how, within a few seconds, the village divides into two opposed, almost hostile sectors. What made people join one or the other of the conflicting camps during the war? Traditional answers are ideology or interest. But here there is no political debate, and both options are equally hazardous; therefore, each group loathes the choice of the opposite group, which may turn out to be the right one. The film is strongly concerned with the schisms that occur within a community during a period of unrest, and it stresses right from the beginning the fact that irrational factors are sometimes as influential as mature reflection.

Galvano surely does not conceive of himself as a new Moses. Yet once he has spoken, and only because he has spoken, he becomes a leader who tells his fellows, including his boss and family, what they must do. What does his charisma consist of? Galvano is in no way much cleverer than the others; when the group leaves the cathedral he is in the lead, but after a night and a day he knows neither where they are nor where they should go, and it is mostly by chance that the group arrives in a quiet place. The Tavianis do not explain why people obey Galvano; they merely emphasize his status by associating his character with a musical theme.

Cinema is more potent than written text in this regard for, by combining images, words, and sounds, cinema can communicate a wide variety of information—both precise facts and vague impressions—simultaneously. Among the four musical themes in the film, the one most frequently used—a quick, joyful march, akin to military music—is first associated with Galvano and then, as he loses his ascendancy over the group, it shifts toward other uses. The group never discusses Galvano's hegemony; there is thus an interesting discrepancy between his apparent authority as represented on the screen and his progressive loss of influence as suggested by the sound track. Charisma is a mysterious, sudden hegemony, likely to vanish as quickly as it has come, but institutional power can make it survive. Again, this is more an assumption than an interpretation, but it obliges us to ponder the origins and duration of political leadership in modern societies: why did the Italians acclaim Mussolini, and why did many of them still back him even after they realized his policy was wrong?

The film focuses on a small community and questions the relationships established in the village. It shows how the richest, comparatively rude bourgeois who live at a distance from their hired laborers and servants, happen to comply with the decision of a domestic; and it illustrates the startling, unexpected split of a seemingly well-balanced, peaceful society. The initial separation is only an introduction to a story whose most important part deals with the exodus of Galvano and his fellows.

Migration is an effective narrative trick that enables writers or filmmakers to follow a group of travelers for a few days while exposing them to various dangers. Yet the journey contrived by the Tavianis does not take place in a remote, imaginary country; rather, it is located in a precise, historically established time and place. Other movies, such as Rosselini's five war films (1945–59) and De Sica's *La Ciociara* (1960), had previously depicted the distressing situation of the civilians under occupation. In these films the Nazis received, at times, the help of a small gang of nasty Italians, but essentially Germans were the villains, and the Resistance was presented as an outburst of national pride. After the war, when Italy was defeated, it seemed necessary to demonstrate that however desperate their situation was, many Italians had not bowed their head. I have already emphasized the fact that the foreigners—Germans or Americans—are given almost no footage in the Tavianis' film; they are present in the background, a threat and a hope, but they do not interfere with the story. If the Germans have decided to punish the village, the slaughter is perpetrated by the fascists. Strapped up tight in their black uniforms, these savage manhunters are the real bad guys of the film; after some villagers have fled from the cathedral, the fascists track them. They catch a fugitive and fling him against a tree trunk until he dies. In the cathedral, the fascists kill elderly people, women, and children, and toward the end, they capture a young woman and rape her. The horror reaches its climax during the final battle. In many movies the last fight marks the triumph of the Good. In this one it is a nightmare that exhausts and destroys both camps, the resisters as well as the fascists. The fascists shoot point-blank at women and old men; they hang Galvano (he is rescued by a woman—one of the many symbols of his decay); they masquerade as resisters and kill their enemies by surprise. Yet once they have decided to retreat, they leave behind their youngest comrade, a rather stupid boy of fifteen. When one of the resisters takes careful aim at the boy, the child rolls about with pain, crying and begging—then the resister shoots him in cold blood.

It could be argued that the resisters have suffered many losses and that the pregnant wife of the murderer himself has been killed by the fascists. Still, there is something utterly inhuman in this scene. It would have been all too easy to present the fugitives and resisters as victims. Instead, the Tavianis have set for themselves the far more difficult task of restraining the audience from instinctively sympathizing with a persecuted group of people. Fascists are the cinematic villains, but evil is not exclusively on their side. There is an interesting discrepancy here between the recourse to a banal device—the opposition of the "bad guys" to the "good guys," one of the best vehicles of classical narration—and the brutal questioning of reprisals. Implicitly, the Tavianis introduce into their picture one of the most controversial debates of postwar Italy: what occured in the Peninsula between 1943 and 1945? The official answer given after the hostilities was that the country had fought a war of national liberation; but many people maintained that Italy had gone through three different wars—an international conflict between the Germans and the allies, an ideological battle between totalitarianism and democracy, and a civil war. When speaking of civil wars, we generally have in mind the English or American examples with their clear-cut oppositions: Roundheads against Cavaliers, North against South. This does not take into account the implacable domestic quarrels that obscured the larger issue most of the time, and this is precisely what the Tavianis wish to stress. All along, we see that the countrymen know each other very well, that resisters and fascists are neighbors and sometimes even relatives, that they may even use proper names or nicknames while shooting at a foe. Such is the essence of a civil war: beyond class, beyond political or philosophical antagonism, we can detect an unpitying hatred, the implacable aversion of people who have been living together for too long and take the pretext of a foreign occupation to settle old scores.

There is even more to the murder of the fascist boy than a shocking act: it is an eye for an eye, a tooth for a tooth, the negation of the Christian moral that is meant to be one of the bases of Italian culture. In a foreign war, tasks and values are perfectly obvious. In a civil war, everything is turned upside down. The film opens with a clandestine wedding: a partisan marries his pregnant girlfriend; while the priest, who should be shocked, congratulates the bride and groom, the father, instead of protecting his daughter, insults her. Under the patronage of the bishop, who ought to do what Galvano does, the cathedral becomes a grave. Shortly before the explosion, while the flock receives communion, two girls comment on the difficulty of swallowing the consecrated bread. During the second day of their journey the fugitives encounter a middle-aged Italian who is also migrating; this man is so tired that he dies under their eyes. Not only do they leave his corpse lying on the road but they steal his provisions. Civilization, along with religion, has faded away; there remains no façade.

A Journey into Wilderness

The Night of the Shooting Stars manages to express a wide range of human lives and primitive feelings by tracing out the momentary connections between a world conflict and the complex, unspoken web of familiarity and aversion that underlies any small community. Yet the film is not a lecture on collective attitudes but rather the story of an exodus told, alternately, by both a child and an adult. The infantile viewpoint has often been used in fiction, especially that of postwar Italy. Rosselini's *Germany Year Zero*, *Paisan* in its Neapolitan episode, and De Sica's *Shoeshine* take their strength from the presence, as witnesses or main characters, of young boys. Two of the most important novels devoted to the German occupation in the Peninsula, Calvino's *The Path to the Nest of Spiders* (1947) and Pavese's *The House on the Hill* (1949), attempt to show how children understood the war; in the latter, the eyes of an insensitive adult who would like to ignore what is happening around him are opened by a gamin, and both novelists share the assumption, also evident in *The Night of the Shooting Stars*, that infants are more perceptive than adults. By focusing on a child, the Tavianis clearly refer to the literary or cinematic fictions launched after the war; but, knowing that the patterns of one period do not correspond to those of another, they refashion the model by making their character into a girl—the small Cecilia. She grasps many things the others do not discern, but her gaze is not all-embracing; at times she seems to vanish, and we observe scenes she could not have seen. There is something intriguing in the presence/absence of the main protagonist, something that prompts spectators to ponder with what and whom the story really deals.

The biblical exodus is a myth of rebirth: after abandoning Egypt and renouncing their ancient life, the Hebrews lay the foundations of a new alliance. The Tavianis do not attempt to reinterpret the tale of Moses, but we cannot help noticing that a symbolic regeneration is enacted at least twice in the film. Before leaving the cathedral, the travelers don heavy, black clothes; at dawn, Galvano orders them to take off their coats and jackets, so that the dark crowd is quickly transformed into a joyful display of bright, contrasting colors. Needless to say, even if summer nights are sometimes cool in Tuscany, coats are unnecessary, especially for those who are obliged to walk fast. The black clothes are therefore emblematic: black was the fascists' favorite color; but saying that the fugitives have escaped the grasp of fascism would not do justice to a disrobing that takes place exactly when the sun rises. During this very night the village has been destroyed, so that now nothing prevents the travelers from severing their roots. The troop sets off again, but the day is hot and they need refreshment; a field of watermelons appears (like manna in the desert), and they all wash their faces with the juice as if in a new baptism. Two days later, the group joins a squad of armed partisans. The men decide they will change their names—to fool the fascists, it is said—but because everybody knows everybody else, this pretext is absurd; it is another baptism, corroborated by the fact that they bathe together in the river afterward.

Are we then allowed to say that the Tavianis, who are attentive to making a politically conscious picture, do not avoid introducing biblical metaphors in their story? This would not be too much of a surprise, given the strong influence of Catholicism upon Italian culture; but we must pay attention to other clues that do not support the hypothesis of an indirect reference to religion. We have already stressed the fact that Galvano's decision divides the village into hostile factions. The two groups gather in opposite corners of the room. The fugitives ought to pray; instead, they have a quick lunch. Thereafter, they will never implore God, not even in the worst moments, during the final battle or when the village is destroyed. On the other hand, those who have remained in the village are such good Christians as to attend a Mass when the cathedral is blown up.

The Tavianis indulge in two contrasting meals—the lay meal, which gives strength for the journey; and the holy meal, the communion, which ends up with the death of the faithful: "civil disobedience" implies religious disbelief. But the conduct of the fugitives, such as it develops in the film, hints at more than a rather trite anticlericalism, and we need the eyes of Cecilia to perceive it. For the girl, everything is different, mysterious, likely to change in a hurry. She is in seventh heaven because she has been taken to a magic world where everybody is nice to her and benevolent, where old ladies give little girls wonderful earrings, and where nursery rhymes protect against all possible dangers. It is true that this is the vision of a child, but the child who apprehends small details that adults do not notice succeeds in creating a sense of wonder on the basis of very simple, seemingly unimportant facts.

Let us return to the first morning, which marks the beginning of a rejuvenated life. As the fugitives refresh themselves with watermelons, someone announces that the fascists are arriving. Everybody takes shelter in the woods (except the man who will be killed against a tree trunk); during the previous night, the escapees had already hidden under trees, and the forest will again provide protection when a plane tries to detect them. But a young Sicilian woman does not like woods and rushes forward, runs through the typical Tuscan landscape, studded with olive trees and vines—and there, amid this magnificent, peaceful scenery, is shot down. This is but one more instance of the already-mentioned reversal of traditional values: the civilized, homely Tuscany has become threatening; the villagers no longer recognize it and are unable to find their way in a country where endless footpaths do not lead anywhere. They roam for hours, and it is only in the woods that they find refuge and comfort. To Cecilia it is a fairy tale, but even adults feel at home under the trees and revel in a return to wilderness. When, in the middle of a bosk, the men decide to change their names, three of them choose the names Orangutan, Lion, and Owl in lieu of their Christian names.

The story of the flight is based on a triviality: in civil war, insurgents are accustomed to taking cover in areas where sophisticated weapons are inefficient; this was adapted by European partisans against the Germans, and later by the Vietnamese. But the Tavianis expand on this very simple fact and make it the focus of a series of mutations and contradictions. Life in the wild obliges people to reinvent themselves: as they sleep together on the ground, as they share the same watermelons, they tend to forget social differences or generation gaps (hence the precious earrings given to a child); they have been freed from legal authorities, from the rules of the Church, and even from the idea of culture. An interesting point is that although they have become wild, they are not savage; the fascists who are unable to renounce their urban, modern surroundings (they use trucks and even a plane but do not enter the woods) are civilized and barbarous, while the fugitives are rustic and innocuous.

Primitiveness implies sexuality. There is no song and dance about sex in *The Night of the Shooting Stars*; a few minutes into the film two boys are already masturbating, while a young woman conspicuously urinates in front of them. Later, a girl explores her naked body. The long break in the watermelon field provides men with a chance to court women, and a tall, wild-looking man makes insistent overtures to Cecilia's mother. She resists at first because she has a husband, at large somewhere in the world; but two days later, as she talks with a young woman about love and sexual relationships after the bath (the second baptism), she drops hints that make it clear that she will accept him, and, although we do not see them, we have been told enough to assume that they make love during the night of the shooting stars. Finally, once the fugitives have reached a quiet place, Galvano goes to bed with a rich woman, demonstrating that, in an upside-down universe, age or affluence are no longer obstacles.

The film emphasizes a gender polarity based not only on the male/female opposition but on a seeing/seen complementarity. Men and women exhibit avowed, patent sexual drives that build up into a strongly eroticized atmosphere. The wild world finds here its completion and its limit; barriers have been removed, but there is no witness to the liberation of sexuality. We see these various scenes because the film displays them. Without using the filter of a gaze, Cecilia, who has introduced us to her enchanted realm, is absent from all the amorous episodes. Oddly enough, there are no boys under ten among the fugitives, and if the girl is willing to get on well with everybody it turns out that she has no connection with any man, except her grandfather. Many commentators have been struck by the last sequence of the movie, and some go so far as to say that it modifies our understanding of the plot. We are back in the room where the adult Cecilia speaks to someone invisible, whom she addresses as "my love"; the camera zooms in and reveals a small baby—no man, no husband, no lover, but only a child. Cecilia stages a sexless continuity of generations: she has a grandfather but no grandmother; a lonely mother, she has given birth evidently without the help of anyone. In the subsidiary plots that enliven the tale of exodus, characters acknowledge a permanent, uncompromising interest in sex, but their lust results in nothing. Galvano and his bedfellow are too old to reproduce; the mother's lover is killed during the closing battle; the longing young woman is kidnapped and raped by the fascists. Sex and procreation are so distinctly separate that I agree with those who consider the last sequence a revision of the interpretation initially proposed for the film: that the upheaval was tremendous but short-lived; it did not last more than the four days necessary to move from one civilized area to another; and its main witness never accepted its most dangerous aspect, the total liberation of sexual drives.

For a good many decades, historians have been anxious to determine whether historical films can help us understand the past. The advantage of movies, where a purely factual contribution is concerned, seems obvious: films offer insight into aspects of the past that are better apprehended through images than through literary descriptions. It is also easy to defend the theory that books are "reconstitutions" of the past and that, in this respect, films are no worse than written accounts. But what happens when cinematographers shift away from the "real," that is to say, the depiction of authentic data, toward the "potential," the exploitation of an actual situation in order to defend a thesis?

The fact that a film is entirely fictional is not, in itself, a shortcoming. The six episodes of *Paisan* are imaginary, but they provide extraordinary insight into death and survival in Italy during the last years of the civil war. The difference between *Paisan* and the Tavianis' film lies in that Rosselini attempted to recapture the atmosphere, and even the scenery, of the time, whereas the Tavianis were less interested in accuracy than in the capacity of cinema to interrogate the dominant vision of the past. Disconcerting though it is, their picture can help historians in at least three different ways.

Placed once again in its own context, the film shows how two leading filmmakers were affected by the combination of left criticism, libertarianism, feminism, and nonconformism that colored much Italian intellectual life in the 1970s and early 1980s. "What is war?" the film asks. And it tells us that war is a time when the consensus that made it possible to live in society no longer works. Those who still rely on the status quo are mistaken; old habits, and especially the belief in the virtues of civilization, must be forsaken. A fascinating aspect of the movie is that it jumbles up, more or less comfortably, moral assessments about power, disobedience, or self-determination with the depiction of an event; the filmmakers try to acknowledge the conventions and standards of the 1980s without relinquishing the deep sense of drama that overshadowed their youth, and they address the contradiction in terms of narrativity, by means of a chronicler who is a child—but not a boy.

Inasmuch as it is a tentative reevaluation of the civil war, the film is also a document that had its role in the debates revolving around the function and significance of resistance in the Peninsula. Many Italians felt uncomfortable with the dominant sentiment that partisans had fought Nazism and Nazism only; but summoning so vague a concept as civil war resulted in another simplification: the poor against the rich. The difficulty was the problem of furnishing a social description with practically no evidence—for police records, when available, do not document the relationships between victims and killers. *The Night of the Shooting Stars* is a conjectural resolution of this difficulty; it is, to a certain extent, an experimentation in history. What could happen in a district already abandoned by the Germans, not yet occupied by the Americans, if forces were approximately equivalent on both Italian sides?

In so experimenting, the Tavianis pose questions that historians have neglected insofar as they have concentrated on the active resisters. The Italian Institute for the History of the Liberation has collected gripping testimonies delivered by ex-partisans. It is time now to interview those who did not rise up in arms; it is time also to move from considerations of political and military history to the detailed analysis of family relationships, authority, and, for that matter, sexual relationships. Historians know how to deal with archives, but all too often they lack imagination—and this is why they have something to learn from cinematographers.

Part Two

VISIONING HISTORY

5

Hiroshima Mon Amour

YOU MUST REMEMBER THIS

MICHAEL S. ROTH

MY INTEREST in the ways in which film affects our understanding of the construction of a past has developed in two different but related ways. On the one hand, I have been working for some time on questions in the philosophy of history, questions that ask not so much whether history is a science or an art as what *kind* of a science and what kind of an art the writing of history is. What do we mean when we say that we know something historically?[1] On the other hand, over the last several years I have been engaged in a study of how the criteria for the *normal* connection between present and past are established through a medical, literary, and philosophical exploration of memory disorders, especially in nineteenth-century France.[2] These areas of research have led me to examine how different cultures (and specific groups with a culture) treat the following questions: *What is the point of having a past, and why try to recollect it? What desires are satisfied by this recollection?* In thinking about these questions in cultural history and the theory of history, I became interested in how photography and film set up criteria for a normal memory, and also in how they explore what it means to have knowledge about the past. *What can film teach us about historical knowing? What can historical knowing teach us about film?* Different film genres have different modes of configuring these questions and thus of proposing answers to them. As I have explored some of these genres and the directors who work in them, the films of Alain Resnais have stood out as an extraordinarily rich body of reflection on the connections among history, memory, and trauma. Resnais's *Hiroshima Mon Amour* (1959), written by Marguerite Duras, is an important exploration of the possibility of living with the past and of living without it. In charting some of the vicissitudes of writing history

An earlier version of this paper was written for a session of the 1991 Twentieth-Century French Literature Association meeting entitled "The Writing of History: Science or Art?" The session was organized by Ora Avni.

as a problem of memory, *Hiroshima Mon Amour* forces the viewer to confront some of the crucial problems concerning the construction of a past with which one can live, especially in regard to our (limited) capacities for representing that past to another.

In the early 1950s Alain Resnais was asked to make a film to mark the tenth anniversary of the liberation of the concentration camps. The result was *Nuit et Bouillard*, a short film whose powerful images of mutilated bodies are juxtaposed with a text warning viewers of the omnipresent threat of the *mentalité concentrationaire*. *Night and Fog* remains one of the most startling, powerful films made about the Nazi period. Recently, when the charges of crimes against humanity were first dropped in the case of Paul Touvier, Minister of Culture Jack Lang asked French television channels to show *Night and Fog*. Its visual, musical, and verbal languages are aggressive in the extreme. There is no place to hide from its assault. In writing about *Night and Fog*, Robert Benayoun recalls Paul Strand's film *Heart of Spain*, in which we are shown a nurse dressing a horrible wound as the voice-over tells us: "You must not look away."[3] The events that were obscured by the night and fog are to be revealed by the piercing gaze of the camera. We get to see the camps *en pleine lumiere* as a warning against the politics and culture that made them possible.

Resnais seems to think that he can burn his lesson into the minds of his viewers. He was asked to commemorate the liberation of the camps, but what would count as a "proper" memory of these places? What are the appropriate images with which to mark this past and our present relation to it? Resnais insisted that he work together on this project with a deportee, because he himself had no authority to speak on this subject. Thus, the text is written by Jean Cayrol, who had been imprisoned at Oranienburg.[4] The authors of the film aim to make not a memorial to the dead but rather "a warning signal." Intolerance and racist militarism were no strangers to France in the middle 1950s, and Resnais means to remind his viewers about the dangers of the culture of totalitarianism.

The connection of horror and memory has recently been given much attention, and what I want to suggest here is that already in *Night and Fog* Resnais is problematizing that connection. He does so by acknowledging and exploring the impossibility of adequately representing the reality of the camps. And if the camps cannot be represented, what does that say about our capacity to remember them? How does memory depend on representation? I quote from the film's text:

> How to discover the reality of these camps, when it was despised by those who made them and eluded those who suffered here? These wooden blocks, these tiny beds where one slept three, these burrows where people hid, where they ate furtively and where even sleep was a threat? No description or shot can restore

their true dimension, that of an uninterrupted fear. One would have to have the very mattresses where they slept, the blanket which was fought over. Only the husk and shade remain of this brick dormitory.

We are shown the "husk and shade," we are shown the skeletons, but we are ceaselessly reminded that we are seeing nothing of the reality of the camps. In the language that Duras would use so successfully in *Hiroshima Mon Amour*: You have seen nothing of the camps. And we are told this as we see on the screen pictures that are almost impossible to look at. For Resnais, the history that is written in *Night and Fog* does not capture the past, but it can provoke us into an awareness of present dangers.

Hiroshima Mon Amour begins where *Nuit et Bouillard* concludes. Resnais was asked to make a documentary about the dropping of the atomic bomb: Hiroshima twelve years later. He decided he could not do it and that in *Nuit et Bouillard* he had already explored why documentary knowledge was impossible. Film offered the temptation to make good on the Rankean claim to provide a representation of the past *as it really was*, and Resnais had already refused (and illuminated) that temptation. The film he would make in Hiroshima would explore what other kinds of connection to the past could be established and maintained in both the most extreme and the most ordinary conditions.

We begin in the banality of a hotel room, where two strangers have spent the night: this could be Paris, New York—almost anywhere. But this is Hiroshima, and there is a friction (Duras calls it a sacrilege) in having the banality of the affair rubbed up against this city whose name is equivalent to horror. The friction is intensified in the early part of the film as we see newsreel film footage of victims of the atomic blast as well as clips from Japanese films made about Hiroshima. She (viewers of the movie will recall the principal characters are not given personal names) claims to have seen Hiroshima, to have recollected its horror, while her lover repeats, *Tu n'as rien vu à Hiroshima* ("You have seen nothing in Hiroshima"). He is insisting that there is no way of seeing Hiroshima because there is no way of remembering it adequately. He is correct, of course, but only in the superficial sense that has come to be all too familiar to us through contemporary theory. That is, he is correct in the adolescent way that the theorist is correct in saying that there is no interesting issue about history writing representing the past, because as a form of *writing* history is always already inadequate to history as experience or even as memory. He is a theorist of memory defending against someone who he thinks believes that she has the presence of the past during her trip to Hiroshima. But he is completely wrong about her. She is no simple empiricist eager to get the past right. The woman who is with him knows that recollection is about the confrontation with absence and forgetting, and that is what she has seen in Hiroshima and everywhere else. She tells him, "So as in love this illusion exists, this illusion to be able never to forget, so too I have had the illusion facing Hiroshima that I would never forget."[5] He is worried about positivist illusions and eagerly wants to deconstruct them. She is already on a different level: seeking an *illusion* of the unforgettable, knowing full well that its illusory qualities are not the only secret to its power. As a sophisticated sufferer, he does not at first want to accept her claim to be *douée de mémoire,* gifted with memory, but he comes to realize that she understands that to be so gifted means to face up to the force of forgetting.

> "ELLE: Like you, I too, tried to struggle with all my might against forgetting. Like you, I forgot. Like you, I desired to have an inconsolable memory, a memory of shadows and of stone. (P. 32)

She remembers her forgetting but knows this is no reason to deny the "evident necessity of memory" (p. 33). This makes all the difference.

In *Nuit et Bouillard* Resnais was struggling with commemorating a history that resisted representation, and he filmed the limits and the possibility of meaningful memory about this past. In *Hiroshima Mon Amour,* he has the even more difficult task of projecting forgetting onto the screen—first, the forgetting of historical memory, the withdrawal of the destroyed Hiroshima from our consciousness; second, the forgetting of personal memory, the evaporation of the traumatic memory of love for the woman in the film; and third, the connection between forgetting and narration.

Tu n'as rien vu à Hiroshima. She has not seen Hiroshima for the same simple reason that he could not have been there for the event. *There is no Hiroshima to see.* What we can see are its traces, in film, in flesh, in stories, and, most graphically, in the stones that have "photographed" the objects that were burned into them. But traces are dangerous for the Japanese man because they can give us the idea that we have seen something of the Hiroshima *of that day.* That day is beyond reach, and coming to Hiroshima a decade later brings us no closer to it.

Now, this might seem like a rather trivial point to make. After all, *any* moment in the past is beyond reach, so why is Hiroshima of special significance in this regard? The significance stems from Hiroshima's status as trauma: as a trauma it draws one to it even as it demands acknowledgment that one can never comprehend what happened there. A trauma is a part of one's past that seems to demand inclusion in any narrative of the development of the present but that makes any narrative seem painfully inadequate. As B. A. van der Kolk and Onno van der Hart make clear, "Traumatic memories are the unassimilated scraps of overwhelming experiences, which need to be integrated with existing mental schemes, and be transformed into narrative language."[6] The "need" for integration stems from the claims that the traumatic past can still make on the person in the present: flashbacks, reenactments, severe anxiety. But there is also a *threat* of integration, stemming from the possibility that the horrific past may, after all, be distilled through "existing mental schemes." The successful integration would necessarily relativize this past in relation to the rest of one's life. The Japanese man discovers that his lover has grasped these lessons of trauma: she makes this clear in her description of her knowing of Hiroshima, and she suggests it in her remarks about her own past when they part on that first morning. He had asked her to describe her episode of madness: "Madness is like intelligence, you know. It can't be explained. Just like intelligence. It hits you; it fills you up, and then you understand it. But when it goes, you can no longer understand it at all" (p. 58). Trauma, too, fills you up, but when it leaves there remain traces that resist any meaningful description. This is the aspect of latency that Cathy Caruth has emphasized as a part of all trauma: "The [traumatic] event is not assimilated or experienced fully at the time, but only belatedly, in its repeated *possession* of the one who experiences it. To be traumatized is precisely to be possessed by an image or an event."[7] One is "filled up" by the flashback or reenactment of the traumatic past, but one can not explain or even describe this belated experience to oneself or another. When the past does not entirely possess the traumatized person, it is inaccessible to him or her. This inaccessibility is closely related to patterns of repetition that Sharon Willis sees at the core of the *Hiroshima*.[8] How to live with this past, which refuses to find a home in the present?

He is an architect, and much of the film shows us the new Hiroshima. It is not a pretty sight. Apart, perhaps, from his home, the new city vacillates between being a tragic tourist spot and a mere denial of any past at all. We can wince at the atomic gift shops and the Hotel New Hiroshima, but what kind of buildings could possibly cover the scars of the past without being scars themselves? What kind of life can be built from a past that refuses translation or assimilation into the present but that will not be forgotten?

She has carried her own trauma in silence for twelve years. In the village of Nevers, the young woman fell in love with a German soldier. The occupier, the enemy, would be shot by snipers as the Germans fled the forces of liberation. And the good citizens of Nevers who had abided this occupation can now turn on those who had forgotten who their enemies were. She speaks to no one about this first, wartime love. It is only in Hiroshima, when faced with this man in this context, that her story emerges. And it is when she tells her story that she fully realizes that the past, this past, cannot be told because it cannot be maintained in recollection. She had experienced an absolute fidelity to the past just after the Liberation. This was her madness, her refusal to live in the present. Then, she became "raisonable"; that is, she began to "emerge from her eternity." When she returned to the world of time—to the world where her hair grew back, where the bells of St. Etienne rang the hours, where the seasons changed, where her lover was dead and she was not—then she accepted living with the memory of her lover. And to live with the memory of something (to be "gifted with memory") is to live with forgetting. But she keeps the process of forgetting (and hence memory) at a distance by never bringing this past to mind—at least, never forming it into words uttered to another. Until Hiroshima.

   How does one live with forgetting? She has left her bitterness behind. No madwoman here; she has a career, children, and lovers. She is, in her own way, an architect, a builder. But perhaps the most important way in which she lives with her forgetting is by not exposing it to anyone else. And when he first asks about her war time love in Nevers, she seems startled. How can he be on to this?:

> ELLE: Why talk about him instead of others?
> LUI: Why not?
> ELLE: No. Why?
> LUI: Because of Nevers, I can only begin to know you. And among the thousands and thousands of things in your life, I choose Nevers.
> ELLE: Like anything else?
> LUI: Yes.
>> *Can one see that he is lying? Surely. She, she becomes almost violent, and trying to discover what she could say (slightly crazy moment).*
> ELLE: No. It's not an accident. (*Some time passes.*) It's you who must tell me why.[9]

How can he be on to this? How can he be on to the importance of this past? After an afternoon in his house—which looks nothing like any of the other interiors we see in the film—they have sixteen hours before her plane leaves for Paris where no one knows the importance of Nevers. Time enough to recount the past? To make one's past count for another?

   As he draws her story out in a Hiroshima bar, she feels herself losing not only the past but also the present. That is, she knows that even the most intense of experiences, even the traumas that seem to call out for recollection, will evaporate from one's consciousness once they are remembered in a form that can be shared, unlike the madness that invaded her as France was liberated, unlike the flashbacks of moments with her German lover that rush into her consciousness without warning. We are not stones that photograph the things burned into us. She faces this as she recounts her past, and he understands in knowing that her story is a tale of what he calls the "horror of forgetting."

That which is unforgettable is that which cannot be remembered, cannot be recounted.

But that is not the only horror here for her. Speaking about the trauma, which is the translation of memory into history, is a violation of the sacred relation to this past that she had maintained for a dozen years. She, of a *moralité douteuse,* had cultivated piety for the preservation of the trauma as something that could never be represented or shared. She had not "integrated" her life into a "coherent whole" because there were events in it that for her belonged apart; when they were lived they filled one up, but they were joined with nothing else. She was not the person who experienced these events; she was subject to them. That is why they could suddenly appear in flashbacks and other forms of possession. Psychiatrists would pretend to offer cures for this phenomenon:

> In the case of complete recovery, the person does not suffer anymore from the reappearance of traumatic memories in the form of flashbacks, behavioral re-enactments, etc. Instead the story can be told, the person can look back at what happened; he has given it a place in his life history, his autobiography, and thereby his whole personality. Many traumatized persons, however, experience long periods of time in which they live, as it were, in two different worlds: the realm of the trauma and the realm of their current, ordinary life.[10]

She lives in these two worlds and finds it enormously threatening to consider "integrating" them, assimilating that early wound to the rest. When she is finally able to speak her past, when she is able to turn the trauma into a narrative success, success is failure and failure is no success at all.

To the extent that she is able to tell her story to him she robs it of its uniqueness; she destroys its aura.[11] We can see that for him to the extent that she is able to do this she gives their own connection a unique status; she creates a new aura. The successful narrative means that the trauma is not the trauma one thought it was. It can be told. It can then be lost. Narrative memory can be forgotten, unlike hallucinations and automatic memories, such as one finds in madness and in flashbacks where the past takes over, and the "pastness" of what one is conscious of evaporates.

> You were not completely dead.
> I told our story.
> I betrayed you tonight with this stranger.
> I told our story.
> It was, you see, tellable.
> I haven't rediscovered for fourteen years . . . the taste
>   for an impossible love.
> Since Nevers.
> Look how I forget you.
> —Look how I have forgotten you.
> Look at me.[12]

The scandal of *Hiroshima Mon Amour* is that nothing is unforgettable and that, on the level of both collective memory and personal memory, to make the past into a narrative is to confront the past with the forces of forgetting. If something is unforgettable, this is, paradoxically, because it could not be remembered or recounted.

Narrative memory integrates specific events into existing mental schemes. In so doing the specific events are decharged, rendered less potent as they assume a place *in relation* to other parts of the past. This is a process closely akin to what Stephen Heath describes as "narrativization" in film: "Narrativization is the mode . . . of a continuous memory, the spectator as though 'remembered' in position, in subject unity, throughout the film."[13] "The final time of film as narrative," Heath writes, "is that of identity, centre perspective, oneness, the vision of the unified and unifying subject, the reflection of that."[14] Heath seems to be thinking of only the most simple of narratives, or simplifying all narratives for polemical purposes. Even one of the most conservative forms of narrative exposition, history writing, allows for more than "centre perspective" and "oneness." But there is an important point here about the integrative function of narrative. Historical writing, for example, necessarily configures the past—any past—into something that can be told. And this configuration has important consequences. As Carl E. Schorske has noted, historians "reconstitute the past by relativizing the particulars to the concepts and the concepts to the particulars, doing full justice to neither, yet binding them into an integrated life as an account under the ordinance of time."[15] Sometimes "doing full justice to neither" can be accepted as a fact of life (or at least of looking back at life). As Robert Dawidoff has noted, however, sometimes the capacity of history to integrate elements into a "meaningful whole" is enormously threatening to those who care for the particulars *as* particulars.[16] Claude Lanzmann raises a similar set of issues in regard to the representation of the Holocaust on film: "It is enough to formulate the question in the simplest terms, to ask: 'Why were the Jews killed?' The question immediately reveals its obscenity. There is really an absolute obscenity in the project of understanding. Not to understand was my iron law during all the years of the elaboration and the production of *Shoah*."[17] This obscenity of understanding is what Hans Kellner has called the beautification of the sublime. The explanatory, or merely domesticating, power of historical discourse "hides the 'primitive terror' behind us, obscuring the possibility that a 'non-sense' lurks behind all 'sense.'"[18] This primitive terror explodes in trauma and is at the heart of trauma's relation to historical representation. Insofar as that representation is tied to narrative, the very quality that makes an experience traumatic (that we cannot take it in through the mental schemes available to us) is lost in the telling. This "loss" can be felt as a cure and as a betrayal, a sacrilege.

In *Hiroshima Mon Amour*, Resnais and Duras explore the question of how one can be fully alive under the burden of a history that is not a stranger to trauma but that has not fully domesticated the traumatic. Insofar as they provide an answer to this question, they suggest that it is through an acknowledgment of the powers of forgetting that one can live with (and with losing) the past. This means that history writing can be fully understood only when one grasps that the writing is a sign of the process of forgetting. Neither the accuracy of science nor the expressiveness of art will in any way allow one to escape losing the past, and the necessary "failure" to prevent this loss remains an important sign of our impoverishment.

From a perspective we might associate with Nietzsche and some of his contemporary postmodern fans, we might think that this is a false, perhaps even a sentimental problem. From this perspective there would be no *problem* of losing the past unless one started with some naive assumption that the past somehow needed to be retained for action (or inspiration) in the present. To be free from the burden of memory as history would not then be a problem of mourning but a promise of liberation. This perspective, coherent and powerful on many levels, is foreign to *Hiroshima Mon Amour* because the perspective denies the power and perhaps even the possibility of trauma. In other words, it denies that parts of one's past remain necessarily and effectively unassimilated to one's

present; it denies that there are parts of the past that resist representation and yet pressure our capacity to act in the present. It is within this resistance and pressure that *Hiroshima Mon Amour* takes place.

After wandering through the new Hiroshima, our characters take separate cabs to an all-night café in the city. The name of the bar is the *Casablanca*, hence the subtitle of this essay. The reader will remember Bogart's character in *Casablanca* as a man with a past—a screamingly silent past until Elsa walks into his gin joint with Victor Laslow one fateful evening and orders two champagne cocktails. It is only then that Bogart's Rick can let the song be played: if she can take it, he can. "You must remember this . . ."

Now, I am aware that in many ways a comparison between these two films could turn out to be downright silly. But the wink to *Casablanca* that Resnais gives us near the end of his film should not be neglected. But not because one can imagine Emmanuelle Riva or Elji Okada saying, "We'll always have Hiroshima"; no, we are given the allusion to *Casablanca* precisely because they see that this powerful romantic claim is (perhaps like all powerful romantic claims) impossible. What these two lovers find themselves sharing is the acknowledgment of the powers of forgetting that their encounter has thrust upon them. Of course, in the film we are shown only the confrontation with forgetting. What it might mean to share in this acknowledgment is left completely obscure or open.

What is the point of having a past, and why try to recollect it? It is crucial to see that *Hiroshima Mon Amour* asks precisely these fundamental questions in the philosophy of history on both a personal level and a collective one. It asks, in other words, why one retains a construction of the past in the face of the relentless pressure of temporal erasure. It acknowledges that this pressure "wins," that there is no way to defeat the power of forgetting. The most powerful form of forgetting is narrative memory itself, for it is narrative memory that assimilates (filters, reconfigures) the past into a form that can be "integrated" into the present. Narrative memory, which is at the core of historical representation both on paper and on film, *transforms* the past as a condition of retaining the past. *Hiroshima Mon Amour* examines the costs of this transformation, this forgetting, and of the remembering that tries to preserve identity, love, and fidelity with full self-consciousness of the inevitability of loss. The injunction from *Casablanca*'s theme melody, "As Time Goes By," still applies: "You must remember this." Only in the effort to remember can one acknowledge the losses in one's personal and political life. I have claimed in much of my other work, and can only suggest here, that this acknowledgment of the past in the present is a necessary ingredient of modern historical consciousness and hence of modern freedom. *Hiro-*

shima Mon Amour shows us that the acknowledgment of trauma and forgetting is also a condition of piety, of the caring attention one can provide to parts of one's past. Whether history is written for accuracy or for expressivity, it is always written against forgetting and perhaps ultimately for either freedom or piety. *Hiroshima Mon Amour* is *douée de mémoire* because it is a film that remembers forgetting.

6

Memories of Underdevelopment

BOURGEOIS CONSCIOUSNESS/REVOLUTIONARY CONTEXT

JOHN MRAZ

> We have to know how to live—with dignity—
> in the age we've been given to live in.
> —*Fidel Castro*

THE SELF and society, private life and social circumstance, individual psychology and historical situation—this is the core of *Memories*, arguably the most important historical film produced in Latin America.[1] Made in 1967 but situated in 1961 and 1962, the work is manifestly historical at the immediate descriptive level. The film opens with the title "Havana, 1961," and the fictional present is clearly identified as the past by framing it between the Bay of Pigs invasion and the Cuban Missile Crisis. These and other historical events appear in documentary format to motivate the film's plot and impel the story's development.

Utilizing the diarylike form of the book that inspired it, the film follows the experiences of Sergio, a member of the bourgeoisie who has decided to stay in Cuba after the triumph of the revolution in 1959.[2] There is very little "action" of the type we normally associate with fictional movies, for the film essentially follows Sergio about in a series of activities: he bids farewell to his parents, wife, and friends, who leave for Miami; he walks through the streets; he meets with bureaucrats to discuss how much longer he can continue living off his rents; and he daydreams in his apartment, fantasizing about sex with his maid, Noemí. He eventually starts up an affair with a young woman, Elena, who comes to his apartment, where they make love. He introduces her to the film's director, Tomás Gutiérrez Alea, at the Instituto Cubano de Arte e Industria Cinema-

I am grateful to Eli Bartra and Robert A. Rosenstone for their critical reading of this article, as well as to Julianne Burton, Carlos Cortés, David Sweet, and Paul Vanderwood for their comments on earlier versions.

tográfica, and they visit Hemingway's house; she later attempts unsuccessfully to coerce him into marrying her.

The movie uses flashbacks to describe the prerevolutionary social context in which Sergio's consciousness was formed—his education, family influences, and work life as owner of a furniture store and apartment buildings. It also portrays his disaffection with that life-style, his desire to be a writer, and his reasons for remaining in Cuba, even though his closest relations leave during the airlift of 1961. The film takes the novel's monologue a vital step forward, however: it "betrays" the book by recontexting Sergio's musings and his social interactions through placing them within the new historical situation, which is presented largely—though not entirely—in documentary sequences.[3] Thus, in an evaluative sense as well, *Memories* is a historical film, for it insistently focuses on the essence of history: the dialectic of social context and individual consciousness.

In order to understand the historical vision of *Memories* it may be useful to compare it to *Hiroshima Mon Amour* (Alain Resnais, 1959), an important film of the French New Wave. This work is particularly appropriate, for Sergio is deeply impressed by a sentence from that movie: "I desire an inconsolable memory." He perceives such a memory as associated with the capacity to relate things, to accumulate experience, to remember the past; this sense of history in developed countries he contrasts to Cubans' underdevelopment.

Certainly, *Hiroshima* offers us historical protagonists, characters whose consciousnesses are the product of their contexts and whose psychologies are the internalization of the external realities they have lived. As with Sergio, the past hangs around their necks like a stone. But the vision of *Memories*—unlike that of *Hiroshima*—is larger than the perspective of its protagonist. The final irrelevance of Sergio's individual fate in contrast to that of a society in profound transformation tells us that, because people are products of their situations, transformed contexts make for a different kind of people. Thus the angst, cynicism, and despair of, for example, the French New Wave can be seen not as a universal condition but as the specific product of a particular situation.

We might contrast these opposing visions of history by calling them respectively "History as Epic" and "History as Tragedy." In "History as Tragedy" people are seen as the product of their contexts. Their structures of consciousness, their forms of perception, their ways of being in and relating to the world have been inexorably shaped by their historical experiences. They are caught, stuck in the past. This is the perspective offered by *Hiroshima* and by the character of Sergio in *Memories*. But the vision of *Memories*, wider and deeper than Sergio's, is that of "History as Epic." Here, we encounter the missing part of the dialectic: people not only are shaped by their context; they actively shape it through will, intelligence, and the commitment to doing what has to be done. When at the end of *Memories* the camera finally moves out beyond Sergio's perspective, it does not move out to nothing, it moves out to everything—to a revolutionary world busy making itself.

But Sergio is not in the process of making himself; he has been made. His entrapment within the past is presented most pointedly in his relations with women. Sexuality is one of the deepest and most resistant expressions of psychological character and thus one of the most difficult to change. Sergio's sexual mentality could be described as imperialist: women are objects of conquest and colonization—underdeveloped colonies to be conquered and transformed. Insofar as they manifest their capacity to act and resist being treated as objects, they are not attractive to Sergio. For example, when Elena returns to his apartment the day after the consummation of their affair and attempts to initiate sexual relations, he is not "turned on" by her.

To carry the metaphor further, women are the object of Sergio's fetishes. They are attractive to him to the extent that they change themselves in accordance with his fetish for the commodities of the developed world—as does his wife, Laura, with "good clothes, makeup, and massages"—or insofar as they represent the developed world, as did Hanna, his German immigrant girlfriend. That is to say, Sergio is interested in women to the degree that they present to him that which coincides with his preformed structures of perception and attraction. Conversely, insofar as women present the material reality of their real beings to Sergio—their "otherness"—he is unable to engage with them because it contradicts the structure of that which excites him: when women return his gaze in the street, he turns away. Unable to relate to living human beings of the female gender, Sergio retreats into fantasies that reveal his own underdevelopment.

Gutiérrez Alea uses this relationship to women as a metaphor for Sergio's perspective on Cuba. Sergio's narcissistic character structure is incapable of confronting the reality of "an object becoming subject"—be that subject a woman conscious of her own desires or a neocolony in the process of making its own revolution. Sergio's rejection of Cuba's underdevelopment is also his refusal to see the revolution. Gutiérrez Alea outlines the relation between underdevelopment and revolution in this manner: "Underdevelopment . . . is interesting because it shows up next to the other side (the positive, vital one) of our reality: the revolution. Both constitute the basic premise of our personality, our future, and our actions. And they go together to the point that to be fully identified with the revolution it is necessary to internalize our underdeveloped condition."[4] Alienated in his relations and unmoved by his immediate context, Sergio remains stuck in a world that is disappearing. Sergio's entrapment in the

past proves the existence of history: in this disjuncture between the fetish-
isms created by his former context and the material reality of his present
situation, we perceive the fact of historical change.

Why, then, is Sergio such an attractive character? As Gutiérrez Alea
explained, he was concerned to effect identification with Sergio. One way
he did this was to present us with an amalgam of two mythic characters
from the developed world's culture: the cinematic hero and the "outsider." The director discussed the specific model he took from capitalist
films as a resource to develop identity with Sergio's values and outlook:
"The protagonist has what every man at some point in his life thinks he'd
like to be or have. . . . He's lucid, intelligent, cultivated, elegant, good-
looking, with a certain sense of humor, and he has all his time for himself—as well as receiving a nice amount of money without having to
work. He also has a luxurious apartment and goes to bed with attractive
women."[5]

But Sergio's alienation—his reflections and meditations at a distance—
also define him as the well-known antiheroic "outsider" of existentialism,
whose ambivalence and detachment are most familiar in the culture of the
First World. Here, although both archetypes serve the purpose of further-
ing identification, Gutiérrez Alea's critique of them as the movie proceeds
makes the audience see with new eyes. The figures have been recontexted:
their traits are now located within a specific matrix and shown to be
historical rather than natural. The alienation effect that Gutiérrez Alea
eventually produces is all the more powerful for having first achieved
identification; he has created an emotive relation with a character that he
then proceeds to annihilate.

Historical fiction ought to humanize social processes and objectify individual psychology. Sergio's compositional importance in the film is like
that of Georg Lukács's "mediocre hero": he situates us in the midst of the
warring social forces.[6] The battle between the bourgeoisie and the revolution is waged in the person of Sergio, who, siding with neither camp,
places us in human contact with both. The great contradictions and crises
of those first crucial years of the revolution are told to us through his
personal destiny, and we see and feel the effects of the antagonisms of
class and nation in human form. Further, the relationship between Sergio
and the revolution heightens our understanding of both phenomena
through the comparison of each with what they are *not*. As Gutiérrez
Alea stated:

Through this character we can discover new aspects of the reality around us.
Sometimes through him, sometimes by contrast with him. His role as a spectator with occasional moments of lucidity sharpens our critical viewpoint. At the
same time, his perceptions of reality, sometimes deformed and always subjec-

tive, also become the object of our critical attitude. And at another level, the confrontation between his world with the "documentary" world that we show (our subjective world) can have some rich overtones.[7]

It is in the confrontation between the individual subjectivity of this "ultimate outsider" and the collective subjectivity of revolutionary transformation that *Memories* most concretely depicts history.[8] Formally, the film juxtaposes Sergio's personal discourse, portrayed essentially in fictional sequences, to the social discourse of revolutionary Cuba, presented largely in documentary and semidocumentary footage. Through this juxtaposition, *Memories* objectifies Sergio's meditations, criticizing and contextualizing his subjectivism and confronting his attempts to retreat into his pre-revolutionary psychological categories and forms of perception with the "fact of change" presented by the new, revolutionary, situation.

The two pans from Sergio's balcony function as a visual frame for the film and inform us of the movement within the work from the individual perspective of Sergio toward that of collective revolutionary transformation. The first pan occurs almost immediately into the film, after Sergio has returned in the afternoon, leaving his wife and parents at the airport. Voyeuristically peering through his telescope at a couple kissing below, he concludes that "everything remains the same." Love is a "universal" theme of humankind, so, from Sergio's viewpoint, if people are loving one another, they must be doing it in the same way they always have. Sergio fails to realize that the revolution is attempting to transform human relations, perhaps even to change patterns of loving. That which remains the same is not the world (at least not the part of it he is in) but rather Sergio's way of seeing it. Sergio's alienation is conveyed as the pan continues, and he perceives Havana as a "city of cardboard." The estrangement apparent in a vision that reduces all to a lifeless facade convinces us of Sergio's role as an "outsider."

But Sergio feels that something is different, for he asks, "Have I changed, or has the city?" We know the answer to that question with the documentary pan with which the movie ends. For this is not a work about the private anguish of an individual in a meaningless universe; it is one about what happens to people caught up in making history through revolutionary practice. In this last pan, at dawn, the film moves definitively out beyond Sergio and his forms of experiencing. *We* see and hear that everything is *not* the same: antiaircraft guns are being pulled to the top of buildings, and troop convoys move along the Malecón to defend the revolution, their reverberation replacing Sergio's monologue. There *is* something out there, something beyond individual subjective ways of seeing, something that shapes and forms perception—something beyond the paradoxical irrelevance of the Sergios.

The dialectical strategy of *Memories* is apparent, first of all, in the film's "multifaceted" visual structure.[9] Documentary footage provides historical background and frames the movie's present between the 1961 exodus in the aftermath of the failed Bay of Pigs invasion and the defensive preparations for the 1962 Missile Crisis. The fictional footage and the monologue narrative present us with Sergio's "mind's eye," how his consciousness realizes itself in his forms of perception: what he looks at and how he sees it. At times, this subjective visual style takes on its most extreme form, the personal point of view; and we see the world as if through Sergio's physical eye.[10] However, even in the midst of Sergio's "mindscreen," a documentary or semidocumentary camera sometimes contradicts his ways of seeing and, at the end of the film, moves out altogether beyond his forms of perception.[11]

The complexity of and contradiction within the film's visual structure can make it difficult for audiences that are accustomed to movies that operate on a single plane of visual (i.e., ideological and psychological) significance. At times, Hollywood filmmakers have used the technique of the subjective camera; *Lady in the Lake* (Robert Montgomery, 1946) is perhaps the most extreme instance. But they have done so most commonly to depict distorted states of perception; for example, Robert Altman portrayed insanity in *Images* (1972), Billy Wilder the effects of alcoholism in *The Lost Weekend* (1945), and Roger Corman the influence of drugs in *The Trip* (1967). Obviously the distortion of perception produced in such unnatural states is contrasted to a "normal" perspective.

That "normal" perception, however, is a function of one's place in history—one's class, race, and sex—is not commonly recognized in cinema, where the dominant form of visual narration is omniscient. Such omniscience is the perceptual rendering of ideologies that consider themselves "universal": they can admit the possibility of altered states of mind but cannot allow real contradiction. Gregory Bateson once remarked, "The rules of the universe that we think we know are deep buried in our processes of perception."[12] The rules of reasonably stable universes insist that perception is "naturally" of a single ideological-psychological-perceptual plane, without recognizing that that plane is in fact the worldview of the ruling class.

The postulates of a revolutionary universe are quite different. Here, in the midst of profound social transformation—with one foot in the past and the other in the future—the forms of perception corresponding to class interests are in open warfare, and contradiction is the rule of the game. Thus, Gutiérrez Alea presents us with Sergio's *Weltanschauung*—normalizing it through the use of realist techniques to encourage identification—while simultaneously contradicting and critiquing his way of seeing. In riding a Brechtian knife's edge of identity/alienation, Gutiérrez Alea and Sergio Corrieri, the actor who plays Sergio, force the audience to feel and reflect on what it is feeling co-instantaneously.[13] Gutiérrez Alea described this process:

> Sergio has a set of virtues and advantages which permit spectators to identify to a certain degree with him as a character. The film plays with this identification, trying to insure that the viewer at first identifies with the character. . . . But then what happens? As the film progresses, one begins to perceive not only the vision that Sergio has of himself, but also the vision that reality gives to *us*, the people who made the film. This is the reason for the documentary sequences. . . . They correspond to our vision of reality and also to our critical view of the protagonist. . . . I feel that it is in this sense that the film carries out an operation which is the most revolutionary, so to speak, the most dialectical with regard to the spectator.[14]

It is crucial to recognize, however, that Gutiérrez Alea is not presenting Sergio's fictional perspective as false and that of the documentary as true. Nothing would be less dialectical. For the director, both are "approaches to reality," and truth lies in the confrontation of perspectives, in the mutual contradictions that lead to an ever deeper and more critical understanding of the historical context in which one is situated. The film "procedure" of mixing fictional and documentary modalities was initiated in Cuba with *Memories* and is characteristic of that country's best cinema during the period 1967–74. In *Memories*—as in *Lucia* (Humberto Solás, 1968), *The Other Francisco* (Sergio Giral, 1974), and *One Way or Another* (Sara Gómez, 1974)—truth and beauty result from the aesthetic tone struck by the formal conflict rather than from the individual parts in themselves. In *Memories*, resonance is produced through the juxtaposition of Sergio's point of view with the documentary elements. But because Sergio's perspective is rendered through realistic camera techniques (hand-held camera, grainy black and white film, natural lighting, etc.), it appears natural, even objective. Thus, Gutiérrez Alea's subtle "denaturalization" of Sergio's way of seeing—providing information as to how such a worldview was formed but never reducing the character or his vision of the world to parody—is what gives *Memories* much of its power and grace.

The film's subtlety led to some misinterpretation and polemics both within and outside of Cuba. For example, confronted with a monologue form—a style in which the film's perspective is almost always that of the protagonist—U.S. critics emphasized Sergio's role as an "outsider" instead of noting how the work contexts his psychology through the use of documentary footage.[15] The documentary and semidocumentary sequences are pivotal in *Memories*, for it is here that Sergio and the audience are confronted with the dialectical "other," the world of history. As Gutiérrez Alea noted, it was the documentary material that allowed them to develop "that line which shows the 'objective' reality that surrounds the character and that little by little closes in on him and suffocates him at the end. That line alternates with the protagonist's own and is basically built with documents."[16]

The documentary thrust is the contextualizing frame that allows us to make sense—historically rather than existentially or absurdly—of Sergio's personal drama. These sequences cover a wide range of forms. There is actual footage of urban uprisings during the late 1950s, of acts of arson by counterrevolutionaries in 1959, and of the Bay of Pigs invasion and the Missile Crisis. There are photographs of starving POWs in the Cuban-Spanish-American War of 1895–98 and of the extreme poverty in the 1930s. There are also postrevolutionary segments shot on the street or in other public places such as the airport, with both hidden and visible cameras that incorporate those present as "extras"; we might call this a semi-documentary form, because the use of such nonprofessional actors lends a documentary feel. A realist aesthetic is achieved as well in fictional sequences through the use of such devices as close-ups of anonymous individuals, the intervention of foreground objects, and the hand-held camera. Finally, the character of Sergio is often presented in a pseudodocumentary fashion as, for example, in the family photos and footage that are used to sketch his personal history.

The credit sequence initiates the documentary structure, and the last two shots inform us of the historical change that is taking place. The film cuts from a dancing *negro* in a straw hat to a black woman who stares fixedly into the camera. The dancing man can be seen as a metaphor for the picturesque image associated with prerevolutionary Cuba and typical of musicals such as *Maracas y bongos* (1932), the first sound short produced in the island. Having awakened the expectations of exoticism, Gutiérrez Alea then initiates his criticism. To be picturesque is to be seen rather than to see, and both women and Third World societies are traditionally viewed as objects rather than subjects. The woman who glares fixedly at the camera will not be made an object for any documentary travelogue about picturesque and exotic peoples and places. Instead, she acknowledges and challenges the camera and, in so doing, forces us as well to recognize its presence.

This sequence also reclaims the African heritage of Cuba, through the focus on the dancing and drums. Gutiérrez Alea was evidently not entirely convinced by the period's "Third Worldism," however, which included criticism of the U.S.'s treatment of blacks and the presence of U.S. black militants at Cuban celebrations. In a later documentary sequence of a panel discussion entitled "Literature and Underdevelopment," he fo-

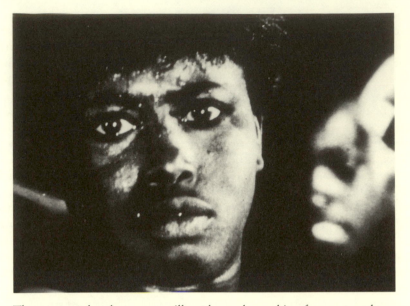

The woman who glares at us will not be made an object for any travelogue about exotic peoples or places. (It is important to point out that this image is a frame enlargement made from a 16mm print of the film. This form of employing visual materials in cinema history has a significant methodological advantage over the commonly used production stills. The latter serve essentially illustrative purposes, whereas frame enlargements permit the analysis of images from the film itself.)

cuses on a black waiter who brings water for the largely white panelists—including Edmundo Desnoes, the novel's author—as they discuss what it means to be a "nigger." Through this image he comments ironically on the persistence of racist structures in the midst of the revolution.

Later in the film, Sergio begins to reflect on Latin American poverty, using words from Castro's "Second Declaration of Havana." The speech had been delivered in February 1962, and, by including elements from it, Gutiérrez Alea is linking the radicalism of the initial triumphal period to the revolutionary revitalization of 1967. The photos in the montage illustrating Sergio's thoughts on Latin America's starving children begin in the Cuban-Spanish-American War and continue to the 1960s. As with the rest of the documentary materials, they are the bedrock with which the film defines itself—in this instance, the chronic ubiquity of two related phenomena in the continent's history: hunger and U.S. imperialism.

Obviously, by including images of the Cuban-Spanish-American War and framing the film's present between the Bay of Pigs and the Missile Crisis, Gutiérrez Alea is pointing to the ubiquitous presence of the U.S.

throughout Cuban history. But, while attacking U.S. imperialism, the director nonetheless respects the Cuban tradition, which, since Jose Marti, differentiates between the rulers and the people of the U.S. For example, several of the photos used in the montage were taken by Walker Evans, who early in his career published a series of images condemning the regime of Gerardo Machado, Cuban dictator during the 1930s.[17]

The documentary sequence about the Bay of Pigs is an intriguing essay on the social structure of prerevolutionary Cuba through a class analysis of the invading forces. The source of the text is a book that Sergio (ever the informed reader) bought earlier, Leon Rozitchner's *Moral burguesa y revolución*. The citation makes a detailed and acute study of the invaders, concluding that their refusal to accept responsibility as a group for the atrocities committed under Batista is characteristic of the previous society's atomism. One trenchant example of the apparent discontinuity—yet real interrelationship—between the bourgeoisie and the torturers is the way that scholars and intellectuals hid neocolonialism and covered up oppression. But if words functioned to conceal reality, then the documentary images of the hungry, the tortured, and the dead demonstrate it conclusively.[18] Here, Sergio's insight about underdevelopment being "the inability to relate things" is applied to the bourgeois predecessors of the revolution.

Formally, the trial sequence of the Bay of Pigs prisoners is interesting for the levels of narration that it offers. Rozitchner's book is an "informed" narrative, sufficiently subjectivized through its presentation via Sergio's voice-over so as not to be taken for "omniscient" narration. Its information provides the context for the "participant" narrative offered by the defendants and their former victims. Here, one of the more revealing testimonies is given by Mario Freyre, the "free enterprise" man of the invaders, who states that he had always been *"una persona perfectamente,* uh-uh [clears throat], *apolitica."* The lie—or self-deception—sticks in his throat and serves as evidence of the sort of nonrelational thinking that the sequence (and the film) is criticizing.

The television footage of a short excerpt from Castro's speech during the Missile Crisis is another key documentary sequence. It is also a brilliant realist strategy, for we are presented with a figure of international significance acting in his historical role. We can compare this to the manner in which famous individuals are often presented in other cinemas, where emphasis is placed on the petty details of their private lives rather than on their historical function. We follow the trifling personal interactions of Alexander the Great, Napoleon, Stalin, or Abraham Lincoln, only to be shocked by the disjuncture between the historical importance of these individuals and their trivial portrayal by actors who reinforce the incredulity of the situation. These figures are famous for their historical roles, not their private lives. In *Memories*, Castro enters at the precise moment of crisis when he is most fully the leader of the Cuban revolution, and solely in order to fulfill his historic mission. The film marches toward Fidel as did history itself.[19]

A marvelously dense statement by Castro in the excerpt defines both this pivotal moment in Cuba's history and the film: "We have to know how to live—with dignity—in the age we've been given to live in." At the center of the world stage, and faced with the possibility of total annihilation in the first phase of a nuclear world war, Castro calls for will, courage, and social consciousness in confronting the danger. These are the same elements on which he had relied in "knowing how" to live under Batista by making a revolution. The character of Sergio, who believes he affects "a certain dignity," points to the density of the statement. Sergio also "knew how" to live in Batista's era, for his psychological structure was attuned to the forms of alienation required by that context: conquest and colonization rather than real human relations, money in place of self-fulfillment, imported culture rather than national identity, and individualism in place of the collectivity which Castro called for in ending his speech: "We are all—men and women, young and old—all one in this hour of danger. And all of us—the revolutionaries and the patriots—will share the same fate. And the victory will be of all." History has moved on and created a new time, a new context in which to live; but Sergio, isolated in his apartment, does not know how to exist in these new forms.

The use of real-life figures in the film underscores Sergio's shortcomings in comparison. Castro, Gutiérrez Alea, and Edmundo Desnoes all provide examples of men from Sergio's generation who, though formed by essentially the same historical circumstances as Sergio, made different decisions and took other paths.[20] Though the film clearly presents a materialist perspective in which consciousness is seen to be the product of concrete historical reality, it also insists on the dialectical role of will and consciousness in that process—perhaps to some extent a reflection of the period's emphasis on subjective factors. Thus, not only does the realism of true-to-life characterization serve the descriptive function of showing what really happened; it is also prescriptive: we learn through these individuals what Sergio ought to do and to have done.

Obviously, these real-life portrayals also serve a distinct role in promoting the self-reflexivity that is central to the film's purpose of creating a critical audience. For example, Gutiérrez Alea appears during the sequence at the Instituto Cubano de Arte e Industria Cinematográfica, where they see the movie bits that were cut out of films by Batista's censors, and he tells Sergio that he is planning to use them in a film collage. Questioned about whether it will be released, the director replies affirmatively; of course, they have already been used in the very film we are seeing.

The presentation of Castro via televised footage is also a crucial realist intervention, for showing him on television makes him even more real than the other actual people. Gutiérrez Alea's appearance was obviously staged, and Desnoes' participation in the roundtable discussion may well have been; but Castro's speech is clearly taken from reality. Further, television is generally perceived as being more "real" than film. The cinematic experience is dominantly fictional, so even when we are presented with the exceptional documentary film, we tend to see it as fiction. But television's news broadcasts, live sporting events, and on-the-spot coverage of real occurrences lead us to associate the form with reality more than is the case with cinema. Obviously, the very fact of seeing a television screen in a film is itself a distancing device, for it calls attention to the fact of the movie. But the ultimate reality—that which is outside us, conditioning and forming our ways of seeing it—is history itself; that is, people like Castro acting in the world to transform reality and forge new ways of being.

It is instructive to contrast the resonance that *Memories* creates between fictional and documentary perspectives with other cinemas, where few attempts have been made to develop such a juxtaposition. In traditional war movies, for example, documentary footage provides "filler" rather than resonance when we are cut from officers on a battleship's bridge to a documentary long-shot of the fleet. There is no confrontation of an "inner" and "outer" world, because consciousness and context are one and the same. A recent example confirms this observation, for *JFK* (Oliver Stone, 1991) also collapses these forms into one another.

One of the more interesting uses of documentary and semidocumentary material is found in Orson Welles's *Citizen Kane* (U.S., 1941). Here, the footage is employed brilliantly to provide an informational base for the stories about Kane that follow. However, its perspective is quickly shown to be that of the sort of "yellow journalism" that Kane himself created—thus, in a sense, Kane's own story about his life and therefore fully as subjective as the stories about Kane told by the other participants. The various perspectives offered on Kane are finally only a series of individually subjective perceptions that make up a context of absolute ambiguity—the proverbial centerless onion. This is the aesthetic expression of atomism, for it denies the existence of the larger collective subjectivity of history.

Historical films have been a central pillar of the Instituto Cubano de Arte e Industria Cinematográfica's creative project since its inception in 1959. In 1968, the official "One Hundred Years of Struggle" celebration led to the production of several outstanding works on Cuban history such as *Lucia* and *The First Charge of the Machete* (Manuel Octavio Gómez, 1969). However, though *Memories* was apparently not as directly inspired by the centennial as were other films, the recounting of recent history in *Memories* is an expression of the emphasis on Cuba's past during the revitalization movement of 1966–68—a period, too, when "underdevelopment was on everyone's lips."[21] By placing the film in 1961–62, Gutiérrez Alea bridged over what we might call the "premature Sovietization" of 1964–65 and established a link between two periods of revolutionary effervescence: the sociopolitical-economic transformation of 1960–63 and the cultural vitality of 1966–68. Both periods were characterized by *guerrillismo* and a radical rejection of the USSR. The director also addressed a key ideological issue of the 1966–68 revitalization movement: Che Guevara's call for the creation of a "New Man," whose transformed being was to be realized through will, voluntarism, and moral incentives.[22] Gutiérrez Alea chose, however, to deal with this issue obliquely by providing an example of what the "New Man" would *not* be: Sergio.

As befits a work produced in a period greatly emphasizing *conciencia*, *Memories* turns about the relationship of personal consciousness and social context. In the fertile loam of the confrontation created between Sergio's archaic psychology and the new reality, *Memories* attests to the inescapable fact of historical transformation.

7

The Moderns

ART, FORGERY, AND A POSTMODERN
NARRATIVE OF MODERNISM

MIN SOO KANG

> "Cheer up," I said. "All countries look just like
> the moving pictures."
> —*Ernest Hemingway,* The Sun Also Rises

NICK HART (Keith Carradine), an artist, cartoonist, forger, and American expatriate living in Paris in the 1920s, sits at a fancy café drawing a caricature of the young Hemingway (Kevin J. O'Connor), who is slumped over a drink at a nearby bar. A dashing industrialist by the name of Bertram Stone (John Lone), a maker of prophylactics and a former apprentice to Houdini, walks in with his beautiful wife Rachel (Linda Fiorentino) surrounded by fawning waiters and other sycophants. Hart (pronounced "Art" by the French) stares at them thoughtfully for a while before he is joined by L'Oiseau (Wallace Shawn), a columnist for the *Tribune* and a gossip monger.

"They won't let me transfer to Hollywood," L'Oiseau complains about his employer. "They just don't see that Hollywood is the city of the future."

"You said the same thing about Paris six years ago," Hart points out.

"The future doesn't just stand still, you know. You should come with me, Hart."

"To Hollywood? Come on, Oisey. Somehow I think it will be more fun to watch the movies than to make them."

"Do you know what is wrong with you?" the journalist asks the cartoonist a moment later.

"No, but I think you are going to tell me."

"You don't know what you want."

Just then Hart recognizes Rachel Stone's face and gapes at her in amazement.

"I'll tell you what I want, Oiselle," he confides in his friend. "I want that woman over there. I want to make love to her for five days. Maybe in a cabin, in a snowstorm. Yeah. And I want to paint her. Then I don't care what happens."

"Good. Then we'll go to Hollywood."

You then realize that you are not in Paris of the 1920s at all. Neither are you in a movie set where a film about American expatriates, about art, forgery, and modernism, is being shot. You are wherever you happen to be, reading an analysis of a movie that begins with a prose description of the first scene.

I

> . . . what is it to-day a french woman said to me
> about an American writer, it is false without
> being artificial.
> —*Gertrude Stein,* Paris France

The task of translating historical events into a cinematic narrative is one fraught with insurmountable difficulties and unavoidable dilemmas. Since film, like music, is a time-based medium, one is forced to squeeze into only a few hours historical experiences that unfolded over years, decades, sometimes even centuries. Traditional historical drama that seeks to present a "realist" narrative of the past by "transporting" the audience to the period of the film's subject must pick and choose the most important cinematic "moments" to put on screen, with the certain consequence of distorting the "lived" experience of the events. Filmmakers who produce postrealist or postmodern cinema, however, have sought to overcome this inherent problem by letting the audience in on the secrets of the distorted mirror to the past presented before them. Through their imagination, movies about the past become movies about the representation of the past, about the unbridgeable gap between the "now" and the "then" and about our impossible desire to become free travelers through time. Once it is established that a particular film will speak not so much of the historical past as of our "desire" for it, a myriad of possibilities, unavailable to "realist' cinema, of what could be "represented" opens up.

One of those possibilities is explored by Alan Rudolph in his 1988 film *The Moderns* in the form of a question: can an idea as broad and amorphous as "modernism" be narrativized into cinematic form? How can the notion of cultural modernity be represented, translated, and emplotted into a two-hour format with a coherent story structure that could be enjoyed without necessarily discerning the conceptual framework of the narrative? A traditional realist film would attempt this by portraying the lives of various modernist artists, writers, or theorists, staying as close to "known facts" about them as possible but choosing to put on the screen what the filmmaker deems the most important events or moments in their lives that elucidate the meaning and significance of modernism. The connection between the Paris on the screen and the "actual" Paris of the 1920s is certainly made in *The Moderns* as one of its main characters is the young Ernest Hemingway; a scene takes place in Gertrude Stein's salon; the paintings of Cézanne, Matisse, and Modigliani play a central role in the plot; and the café culture of the city is portrayed in American expatriates' dimly lit hangouts, where numerous scenes take place.

Yet there are further dimensions to the narrative of *The Moderns* that undermine this simplistic identification of the represented past with the past itself. Not only is strict adherence to historical facts abandoned in order to emphasize the "mood" of the unfolding scenes and to bring out the conceptual problems delineated through the plot; certain devices are used throughout the narrative that act as signals to alert us to the "artificiality" of the cinematic space.

Each sequence begins with black and white footage of Paris in the 1920s, followed by the opening scene, which slowly fades into color before the action begins. At the conclusion of each sequence, the scene fades back to black and white, followed by more footage, providing strict frames of "reality" reference for the fictional plot. This is further emphasized by the fact that all the footages are of outdoors, with long shots of streets, buildings, and crowds, whereas most of the "fictional" scenes take place in dimly lit interiors with close shots of the characters.

Where footage is not used, paintings are substituted, emphasizing the artificiality of the space in an even more provocative manner. As Nick Hart gets into the car of the rich divorcée Nathalie De Ville (Geraldine Chaplin), jazz music reverberates in the street just as a huge poster of black musicians appears around a corner and heads straight toward the camera. Hart and Nathalie talk of love and art in the car while we notice odd, cubist shapes outside the car's oval rear window. In Nathalie's lavish living room, decorated with the crucial paintings by Cézanne, Matisse, and Modigliani, they drink champagne to the tune of a soulful chanteuse on the record player and strike a bargain that propels the plot forward. As they kiss and begin to make love on the couch the camera pans up to a large rectangular window, upon which the sheer white curtains flutter gently aside to reveal the outside world as another vast modernist painting. Once again, the painting fades to black and white before cutting to another footage of Paris.

In another scene, the surrealist poets, jazz musicians, and other "moderns" sitting with their liquors and coffees in a café are mysteriously joined by punk rockers and other assorted bohemians of the late twentieth century who are gathered around a bar, staring intently at the camera as if watching television.

With the artificial space thus established as the background of the narrative, the idea of "modernism" can be represented and examined. Given the complex and deliberately contrived plot as well as the unrelentingly evocative mood of the scenes, however, the meditation on modernism is much more than just a series of portraits of "moderns" living and working in the city central to cultural modernity. While seeking to "reinvent" rather than "capture" the feel and ambience of the period in a romantic manner, complete with jazz music, low lighting, passionate situations, and snappy, suggestive dialogue, the film questions and undermines various aspects of modernism, just as the self-reflexive devices used throughout the film questions and undermines the "reality" of its space. Ultimately, this story of love thwarted and then regained, of art and forgery, and of purity and artifice amounts to a postmodern critique of modernism.

It is a tale told from hindsight, at the ash heap of the great movement that burst out at the end of the nineteenth century, survived through the First World War, and bloomed during the interwar period only to die slowly of exhaustion and suicide in the decades following the demise of fascism. It is an artificial narrative of a grand gesture that would not admit to its own artifice. It is a love story of a man who cannot help loving the most deceptive of women. It is about postmodernity's ironic attachment to modernity.

II

> Now this was very important because once
> again this made a background of unreality
> which was very necessary for anybody having
> to create the twentieth century.
> —*Gertrude Stein*, Paris France

There are two main plot lines that carry the story forward in *The Moderns*. In the first, Nathalie De Ville hires the reluctant Nick Hart to forge the three paintings from the collection of her ex-husband. Once this mission is completed and Hart paid off, she intends to give the copies back while donating the originals to a museum in New York. The plot thickens when her ex-husband dies shortly after Hart completes his task and Nathalie reneges on her contract with Hart, compelling each of them to take extreme measures in order to get satisfaction.

In the second plot line, Hart recognizes Rachel Stone as his own wife,

who left him many years ago without leaving a word. With the ruthless
Bertram Stone, who is reputed to have once killed a man, always watching with his sinister gaze, Hart and Rachel begin a dangerous affair. At
the suggestion of Gertrude Stein, Hart and Stone fight a duel in the form
of a three-round boxing match, with Hemingway manning the bell.

When Hart refuses to return the originals until Nathalie pays him for
the work on the forgeries, she sends a couple of thugs to steal back the
paintings. His copies, however, are so convincing that the thugs steal
those by mistake. In the confusion and the caper that follows, Nathalie
sends the copies off to New York while Hart, with the help of his art
dealer and defrocked nun Libby Valentine (Genevieve Bujold), sells the
originals to Bertram Stone. When the latter puts on a showing of his cultural assets, Nathalie declares the paintings as forgeries, finding support
from a pair of art critics who find all kinds of things wrong with them,
including the nipples of the Matisse. In a fit of rage, Stone destroys the
three works by slashing them with a knife and throwing them in the fire,
compelling one of the critics to declare, "Another dadaist provocation!"
Much later, Hart visits the New York Museum of Modern Art and sees
his own copies displayed as the originals. Standing before his pseudo-
Cézanne, he listens to an instructor lecture to a group of students about
the work: "This is a work of rare emotional delicacy. This revelation
cannot be taught or duplicated. Only the greatest artist can achieve what
has happened here. And only then in that rare moment in time. So let's
silently observe this."

"Come on, I'm bored with these pictures," L'Oiseau complains to
Hart. "I want to go where the pictures move."

III

That was the trouble with the sur-realist crowd,
they missed their moment of becoming civilized, they used their revolt, not as a private but
as a public thing, they wanted publicity not civilization, and so really they never succeeded in
being peaceful and exciting, they did not succeed in the real sense in being fashionable and
certainly not in being logical.
—*Gertrude Stein*, Paris France

The much-discussed question of great art and forgery is a particularly
intriguing problem for critics and theorists alike for it presents a crucial
challenge to how we identify, observe, and trade art in our society. Denis

Dutton, in a collection of essays on the subject, tells us for example that "the initial spark for *The Forger's Art* came from students in my aesthetics classes persistently demanding to know why forged paintings must be considered inferior to originals, when 'nobody can tell the difference.'"[1] Or, more concisely, as the title of an essay by Alfred Lessing in the collection asks, "What is wrong with forgery?" Despite a wide variety of analyses that have been made to answer this difficult question, Michael Wreen among others has pointed out that there are essentially two main positions that one can take on the relationship between great art and forgery.[2] The first and more traditional stance is that no matter how perfect the forgery, it is inherently flawed in an aesthetic sense. This may be because it claims originality in methods or execution when it is actually derivative, because it distorts the history of art through false attribution, or because it violates the special relation one has in communing with an artistic object that has the reputation and aura of "greatness."[3] The second stance, which is informed by contemporary criticism, is that forgery is really about the violation of institutional standards in the exchange of symbols, whether in art as commodity or in the gazer's relationship to the artifact labeled "great." What is wrong, in that case, with a forgery of a Cézanne is not in the painting itself but in the way that the work attaches false labels to itself as it enters the semiotic marketplace that has a priori loaded the signifier "Cézanne" with a certain amount of value. The consequence of this idea to the traditional notion of "objective aesthetic criteria" and of "greatness" in art is devastating because it sees both as inextricably linked to the historical, social, and above all economical context of their production. In locating the problem of forgery in the distortion of its "exchange value," it undermines the "essentialist" notion of aesthetic value in art.

Given the plot line concerning the forged paintings, it would seem that *The Moderns* takes the latter position in seeing Hart's work as a success of one artifice in a world of artifice. As long as no one discovers that the paintings are forgeries, there is no reason why they cannot be "great." Yet given the subtle suggestions made by various "twists" in the story, the meditation on the value of art and forgery in the film turns out to be of a much more complex order. It is, after all, Bertram Stone, the vulgar villain of the story who wants to buy a cultural reputation, who says when his paintings are declared forgeries, "I don't give a damn for your silly opinions on the value of art. There's no value except what I choose to put on it. This is art because I paid hard cash for it. Don't you understand? Your precious painters mean nothing to me. I could have Nathalie's mutt shit on a canvas and if I pay five thousand dollars for it, you critics would call it a masterpiece." Even as the critics protest at his words and accuse him

Variations of Cézanne, Matisse, and Modigliani raise a question of artifice—but who is forging whom?

of having "missed the whole point," we as the audience know that it is they who missed the whole point when they failed to recognize the paintings as the originals and stand idly by as Stone destroys the works in front of them.

Yet it is Nick Hart for whom we are made to feel sympathy in the drama, and he obviously has nothing but contempt for Stone's philistine attitude toward art. As he stands before his own pseudo-Cézanne at the museum, the eloquent praise of the art instructor does not seem wholly unjustified, in that the painting may be still great whether it was created by Cézanne or by Hart. There are at least three conflicting ways in which one can read the situation—first, that the painting by Hart, however convincing, is not a Cézanne and therefore not "great" (in which case the art instructor would be entirely wrong in his aesthetic judgment, which is wholly arbitrary and based on academic snobbery); second, that Hart produced such a perfect copy that he managed to replicate all that is great in the original (in which case the art instructor would still be right except in his claim that the greatness can never be taught or duplicated); or third, that Hart himself is a great painter who came up with a great painting of his own that is a "variation" of Cézanne (in which case the art teacher would be entirely right except in his thinking that it was created by a man named Cézanne and not Hart). What makes the film a postmodern critique of modernism is not that it crudely rejects modernist values of "greatness," "purity," and "art for art's sake" but that it delineates the dilemma between "art as art" and "art as commodity." By exposing the possibilities as well as the limits of both positions, it presents the audience with a paradox and allows us to make up our own minds about the question. Are we, for instance, to take the side of the art critics who insist on the intrinsic "greatness" of great art but complain about the nipples of the Matisse, or that of the industrialist who is interested only in the monetary value of the works?

Even Hart himself seems altogether unclear about the question as he becomes embroiled in the complicated affair. While Libby Valentine haggles with Stone over the three paintings, he makes love to Rachel in the bathroom upstairs. Afterward, he rejoins Stone and sells him one of his own original works, featuring winged cherub-heads and a half-naked woman resembling Rachel in the throes of erotic ecstasy. Later, on a dark, fog-filled night, Rachel disappears into the city while Hart and Stone wrestle over a pistol. When they realize that the woman of their desire is gone, Stone commits suicide by jumping into the Seine, forcing Hart to swim after him. At the feigned funeral of L'Oiseau, in whose empty coffin Stone's body was secretly placed, the astonished Hart stares aghast as the dead industrialist who was Houdini's apprentice emerges from the grave and frees himself of chains and a straitjacket before walking off with a great, liberated smile on his lips. Finally, as the train bearing Hart and L'Oiseau away from Paris starts moving, Hart notices a billboard upon which his own painting that he had sold to Stone has been transformed into an ad for prophylactics. "Touché," Hart concedes with an ironic smile. The birth of pop art—the end of art for art's sake and the beginning of art as commodity—touché indeed.

IV

> That is why writers have to have two countries,
> the one where they belong and the one in which
> they live really. The second one is romantic, it is
> separate from themselves, it is not real but it is
> really there.
> —*Gertrude Stein,* Paris France

In the science-fiction television series "Star Trek: The Next Generation" there is a room on board the Starship Enterprise called the holodeck. By activating a program in the computer, the room transforms itself into a three-dimensional representation of any place the user may wish to visit. Besides some practical uses, such as performing technical simulations, the holodeck is used mostly for the crew to take short vacations on their favorite spots in the known universe, revisit places in their past with simulated people they have known, or to fulfill fantasies in made-up lo-cales. As the main characters of the show often go to mid-twentieth-century America to play parts in private detective dramas, there is no reason why they cannot visit Paris during the 1920s and meet simulated versions of Ernest Hemingway and Gertrude Stein. The world inside *The Moderns* oddly resembles that of the holodeck, not only because of the self-reflexive devices used to point to its artificiality, as discussed earlier, or because so much of the fast-flying dialogue seems to be a series of inside jokes with the late twentieth-century audience, but also because the protagonist seems to be oddly misplaced in the environment. "Ah, Hart, among the throng but not of the throng," as L'Oiseau's first line in the film indicates.

Hart's own works (painted by Frank Mulvey), a few of which are shown throughout the movie, are distinctly postmodernist in character, consisting of representational figures involved in frankly erotic scenes. They are, in fact, reminiscent of the de-idealized nudes of Eric Fischl as well as of the truncated bodies of James Rosenquist, whose works were inspired by billboard ads. In the reversal of direction in influence, it makes perfect sense for one of Hart's works to become an ad at the train station. It is a stationary picture that moves as the train moves—the natu-ral progression of art toward commercialization and pop, from the static image of a painting to the mobile one of cinema. Nick Hart with the silent *H*, in other words, is a postmodern artist slumming in the holodeck of modernist Paris, seeking to find that "purity" and original "greatness" that never was—who, overcoming his initial disgust at movies and for-gery, succumbs to both, returning eventually to the nonreality of his own time, ironic rather than cynical, sentimental rather than bitter. Hart's re-luctant but unquenchable love for Rachel is a metaphor for postmoder-nity's unceasing nostalgia and obsession for modernism, despite full knowledge of the latter's deceptiveness, blindness, and ultimate self-delu-sion. Hart gets the girl at the end because it would be tragic for him not to, and tragedy is not a genre fit for the postmodern. It is rather ironic that he gets the girl after everything that has happened, and sentimental in the sense that every postmodernist is madly in love with what he or she knows perfectly well to be an artifice and a lie.

When all is said and done, the letters MODERN in the sign NEW YORK

MUSEUM OF MODERN ART stand out as the reunited lovers and L'Oiseau get into a car and head toward Hollywood, the center of the twentieth-century holodecks that are movies.

V

> Look, if you can't write why don't you learn to
> write criticism?
> —*Ernest Hemingway,* A Moveable Feast

(A telephone conversation with the editor after the submission of the first draft of this essay.)

EDITOR: I liked it okay up to the point where you started discussing the problem of forgery in art. I thought you went a bit astray in focus from there.

MSK: In what way?

EDITOR: Well, I had trouble understanding exactly what you were trying to say. Do you really mean to say that all of modernism was really one big act of forgery? Picasso, Joyce, and the whole group were just a bunch of fakers?

MSK (uncomfortable): I don't know. I was just trying to make sense of that whole business with the forged paintings in the movie, you know. Then I did some readings on forgery, and so on. The thing is, I guess if I follow my own argument to its logical conclusion, I would have to conclude that modernism was about the creation of artifice that tried its best to hide that fact from the viewer.

EDITOR: From a postmodern perspective.

MSK: Yes. That's why I still feel uncomfortable saying it. I don't know if I buy it.

EDITOR: But don't you think it's really postmodernism that's about nothing much at all? I mean, just what the hell *is* the postmodern, anyway?

MSK: Well, as I say in the essay, it's all told from hindsight. Besides, it's all just the opinion of one movie as expressing the opinion of the filmmaker, and my opinion as to what that opinion is. Now I'm confusing myself. See what throwing around all this postmodern jargon does to one's thinking process?

EDITOR: Writing about an autonomous work, especially a movie, can never be more exciting or enlightening than the original experience of it.

Msк: Precisely! I mean, this whole review and analysis business is all rather parasitic, isn't it? You take a work with all its wonderful enigmas and ambiguities and try to draw some kind of cold coherence out of it. A bit like Procrustes chopping off anything that doesn't fit into the neat argument one is trying to make about the work. A film, after all, consists of images in motion, and trying to explain what it all means in a verbal format is a bit like trying to explain a joke—one may learn something from it, but it's never funny. It loses the whole point of the exercise.

EDITOR: Well, I can't disagree with any of that, but it still doesn't solve the problem of your essay, which does lose its point toward the end. You can't just write an essay on how stupid it is to write an essay.

Msк: I know, but maybe it could raise some interesting points if it's done right. I mean, people are quite gullible. They might even think that we actually had this conversation I am writing at the moment.

EDITOR: But we did.

Msк: Well, sort of. We talked about in a similar way over a given period of time, and you may even have used some of the words and phrases I've put into your mouth here, but I am really just using you as a fictional construct to sound off some ideas about having to write an essay of this sort.

EDITOR (ironic): So I am just a literary device.

Msк: You know what I mean. Besides, you will be the ultimate judge of whether any of this is really relevant. The real you, I mean.

EDITOR: But don't you realize that you are just digging a deeper hole for yourself? Haven't you strayed off even farther ever since you decided to include this little dialogue of yours?

Msк: But have I? I just finished talking about the problems raised by forgeries and how the film wants to play them out. And this little "telephone conversation" itself turns out to be a fake. As I said before, people are gullible, and they are likely to take this whole essay as an attempt say something "true" about the movie when it itself is just an artifice, a crude forgery of the original that only a fool would take for the real thing.

EDITOR: In that case, why the hell should I include it in my book at all?

Msк: Well, I did point out some of the ways that the movie suggests how history, or historical ideas, could be represented on film. But I didn't make any statements as to whether I think *The Moderns* succeeded in carrying those suggestions through. That, I honestly think, is beside the point.

EDITOR: I still don't know. Sounds a bit like a desperate search for a justification to me.

MSK: Now, why do you say that?

EDITOR: Sure, an original way of writing an essay on a film aside, what has the subject of an analysis of this sort ever been about but itself?

VI

> If you are lucky enough to have lived in Paris as
> a young man, then wherever you go for the rest
> of your life, it stays with you, for Paris is a
> moveable feast.
> —*Ernest Hemingway to a friend, 1950*

A variation on the theme of deception—L'Oiseau talks throughout the movie about committing suicide. Finally, he manages to fake his own death in order to get out of his contract with the *Tribune*, showing up at Hart's apartment dressed as a woman after the report of his alleged death. The two of them watch his funeral from afar in a car, L'Oiseau weeping at the emotional occasion, saying, "Look at them. If it weren't for me, people would have thought 'surreal' was a breakfast food."

"You know, Paris has been taken over by people who are just imitators of people who are imitators themselves," he goes on to point out to Hart at the train station on their way out of Paris. "It's become a parody. It's finished. It's over. Believe me, Hollywood is going to be like a breath of fresh air." In New York he runs into a woman who grew up and went to school with him, yet he disregards her by snapping, "Je ne connais pas anglais."

Hemingway, who throughout the film is drunk and annoyed at everyone, ponders various titles that he could use for a book on his experiences at Paris—a "traveling picnic," a "portable banquet." As Hart's car pulls away from the museum at New York, the writer arrives with a friend, saying, "John, if you were lucky enough to have lived in Paris, if you were lucky enough to have been young, it didn't matter who you were, because it was worth it. And it was good."

David Stein, the famous real-life forger who executed numerous Picassos, Chagalls, Degas, and Villons among others, and who managed to fool some of the most eminent art critics during the 1950s and 1960s until his capture and indictment in 1969 painted the "variations" of Cézanne, Matisse, and Modigliani used in the film, in addition to playing one of the art critics who mistakes the originals for forgeries.[4] Are we to conclude then, that, there were never any originals or that there were never any forgeries to begin with? Once again, the paradox of art as delineated by

the film—to believe in untenable standards of greatness or to acknowledge the possibility that forgeries and other artifices could be great.

> We had installed electric radiators in the studio,
> we were as our finnish servant would say get-
> ting modern. She finds it difficult to understand
> why we are not more modern. Gertrude Stein
> says that if you are way ahead with your head
> you naturally are old fashioned and regular in
> your daily life. And Picasso adds, do you sup-
> pose Michael Angelo would have been grateful
> for a gift of a piece of renaissance furniture, no
> he wanted a greek coin.
>   —*Gertrude Stein,* The Autobiography of
>   Alice B. Toklas

8

Radio Bikini

MAKING AND UNMAKING NUCLEAR
MYTHOLOGY

CLAYTON R. KOPPES

THE CASUALTIES of nuclear warfare began, horribly and dramatically, at Hiroshima and Nagasaki, but they did not stop there. They have extended to thousands of innocent people, many of them participants in nuclear weapons programs. They have included not only the victims of a nuclear weapons plant explosion in the Soviet Union but the docile residents downwind from the Nevada test site and American servicemen exposed to radiation in the course of duty. As always in matters of national security, truth too has been a casualty. The ultimate power of the bomb impelled governments to construct politically useful meanings that legitimated and normalized the bomb. Crossroads, the first postwar atomic tests, took place at Bikini atoll[1] in July 1946. Crossroads was as much about the construction of official nuclear meaning as it was about building bombs.[2]

Not only does Robert Stone's brilliant documentary *Radio Bikini* (1987) expose the dangers and cover-ups in the official story of Bikini; it also creates a path-breaking approach to history and film. Stone challenges the official story by employing cinematic techniques to show how the government used film to create approved nuclear meaning. The federal government deployed its control of atomic information to define the terms of the contest for meaning. Official control of nuclear information, from ultrastrict limits on access to data to careful staging of nuclear demonstrations, made it hard to penetrate the official construct. Eager to participate in one of the great stories of the age, the media collaborated readily. By focusing on this early stage of the development of nuclear discourse, Stone illuminates how nuclear discourse has been built on a foundation of suppression and distortion of information.

Stone uses film to give voice to those who have been shut out of official or respectable discourse. He interviews those who were marginalized or excluded from the contemporary discourse at Bikini; their testimony contradicts the official line. He exhumes footage from military film archives that shows how the process of approval and selectivity distorted understanding for official purposes. Stone demonstrates that the message's feigned naturalness rested on ignorance, distortion, and cynical manipulation. In *Radio Bikini* we are all nuclear casualties—and victims of nuclear mythology.

Radio Bikini opens in paradise and peace. Palm trees are silhouetted against an iridescent orange and lavender sunset; the surf breaks smoothly on the crescent beach. This is the landscape of Gauguin, of Maugham and Michener, of Club Med's commercialized pleasure. But something is radically wrong. Stone's music unnerves us; it is haunting and elegiac, the cadence of a dirge. The beach is deserted. All of Bikini is abandoned. It is a radioactive wasteland, a landscape of death.

Nor is this a time of peace. Stone cuts to the familiar black and white newsreels of V-J Day celebrations. "JAPS SURRENDER," trumpets the billboard. Servicemen sweep exuberant young women into their arms and dunk their friends in fountains. But Stone slows the newsreels to the pace of the opening dirge, creating a choreographed foreboding. We know how the war ended. Harry Truman, ill at ease and unprepossessing, reads the official announcement of the atomic bomb. His curious prose naturalizes the bomb (it is a "harnessing of the basic force of the universe"), implies that its development was a routine scientific discovery turned to obvious application ("having found the bomb we have used it"), and represents our purposes as congruent with the Almighty's ("we thank God it has come to us"). The cataclysmic violence that ended the war flowed inexorably into a violent peace.

There was no escape. Could there have been a place and people more remote from the atom's international rivalries and big science than Bikini? The people of the tiny atoll had not seen a camera. But their seamless history was rent into prebomb and postbomb eras in 1946 when the navy loaded them on ships for Rongerik and left them doomed to wander indefinitely as refugees among the Marshall Islands. Their eviction, even their farewell visits to family gravesites, was carefully recorded by navy cameras. But the Bikinians' voices were silenced in 1946. They obliged with stunts for the media. A group incongruously sings "You Are My Sunshine" in Marshallese, and their "king" observes the second test from a naval vessel. But only through Stone's interview with their chief, Kilon Bauno, do we learn of the ineffable sadness that enveloped them—no one ate for days—as they looked back on their island and saw their homes in flames. The navy had not waited for them to sail out of sight before torching their dwellings. For the Bikinians it was the apocalypse.

The contrast between the complex industrialized society that made the bomb and simple, peaceful Bikini offered an irresistible trope. Contemporary reporters often used it to point up the islanders' supposed backward-

ness and naïveté. One radio announcer says, without irony, that the islanders are "not too wise in the ways of our civilized world." (Another
announcer notes that they do not understand atomic weapons, but "at
least they admit it.") Stone employs these irenic images, too, but he does
so to invest *Radio Bikini* with a mythic quality. Rather than implied progress, his contrasts underscore global contamination and degeneration.

Even as navy officers speak to the Bikinians they are constructing nuclear meaning for a world audience. An officer repeats his lines over and
over to get his inflection and gestures just right for the movie cameras.
Stone uses the navy's outtakes, which show the officer, encircled by un-
comprehending Bikinians, repeating: "Tell them please, James, the
United States government wants to turn this great destructive force into
something to benefit mankind." To support its image making, the navy
lavished 208 movie cameras and 11 tons of film on the tests.

The central feature of the official nuclear myth was casting American
purposes as universal. The conflation of American purposes with "something good for mankind" justified almost any sacrifice. It was as if America held the bomb in trust for humanity.[3]

Constructs of scientific rationality bolstered the attempt at universalization. Naval officials and scientists clothed Crossroads in the familiar,
disarming discourse of scientific progress. Media reporters picked up
their cue and referred to the tests as a gigantic scientific experiment. The
awesome nature of nuclear power made that enterprise more frightening
but also more imperative; to fail to pursue it was a dereliction of duty. An
officer, shifty and evasive before the camera, strings a chain of clichés:
"Experiment provides experience. Experience fortifies theory. Knowledge
is power. The way is clear, the challenge strong, the duty inescapable. We
must have the facts. Common sense calls for the facts—now."

Beyond this disinterested search for scientific truth lay the image of the
bomb as shield and its keepers as guardians of the republic and the home.
If international control of atomic energy failed to materialize, it would be
every nation for itself. Over the horizon lurked the specter of a nuclear-
armed Soviet Union. Vice Admiral W.H.P. Blandy, who supervised the
tests, warned Americans not to allow "your homes [to be] protected by a
military force that was inadequate and obsolete." He vindicated Crossroads as providing information to make the United States "better prepared than any other nation" if nuclear weapons had to be used. America's duty was to advance universalization, rationality, and protection.

This was a masculine undertaking, the male as rational being and war-
rior-protector. Forty-two thousand men and twenty-two women sailed in
the American armada. Navy cameramen employed the clichés of the Hollywood buddy movie: men drink beer, roughhouse with one another,
play volleyball, and whistle at the girls. As innocent as a Sunday after-

noon with the guys in the park, these scenes normalize the deeply abnormal. Women serve as passive props. A bomber is christened *Gilda*, after Rita Hayworth's hit picture of 1946. A woman stands for a ritual radio interview (the announcer is glad to see "a little femininity out here") and assures her mother she's in no danger.

Hierarchy pervaded the operation. Risk was calibrated by rank. By subtly signaling class distinctions Stone counters the official universalized dogma. Congressional observers were kept twenty miles from ground zero, provoking a congressman to remark tastelessly that the navy did "not consider us expendable." But ordinary sailors were. Some were stationed on ships only nine miles from the target. Precautions were minimal. "We really and truly didn't know what was coming off," says John Smitherman, a self-styled country boy who is interviewed in the film. Perhaps the officers were told about radiation dangers, but he could not recall any such information for ordinary sailors. In the most aristocratic of the services, the officers were drawn from higher status groups; the men were mainly working-class and often rural. The average sailors' speech and subservient demeanor betray their origins and rank.

The construction of meaning around Crossroads occurred against the background of discussions of the international control of atomic energy at the United Nations. Stone devotes relatively little time to this issue—perhaps appropriately, because these discussions degenerated immediately into a sterile standoff between the United States and the Soviet Union. Pompous, platitudinous Bernard Baruch intones that we are here "to make a choice between the quick and the dead." Molotov responds that the Soviet Union has no plans to build atomic weapons. Most written accounts foreground the competing control plans and treat the tests as a background consideration. By reversing this emphasis Stone suggests that power politics went on as usual, with scant regard for the human tragedy being played out at Bikini.

Some people, notably the nuclear physicists who organized into the Federation of American Scientists, tried to stop the tests. But their efforts come across as inept and puny against the national security state. Their slogan, "One World or None," reenacted the dichotomous thinking of Baruch's "quick and the dead." Crisscrossing a path in front of the Pentagon, the "One World or None" demonstrators are visually overwhelmed by the gray monolith. They are literally and figuratively outside the discourse of power.

As the date of the first test, code-named Able, drew closer, image management went into high gear. The military shrewdly extended to the media the irresistible opportunity for on-the-spot coverage. With the navy in control of movement in the entire region, the media accepted a tacit exchange—access for favorable coverage. Even had the media been

Factually and symbolically outsiders of the discourse of power, protesters picket the Pentagon's decision to conduct nuclear tests at Bikini.

inclined to seek independent information, it was not available in the Bikini region. Distant contrarian sources, such as the Federation of American Scientists, tended to be marginalized by naval pomp and official authoritativeness. The media reveled in the spectacle of the bomb; national radio networks interrupted regular programming for eyewitness play-by-play. Ill equipped to treat the issue with complexity, radio announcers fell back on sports frames and metaphors. Crossroads became a giant demolition derby.

A special station, Radio Bikini (which inspired the name of Stone's film), was set up to broadcast blow-by-blow accounts. An announcer remarks that this is the first radio station to broadcast from Bikini and will "no doubt be the last." Sailors are paraded before microphones for ritual human-interest interviews in which they attest to their good treatment and safety. Newsmen phone the mother of the pilot whose superfortress carries the bomb; she expresses pride in her son and asks for God's blessing. U.S. officials repeat their rationales for the tests. Admiral Blandy, resplendent in dark uniform and gold braid, tries to quell legitimate fears by ridiculing the outlandish ones (e.g., the explosion will punch a hole in the ocean floor through which all the water will run out). Of the substantiated fear—radiation—the naval medical officer delivers the blanket assurance that "every precaution" will be taken for safety.

A parade of scientific and military observers from around the world file past the receiving line of naval secretary James V. Forrestal and assorted navy brass. The observers shake hands and sometimes bow, as if in homage to their new rulers. Sheep are confined on the target ships' decks in order to measure radiation effects. They are about "to draw their last breaths for humanity," says a radio announcer. As the "Ave Maria" is sung at a shipboard church service, Stone juxtaposes sailors shearing the sheep.

The Able bomb explodes in a tower of steam and smoke. The Baker bomb, detonated in the water, is more visually impressive.[4] Mixing with the clouds of steam and smoke, a column of water thunders a mile high and showers the unprotected sailors with radioactive water and debris from the lagoon. Stone lingers on the spectacle, reflecting the mixture of horror and fascination we feel in witnessing atomic destruction. Issued no eye protection, the sailors obediently put their heads down and cover their eyes with their arms at the moment of the blast. Then they look up, awe-struck, from their front-row seats.

Smitherman explains that, being from the country, he would never have had a chance to see anything like that.

Oddly enough, the damage to the target ships, while substantial, lacked the visual impact of Hiroshima and Nagasaki. Some superstructures were wrecked, turrets were twisted, and hulls were blackened. Yet the ships still rode at anchor. (The submarine *Skate* even sailed away from the reef under its own power.) From their more distant vantage point congressmen were less impressed. "It resembled a giant firecracker," said one. The bomb was an auditory dud. Congressman Clair Engle of California contributes to the trivialization of the bomb with the fatuous observation that he isn't ready to dispense with the army and navy and start lobbing "atomic baseballs." Crossroads' images helped reduce public fear of the bomb and convert it into the shield of the republic.

The tests' immediate drama exhausted, the media went home. But the horror had only begun. Stone stays to explore the effects of the insidious killer, radiation. He deploys the navy's own footage to indict the service's negligent, if not criminal, exposure of its men. Only ten hours after the explosion, they are ordered to ground zero. He reintroduces the film's opening elegy, like an operatic fate motif, as the men scramble aboard the ghost ships wearing thin cotton T-shirts and ordinary pants. Scientists wearing protective clothing run Geiger counters over the men's bodies. The men strip out of their clothes and pile them neatly for disposal.

But shedding their clothing compounds their danger. They shower in water ingested from the radioactive lagoon and sleep in their shorts on deck in the contaminated atmosphere. Their drinking water comes from the lagoon. They pull fish from its waters. A viewer wants to snatch the fish away and say, Don't you know you shouldn't eat that?

Smitherman narrates these experiences in his dignified, polite, laconic manner, still revealing traces of his East Tennessee country accent. We see him in a tight head shot. His face is contorted. He explains that on the way back to Pearl Harbor he became ill and had to take bed rest. After a long hospital stay there he received a medical discharge. Eventually his left leg swelled up as big as a man's waist and burst open; it had to be amputated. Then his right leg too had to be removed. The camera pulls back slowly to reveal his wound, his trouser leg neatly tucked on the seat of his wheelchair. His left hand is grotesquely swollen, the fingers the size of giant sausages. He was not unusual. He recalls that many of his friends from Crossroads suffered similarly and died. A few months after the interview John Smitherman was dead.

Smitherman and his friends dead, after decades of suffering. The Bikinians still homeless, with no one who has known Bikini able to return. The casualties of the nuclear age are not simply the people of Hiroshima and Nagasaki but all who have been hostages of nuclear policy. Even though nuclear weapons have not been used in subsequent warfare, they have exacted a mounting toll of victims. We are all, like the sailors and the islanders, in varying degrees diseased, homeless, and misled.

Stone's achievement is to use the techniques of myth creation to undo the mythic message. By showing officers rehearsing their scripted lines he demonstrates that the feigned naturalness of their speech was carefully constructed. By contrasting the consequences of radiation with officials' glib assurances of safety he indicts their ignorance or callousness. The real news of Bikini was not the immediate damage from the blasts but the pervasive threat from radiation. That peril the government strove to minimize.[5] The media, focused on the immediate and dramatic, showed little interest in radiation's more difficult (and officially downplayed) tragedy. *Radio Bikini* tells a mythic story, of power's contamination of innocents. It is a parable of the nuclear age.

Radio Bikini is a model of how to approach history and film. Stone combines historical method—in this case archival research into film sources—with cinema technique. He avoids the temptation to put a book on film. Although there is an inescapable authorial voice, he does not use a narrator. The talking heads are limited to Bauno and Smitherman. Stone takes seriously the central strength of film, letting visual images carry the story and letting people talk for themselves; he trusts the audience to put the fragments together.

This technique has its limitations, to be sure. Unlike conventional documentaries it does not strive to be "comprehensive." A more typical approach might provide more hard information of a familiar historical sort. For instance, in *Radio Bikini* the origins and role of the scientists' opposition is murky. It would be helpful to know that they represented leading scientists from the Manhattan Project who tried to carry their concern about nuclear weapons into the political arena but largely failed; yet this information is better conveyed in print. By his choice of newsreel images, however, Stone clearly displays their ineptitude and impotence. His strategy is to *show* a single emotional point, not tell.

Stone's approach leaves many questions unanswered. He does not try to explain Crossroads' geopolitical context; his aim is different. The extent of radiation disease among American sailors and Marshall Islanders is not explored, nor is the degree of knowledge about radiation in 1946 made clear. One can imagine another documentary, and a very good one, addressing these questions. These issues are probably better suited to print. For a complete picture of Crossroads, *Radio Bikini* needs to be studied in conjunction with printed sources such as David Bradley's classic log of the tests, *No Place to Hide*, and Paul Boyer's history of the atomic bomb's impact on American thought and culture, *By the Bomb's Early Light*.[6]

Stone's approach would not work for all subjects; the subject needs to have sufficient weight to sustain his mythic quality. But for the Crossroads tests Stone has crafted a model of how to serve history by giving voice to the voiceless and turning the techniques of official mythmaking against its creators.

Part Three

REVISIONING HISTORY

9

Repentance

STALINIST TERROR AND THE REALISM OF SURREALISM

DENISE J. YOUNGBLOOD

FOR 150 YEARS, art served as a substitute for political power in the Russian empire and its successor state, the USSR. For most of the 53 years between the Cultural Revolution of 1928–32 and Mikhail Gorbachev's accession as first secretary of the communist party of the Soviet Union in 1985, art in the USSR had been "tongue-tied by authority."[1] Therefore, it is not at all surprising that for most Soviet intellectuals the *glasnost* era was symbolized not by politicians, speeches, and congresses—but by a novel and a film: Anatolii Rybakov's *Children of the Arbat* (Deti Arbata) and Tengiz Abuladze's *Repentance* (Monanieba [Georgian]/Pokaianie [Russian]).

That these two works are historical, focusing on the terrible 1930s, is also no surprise, given the centrality of the reexamination of history as a foundation for *perestroika*.[2] Yet neither *Children of the Arbat* nor *Repentance* is a product of *glasnost*. Rybakov wrote his epic novel in the 1960s and 1970s "for the drawer"; Abuladze wrote and produced *Repentance* from 1982 to 1984 for Georgian television, under the protection of a powerful patron, Eduard Shevarnadze.[3] Otherwise, these two iconographical works seem to have little in common. *Children of the Arbat* is firmly situated in the tradition of Russian realism (with some vestigial remains of socialist realism). In its scope and structure (especially its blend of fictional and historical characters), the novel pays conscious homage to Lev Tolstoi (especially to *War and Peace*), and it was warmly embraced by Russian readers as "theirs." *Repentance* is an altogether different matter—a Georgian slap in the face of the hallowed Russian realist tradition, sanctified in the Soviet period by the official

I am grateful to Peter Kenez, Thomas Sakmyster, and Josephine Woll for their thoughtful critiques of an earlier version of this essay and to Andrew Horton for sharing unpublished material with me.

aesthetic of socialist realism. Only tenuously "historical," extravagantly surrealistic, irritatingly mannered, and difficult to grasp, the film was a sensation.

Inside the USSR, *Repentance* provoked paradoxical reactions. The film received officialdom's highest accolade, the prestigious Lenin Prize, in 1988, but audience responses ranged from tears and passionate admiration to noncommittal shrugs to outright hostility.[4] *Repentance* has been lauded as a "strange but great picture"—and excoriated as a "political porno film" that sensationalizes and trivializes its material.[5] Outside the USSR, the movie received lavish praise from critics, garnered film festival prizes (including several at Cannes and Chicago in 1987) and was extensively distributed, a rarity for a Soviet film.

As befits a work of its richness and complexity, *Repentance* is a film open to varied readings, yet unexpectedly (given its stature in the history of Gorbachev's cultural revolution) it has rarely been analyzed in depth. Most often considered as political or moral exegesis, the film has also been studied as a specifically Georgian work, the final installment in Abuladze's trilogy of Georgian "nationalist" films.[6] But despite its obvious engagement with burning questions of the *Soviet* (as opposed to Georgian) past, no one has explored it as a serious work of Soviet history.[7] Though R. W. Davies reports that at least one Soviet professor was moved enough by *Repentance* to declare that "he was going to make big changes in his lectures on the 1930s,"[8] most Soviet critics have explicitly rejected it as a historical film, finding its self-conscious surrealism fundamentally antihistorical. As Igor Aleinikov put it:

> Unfortunately, the film is not even an adaptation of Solzhenitsyn. It is not a TV serial with a full list of the victims and the killers of Stalin's regime. . . . The time for solving the aesthetic issues of the material of the 1930s is not yet here. The urgency is to call a spade a spade first; otherwise the historical issues will not be clear for the majority of the audience.[9]

Film as a medium is poorly suited to the transmission of factual information if it is to remain true to its own aesthetic imperatives. Yet this kind of pedantic criticism—making factual accuracy (or inaccuracy) the chief criterion for judging the merits of a historical film—has been around a long time. In the 1920s the Soviet poet Vladimir Maiakovskii, ardent defender of facticity in historical films, led the charge against movies as diverse as the costume drama *The Poet and the Tsar* (about Pushkin) and Eisenstein's revolutionary masterpiece *October*.[10] A few comparatively recent historical movies, like Daniel Vigne's *The Return of Martin Guerre*, have more or less succeeded in passing the litmus test for "accuracy," but *Repentance* is not one of them. There can be no argument about *Repentance* on this score: it is not "factual," and indeed Abuladze seems to go out of his way to avoid any such accusation. The NKVD, of course, did not make their nightly rounds decked out in full suits of armor. Soviet artists' wives in the 1930s likely did not wear red satin gowns and ermine headbands. Police interrogations did not take place in sunny, abandoned gardens with inquisitors dressed in tails playing grand pianos.[11]

Yet *Repentance* is most definitely "real." It succeeds, moreover, as a true representation of the epoch it depicts *because* of its surrealism, not despite it.[12] No period in Soviet history (and perhaps in all of history) was more surrealistic than the Great Terror, a time when black was white and day was night. The transcripts of the show trials demonstrate this, contemporary newspaper accounts demonstrate this, survivors' memoirs demonstrate this—and so does *Repentance*, as vividly and profoundly as any other source. Abuladze utilizes the tools of a master filmmaker, but he thinks like a historian in this picture. Through the construction of his cinematic "metanarrative," he has brought the *mentalité* of the 1930s to life. As one sympathetic and perceptive Russian critic put it, "The historical parallels are not obvious but grasped inwardly."[13]

For these reasons alone, *Repentance* should be considered a landmark historical film, but it is far more than an imaginative re-creation of the Stalinist Terror and an exploration of the mentality of terror. It is also a film about history, the persistence of memory, and the relationship between the past and the present. That this was early recognized is demonstrated by the way *Repentance* was introduced to the audience at a preview for Moscow's literati. A critic quoted none other than Lev Tolstoi (an artist quite remote from Abuladze in style), but as philosopher of history rather than as legendary realist writer: "We say, why remember? Why remember the past? It's no longer with us, so why recall it? What do you mean, why remember? If I were gravely and dangerously ill and recovered or got over it, I would always recall life with joy. I wouldn't remember it only when I got sick or became more ill and so wanted to fool myself." Abuladze, who was present at the screening, laconically responded to this unusual tribute by saying: "After hearing Tolstoi's words, what can one say? Let's watch the film."[14]

So let's "watch" the film by deconstructing it.[15] In so doing, we will see revealed not only Abuladze's understanding of Stalinism but also a sophisticated engagement with the problems of historical interpretation. Abuladze's approach to the story is "structuralist": the chronology (or sequence of events) is critical, and he eschews seamless transitions for discrete episodes that function like chapters. The narrative heart of *Repentance* is the protracted flashback that occupies more than half the film's two and one-half hours' running time. Flashbacks are standard devices in historical films, but Abuladze's use of the flashback is as unconventional as everything else he does in this picture.[16] *Repentance*'s flashback is complicated, as we shall see, by the existence of not one but *two* framing narratives, a fact that is not obvious until the very end of the picture and that has a serious impact on interpretation.

The film's surrealism is carefully constructed and transmitted in six main ways: plot details (beginning with the appearance and reappearance of the corpse); symbols (unnaturally large figs hanging like microphones in the conservatory); costumes and mise-en-scène (Guliko's appearance in court in a black sequined dress with white fur boa); eclectic music (ranging from the "Moonlight" Sonata to "Sunny"); mordant humor (Varlam's corpse cavalierly tossed into the paddy wagon); and purely cinematic techniques (exaggerated camera angles, unexpected shot perspectives, and unusually long takes). The overall effect is to keep the audience constantly unbalanced, so that we will see, feel, and think in new ways about familiar material.

That *Repentance* will be completely out of the ordinary is evident from the opening shot, a close-up of a woman's hands making a marzipan flower. The scene that follows confirms this initial impression and beautifully illustrates how Abuladze establishes the atmosphere and succeeds in keeping the viewer perpetually off guard. The marzipan flower is destined for an elaborately decorated cake, which the baker hands out the window to a woman, who (despite her modern clothing) is picked up by a horse-drawn carriage. The baker has a visitor, who is eating cake and chatting with her when he suddenly reads in the newspaper that a "great man" has died. Listening to his emotional expostulations with evident lack of interest, the baker simply remarks how lucky he was to have known "such a man." A close-up of the obituary notice is followed by a cut to the funeral of the late, great Varlam Aravidze.

Abuladze sustains this oddly unsettling mood at the funeral. The camera pans the flowers on the casket and then, very, very slowly, the faces of the mourners. Expressions of grief are highly stylized. A diminutive bearded man dressed in worker's garb appears; he is applauded and identified only as "our benefactor." He reads a bizarre poem intended as the funeral oration. The guests join hands and sing "Samshoblo," a Georgian Menshevik anthem.[17] The transition to the next sequence, the funeral procession, is another abrupt cut, to the face of Guliko Aravidze (wife of Varlam's only child, Abel),[18] then to flowers, then to the coffin being carried down a staircase—further examples of the constant and unsettling changes of perspective.

The pacing is so slow and the "action" so meaningless that by this point, the viewer is impatient for something to happen. Abuladze obliges. That night Guliko, investigating her howling dog, discovers Varlam's corpse propped against a tree in the garden. He is reburied in an eerie

nighttime procession. The next morning, he has reappeared, again lean-
ing against a tree. The police arrive in a comic opera scene to "arrest"
Varlam for their investigation (very characteristic of Abuladze's use of
black humor, not only to mock but also to relieve tension). When Varlam
reappears, he is sitting on a bench, the chain used to lock the cemetery
gate wrapped around his neck. The police and the two Aravidze men,
Varlam's son, Abel, and his grandson, Tornike, stake out the cemetery.
Tornike shoots and captures the miscreant, who appears to be the baker
we saw in the opening scene.[19]

Her name is Keti Barateli. Dressed in a white suit with elaborate white
hat (the woman in the white hat?), Keti arrives at court for her trial,
flanked by armored guardsmen. The head judge, who looks bored, plays
with a rubik's cube. Keti, asked to enter her plea on the charge of mali-
cious mischief (for disturbing the corpse) makes a startling announcement: "I confirm the fact but do not admit guilt. . . . For as long as I am
alive, Varlam will not rest. The sentence is final." She proceeds to tell her
story: "You must all want to know why I'm pursuing the deceased. . . . I
have no choice." And like a good historian, she poses the central question
and establishes the context for the transition into the past: "And so, who
was Varlam Aravidze? I was eight years old when he became mayor of
this city . . ."

Now we see Varlam Aravidze clearly for the first time, standing on a
balcony watching his inaugural parade, decked out in generic dictator's
garb: a fascist-style uniform and a Hitlerian moustache. Early suspicions
are confirmed: in appearance and mannerisms, he bears a stunning resemblance to Lavrentii Beria, native son of Georgia, who was party chief
in the Transcaucasus during the Great Terror and who at the end of 1938
became head of the NKVD as a reward for his "outstanding" service.[20]
This is not to say, however, that Abuladze intends to establish a direct
parallel between Varlam and Beria. Such a parallel would be far too limiting; Abuladze is no reductionist who finds simple relationships between
cause and effect.

We begin to understand how carefully crafted the protracted introduction to the story is—that the fantastic details are not so fantastic after all.
Varlam was lauded at his funeral as a "modest man" who "had an outstanding gift for turning a foe into a friend and vice versa . . . a gift of the
chosen." This was Stalin's persona; this was Stalin's "gift." There is no
death for Varlam Aravidze. He is the "undead"—the embalmed corpse
"sentenced" to remain on public display—like Stalin.

And the trial of Keti Barateli? It is a show trial, with the same aura of
unreality that characterized the actual events of the 1930s. Her statement
"I confirm the fact but do not admit guilt," echoes the bizarre confessions

of those accused at the show trials, for example, Bukharin's: "I refute the accusation of having plotted against the life of Vladimir Ilich [Lenin], but . . . [I] endeavored to murder his cause."[21] Indeed, the very title of the film provides another connection between the events of *Repentance* and the show trials, where the words *repent, repentant,* and their synonyms made frequent appearance in confessions.[22]

The flashback is constructed in two parts, with the fulcrum a long scene that begins with Varlam's arrival at the Barateli apartment and ends with Sandro Barateli's arrest. The first part consists of four scenes of approximately equal length and weight, and the historical content of each is powerful, whether manifested directly or indirectly. At every juncture, Abuladze takes on the icons of Stalinism.

The opening sequence, showing Varlam's inauguration as mayor, is a farcical one strongly reminiscent of Fellini. The day is lovely, warm and sunny. Varlam waves and smiles benignly as people give speeches in his honor; a secretary sits on the balcony busily transcribing these words (which we cannot hear) for posterity. But a water main has broken, and the action at the main, as the workers struggle unsuccessfully to stem the flood of water, becomes the unintended focal point of the "celebration." Everyone, including Varlam, is soaked—and yet they stoically continue the revelries. No matter the reality, as the ubiquitous slogan of Soviet power had it, "communism will conquer"; adhering to the form is more important than the substance.

The eight-year-old Keti Barateli is standing on her balcony, blowing bubbles and watching the unexpectedly comical festivities, when her father, Sandro, sternly orders her in. As Sandro closes the balcony window, we see in Varlam's gaze a subtle but sinister change of expression.[23] These two men, who will become bitter antagonists in the struggle between art and authority that follows, appear to make eye contact (though they are never shown in the same shot). The lighthearted mood evaporates like Keti's bubbles, never to return.

The next scene, which takes place in a church being used as a vibration testing laboratory, establishes the conflict between religion and science, between culture and political power, which is central to the flashback (and paradigmatic to Soviet history). As the Baratelis (Sandro, Keti, and the madonnalike Nino) wander wonderingly through the church, we hear, quite incongruously, a doomsday speech by Einstein on the radio followed by a program of cheerful 1930s' song-and-dance music.

Sandro is handsome but otherworldly and obviously an intellectual (Edisher Giorgobiani is the kind of actor who could never have been cast as a protagonist in a socialist realist film). This man turns out, quite fittingly, to be an artist, a dangerous occupation in Stalin's time, with profound political reverberations. Sandro takes his moral and social responsibilities as artist quite seriously; his cause is saving the church and its frescoes from the depredations of the vibration experiments. In the company of two elderly "bluebloods" with biblical names (Mose and Miriam), Sandro has an audience with Varlam (in a lush, almost tropical garden) to discuss the disposition of the laboratory. That this plot line is similar to that of *Out of the Way!* (Khabarda, 1931), an antireligious comedy by Mikhail Chiaureli, the Georgian who became Stalin's favored director, is surely no accident.

Varlam's first reaction to Sandro's pleas on behalf of the church serves as a tocsin: "So you're opposed to science and progress" (watchwords of Stalinism)—but Sandro is not deterred. He refuses to be silenced. He speaks persuasively about the preservation of culture as spiritual nourishment for the people, whereupon Varlam nods sympathetically, saying of the church, "It's our history, our pride" (the first of several admiring references he makes to the past).

Yet Varlam is willing to go only so far in respecting the artifacts of the past, pointing out that financial considerations make this odd arrangement a necessity. When Mose persists, claiming that "the city will be blown up," Varlam suddenly and dramatically destroys the order permitting the laboratory to be situated in the church, and begins to talk about history again, in the form of genealogy.

He insists that he and Sandro share an illustrious ancestor (one Tarasi Taraskoneli), then smilingly reminds Sandro of the incident on election day with these chilling and prophetic words: "I notice everything. So beware of me. Some blow bubbles while others track down enemies of the people."

Varlam becomes unaccountably agitated, talking about the "sluts" and "criminals" populating the nation, ending his tirade screeching in Russian: "IS THIS NORMAL?!" (one of only three times the Russian language is used in the film).[24] The camera sweeps upward, and we notice for the first time that the scene is not located outdoors (in a free and open area) after all. They are sitting instead in a closed space, in a conservatory guarded by medieval knights walking on the glass ceiling.

The ominous implications of this sequence are borne out in the next, which takes place in the office of Mikhail Korisheli, Sandro's longtime friend, apparently the party secretary and certainly a "true believer"—one of those fervent communists who perished by the tens of thousands during the Terror. Mose and Miriam have been arrested, and Korisheli telephones Varlam. Relieved to hear that "Varlam looked into the case and released them," Korisheli, with some amusement, wags his finger at Sandro and twits him as a "strange fellow." Sandro's somber face and the room shrouded in darkness belie the optimism of Korisheli's words and mood.

These four episodes set up the turning point in the flashback. Their slowly building sense of doom then explodes in a scene remarkable for its skillful combination of realism and surrealism. The doorbell of the Barateli apartment rings, and Keti skips to answer it. She flings open the door to Varlam, his son Abel, and his dim-witted flunkeys Doksopulo and Riktafelov, as Sandro, his wife, Nino, and their guest Elena Korisheli (Mikhail's wife) exchange concerned glances (arrests occurred at night, almost without exception). Varlam is wearing a Cossack cape over his uniform; Doksopulo and Riktafelov are in tails. They are singing bel canto and present Nino with flowers and Keti with a caged bird.

Varlam's mood is jovial. He apologizes for the inadvertent arrest of the "old couple"; the trio sings again; and Varlam turns to admire Sandro's paintings, which line the walls of the apartment covering almost every available space. Varlam looks searchingly at the paintings, and his admiration is obviously sincere as he tells Sandro, "This is the kind of art we need—serious, thoughtful, and deep," and "Artists like you must be with us now." Varlam also, however, labels the work "intimate boudoir art" and "an escape from reality" (words that were a death sentence for Soviet artists in the 1930s and beyond). And when Sandro protests against the role that Varlam wants to assign him as an enlightener of the people, Varlam is plainly annoyed, but he remarks (in Russian for the second time), "Modesty is a fine quality in a man" (another allusion to Stalin's well-known "modesty").

The impromptu musicale continues, and even the skeptical Sandro is able to laugh, applaud, and enjoy himself. The trio is in fact quite brilliant; this is no "amateur hour" presentation. Varlam reveals himself to be not the ignorant thug we have supposed but someone far more disturbing: a highly cultured, perceptive, and complex man who looks on his minions with a great deal of disdain. As he prepares to leave, Varlam smilingly accedes to his listeners' request for one last song. He does not, however, sing. Rather, he recites (and quite movingly) a poem that, were the author not William Shakespeare, one would say had been written to commemorate the evils of Stalinism. Certainly we are to understand the sonnet as the quintessence of Abuladze's interpretation of Stalinism, for every word rings true to the story that is unfolding:

> Tired with all these for restful death I cry,
> As, to behold desert a beggar born,
> And needy nothing trimm'd in jollity,
> And purest faith unhappily forsworn,
> And gilded honour shamefully misplaced,
> And maiden virtue rudely strumpeted,
> And right perfection wrongfully disgraced,

And strength by limping sway disabled,
And art made tongue-tied by authority,
And folly, doctor-like, controlling skill,
And simple truth miscall'd simplicity,
And captive good attending captain ill,

Varlam leaves the final two lines of the sonnet unspoken, but we know from the expression on Sandro's face that he could supply them:

Tired with all these, from these I would be gone,
Save that, to die, I leave my love alone.[25]

Shepherding his son and followers together, Varlam bids his reluctant hosts goodbye. ("Routine is routine," he says cheerfully in Russian for the third and final time, referring perhaps to the prosaic workings of the Terror.) Laughing, the four visitors—"needy nothing trimm'd in jollity"—jump out the window, and we hear the sound of horses galloping away. As Sandro is rather inexplicably pronouncing Varlam a "buffoon" (he has revealed himself as anything but in this scene), the doorbell rings once again, foreshadowing doom. Varlam has come to return the crucifix Abel pilfered. (The two children spent the evening talking about Jesus and heaven.) Varlam kisses Nino's hand and says with heartfelt emotion, "Count me on the list of your many admirers, dear Nino." Cut to Sandro, playing Debussy's elegiac "Les pas sur la neige" on the piano, a piece used in another Soviet film featuring a similarly Christ-like figure, Larissa Shepitko's *The Ascent* (Voskhozdenie, 1977). Sandro, "captive good attending captain ill," knows he is dead from this moment on.

As Sandro plays, Nino dreams the nightmare that is about to befall them. She and Sandro are running through sewers, through city streets, through a field on the hills high above Tbilisi with Varlam and his knights in hot pursuit. They are buried alive in the newly ploughed field as Varlam sings and laughs. As she awakens, she urges Sandro to run away, but Sandro, resigned, tells her there is no point, that they would be "tracked to the ends of the earth." The doorbell rings for the third and final time. The knights (one of whom, as we see behind his iron mask, is Doksopulo) have arrived, muttering the incantation "Peace unto this house." The nightmare is real; peace will be no more. The interlopers take Sandro away and strip the apartment of his paintings, while Doksopulo bangs discordantly on the piano that Sandro had been playing so beautifully moments before. "Right perfection" has been "wrongfully disgraced."

This long transitional scene in the apartment—the longest sequence in the film—encapsulates, as does the sonnet, the major themes of the film: the struggle of humanity against abstract idealism, of essence against appearance, of art against authority. And yet there is no "simple truth" to

"Needy nothing trimm'd in jollity": a merry Varlam mystifying
Keti on that fateful night in the Barateli flat. Copyright © 1984 by
Metro-Goldwyn-Mayer Pictures. All Rights Reserved

be found. As though acknowledging this, the tone and pacing alters considerably, to a gritty realism and quick shifts of location.

Following Sandro's arrest, there is a cut to Korisheli's office, as the outraged Korisheli, still unaware and unafraid, demands to know the reasons for Sandro's arrest. Varlam calmly reads from a letter denouncing Sandro, a document replete with the stock phrases of the denunciation ritual, painfully familiar to anyone who knows the rhetoric of Stalinism: "This pompous artist is a hooligan . . . an individualist . . . an anarchist. . . . His art is a menace to our society." Korisheli, the true believer, angrily informs Varlam that "those who write this are enemies of the nation," to which Varlam, the true democrat, sorrowfully responds that by arresting his "close relative" (Sandro), he has fulfilled the will of the people, adding that "in this matter I must support the majority." Korisheli is at last unmasked as an intellectual and an elitist (like most Old Bolsheviks) when he retorts: "An intelligent person is worth one thousand idiots." Varlam, unmoved, replies in a classic example of Stalinist transference: "He's our foe, and we're his victims." Enraged, Korisheli slaps Varlam and breaks his pince-nez glasses, thereby sealing his own fate (as we can see recorded in the slight twitch on Varlam's face).

This dramatic scene is followed by a cut to the prison—a long line of women and children waiting to learn, from a never-seen bureaucrat, the fates of their men. Nino and Keti are told that Sandro has been "exiled without the right to correspond," the standard euphemism during the Terror for the death penalty,[26] though Nino does not yet know this. Nino runs to party headquarters; Korisheli has also been arrested. In anguish and frustration, she smashes one of Varlam's posters; Varlam is, of course, there watching her. (He, like Stalin, is everywhere.) She falls to her knees, begging him to save Sandro, but with a look of subtle satisfaction, he moves on. It is obvious that this desirable woman ("maiden virtue rudely strumpeted") would have done anything for him; by rejecting her, his power over her is complete.

The final episode in this series of relentlessly realistic scenes takes place at the railway station. A little boy has informed Nino and Keti, who are sitting listlessly in their darkened, denuded apartment, that a shipment of logs from a labor camp has just arrived and that sometimes the exiles carve their names on them (yet another historically accurate detail). Nino and Keti rush to the yard, slogging through the mud, running from one log to another in the company of a few other women and children. They, of course, find nothing (since Sandro has not been exiled), but there is a lingering medium shot of a woman crying, stroking, kissing, and talking to her log, a shot held so long that its emotional intensity is absolutely unbearable. Nino and Keti disconsolately walk away.

At last, Abuladze returns to the surrealism that has characterized most of the film, and the viewer realizes that this style has another advantage. Yes, surrealism is formally suited to the expression of the Terror, but it also serves as a shield against the intense pain of these events. So we experience a real sense of relief when the location shifts to a sunny neglected garden, with a man and woman in evening wear playing the Mendelssohn Wedding March on a white piano. It is Sandro's interrogation. As Sandro appears in a torn, bloodied shirt, the woman becomes a living statue—of Blind Justice. The cheerful inquisitor informs Sandro that he has been arrested because Mikhail Korisheli, head of a secret organization, has implicated him. We know that such a sequence of events cannot possibly be true, since Korisheli was arrested after Sandro (not that the

truth ever mattered at this stage of the proceedings). Sandro defiantly
(though naively) replies that "if men like him are being arrested, you
might as well arrest the entire country." The interrogator regards Sandro
with an indulgent smile and offers to produce Korisheli.

A gray-faced, obviously disoriented Korisheli staggers in. He mechanically confesses his crimes to the shocked Sandro: he plotted with his
2,700 conspirators "to dig a tunnel from Bombay to London" and "to
poison corn to annihilate the population." He takes Sandro aside and
feverishly explains his plan—and why, true believer to the end of his life,
he had informed on Sandro: "We must accuse as many people as possible—and call them enemies of the people. . . . We'll expose the male-
factors who are deliberately misleading the government. . . . We must
sign everything and reduce it all to complete absurdity. . . . We'll sign a
thousand stupid statements." As Sandro watches and listens in horror,
Korisheli's lips tremble, and his haggard face crumples. The wretched
man ("purest faith unhappily forsworn") is overcome by tears, impotent
rage at his plight, and hysteria. Once again, as so often in this film, we see
the line between unreality and reality blurring and disappearing in a way
totally suited to the material. Was anyone arrested for attempting to dig
a tunnel from Bombay to London? Perhaps not, but as all available evidence indicates, it is too close to the truth for disbelief.[27] Korisheli's nam-
ing of names is definitely the truth—many party faithful, "gilded honour
shamefully misplaced," implicated others for this very reason.

Varlam, in the meantime, is giving speeches on his balcony, his previous persona of thoughtful, reasoned kindliness abandoned in favor of
crazed bombast. His language is now purest Stalin-speak:

> We must be vigilant and prepared to unmask enemies. . . . Four out of every
> three persons are enemies! . . . Numerically, one foe is greater than one
> friend. . . . Our motherland is in danger! . . . It's difficult to catch a black cat in
> a dark room, especially if there's no cat there. We are faced by a most difficult
> task, but nothing can deter us. If we want to, we'll catch the black cat in the
> dark room, *even if there's no cat there.*[28]

Cross-cut to Nino, who meets with Elena Korisheli, like her husband Mikhail still a true believer despite all the evidence at hand. Elena feels that
Sandro's and Mikhail's arrests were a mistake, but even if the errors were
never uncovered, the sacrifice the women were making would be worth it,
since "we're serving a great cause." Her face shining with fanaticism, she
begins singing the Schiller "Ode to Joy" from the Beethoven Ninth Sym-
phony. The jubilant, exalted music continues as we see Sandro confess-
ing, and being condemned and finally crucified.

At the moment of his death, the church (the symbolic foundation of
this tragic conflict) is dynamited, the triumph of political authority over

culture. The past has been obliterated, reduced to rubble. Nino, awakened by the blast, pulls Keti close to her and tells her that Sandro is dead. Nino goes to Elena's, but it is too late. Elena has been arrested as well, and Nino's despair is complete as she sits weeping on the steps outside the abandoned Korisheli apartment. In the meantime, we are treated to a little, quite necessary black comic relief in which Varlam finds that the Terror, "doctorlike," has assumed a life of its own. Thus, he is forced to accept the folly of Doksopulo's "truckful of enemies": everyone named Darbaiseli has been rounded up and arrested, an ironic reference to the arrest quotas of the Terror.

And then, at long last, it is Nino's turn. Keti is torn from her, screaming and crying, as we see Nino's hands vainly stretching through the bars of the horse-drawn van (a turn-of-the-century Black Maria). "That was the end of Nino Barateli," says the middle-aged Keti, back in the courtroom, and that is the end of the flashback.

The flashback personalizes history, as flashbacks often do, and that is an important contribution, especially in this case. The catastrophe that took place in the USSR under Stalin can all too easily become a mind- and soul-numbing matter of numbers. In Tofik Shakhverdiev's 1989 documentary *Is Stalin with Us?* (Stalin s nami?), one contemporary Stalinist notes in all seriousness that while he does not believe 20 million people died at the hands of the state, if it were true, that would represent "only" 10 percent of the population.

But *Repentance* is not just about the Aravidzes and the Baratelis, hence the stylized "everyman" shape of the parable and Abuladze's refusal to use real names.[29] Every detail of this tale, fantastic or mundane, was repeated countless times from 1936 to 1938 as eight to ten million people were arrested, most of them, like Sandro and Nino Barateli, never to be seen again. Abuladze's description is a complete one, despite its deceptive simplicity: he has shown us the support the regime enjoyed, the extent of the collusion and collaboration that fueled the engine of terror, the creeping paranoia and ruthless illogic of the witch hunt, and the way "class conflict" was manufactured, with the "people" on one side, and artists and intellectuals on the other. Perhaps most importantly, in the person of Varlam Aravidze, Abuladze and Avtandil Makharadze have given us a chilling and thoroughly believable portrait of the inscrutable mask of twentieth-century terrorism.

With so many witnesses dead, it is mainly those hopelessly implicated (whether through action or through inaction) who are left to remember. How can the past survive under such circumstances? *Repentance* has been presented as Keti's story, but we must keep in mind that it is only infrequently told from Keti's point of view. There is much we see that Keti did not, and that it is highly unlikely her parents would have told her.

How does she know the story she told? Through research? Through imagination? Through collective memory? Is her story therefore suspect?

These are questions that cannot be answered by reference to the flashback alone, and we must return to the film to see the way the framing story plays itself out. In the second part of the framing story, it rapidly becomes apparent that Varlam's grandson Tornike is a key figure, not the peripheral character he seemed at first. He is the Keti of the next generation of the tragedy. Tornike has appeared since the beginning of the movie as a voyeur, or witness; in the opening scenes as the corpse is discovered and rediscovered, we see him constantly in the background, quietly observant. During the police stakeout, he is the only one alert and aware. (His father and the police chief have gone to dinner, and the other policemen are crouched behind a tombstone, drinking and joking.) At the trial, there are frequent cuts to his ever vigilant countenance, none more important than that at the end of the flashback.

As the courtroom erupts in exclamations of disbelief and shouts of "She's insane!" Tornike looks shell-shocked. He immediately sinks into a reverie in which he imagines his grandfather blindly staggering about in a towerlike enclosure, mortally afraid of the light (the light of the truth that has just been revealed). After the trial recesses, Tornike accusingly asks his father Abel: "Did you know all that?" It is a rhetorical question, since Tornike, like the viewer, is now aware that there is much that Abel knows. Keti and Abel are, after all, acquainted (on that fateful evening in the Barateli flat, Abel even kissed her and promised to return soon), but Abel has taken some pains to conceal this fact. Abel's response to his son's question is a troublingly evasive justification, but one oft-heard in "real" life: "Those were complicated times. . . . It's difficult to explain now. . . . The situation was different then." As Tornike persists, Abel becomes defensive, arguing that Varlam "never personally killed anyone" and asking, "What are the lives of one or two people when the well-being of millions is at stake?" Desperate, Abel pleads with his son: "What am I guilty of?" and receives the answer he does not want to hear: "You justify Grandpa and follow in his footsteps."[30]

At home, Tornike dreams his second dream: he sees his mother, Guliko, dancing provocatively and mockingly around Varlam's corpse (another sign of disrespect for the past and for the story that Keti has told). In a nearby room, the Aravidze clique, now clearly depicted as a kind of mafia, plots to rig the outcome of the case. Abel knows that Keti is not insane and is reluctant to manipulate the trial, but the hard-bitten Guliko prevails. They will coerce a court psychiatrist, who is one of "theirs," to declare Keti unfit to stand trial. As Abel listens to the court pronouncing Keti insane on the basis of the fabricated "new evidence," his own sanity is in doubt. That night, he goes down to the cellar of his palatial home, where he has a long conversation about good and evil with a figure, shrouded in darkness, who is eating a raw fish. It turns out to be Varlam—openly contemptuous of Abel's doubts. As the camera pans around the gloomy cellar, we see a stunning sight. Sandro Barateli is more than a memory: Varlam may have ended Sandro's life, but he preserved Sandro's art, which is now stacked against the walls, decaying in the damp cellar, seen only by the Aravidzes.

Is this strange scene no more than Abel's nightmare? It would seem so, but at the final session of the court the next day, Guliko, in disgust, removes a fish skeleton from Abel's limp hand. He says, to no one in particular, "My life's over." Keti's final statement, before being committed to an asylum, is determined and defiant: "Aravidze is not dead. He's alive and continues to corrupt society."

Tornike believes this, too. After visiting Keti in prison, a surrealistic scene in which he begs her forgiveness, he returns home to confront his father for the last time. Abel, as musically gifted as his father (and Sandro), is pensively playing the "Moonlight" Sonata (well known to Soviet audiences as Lenin's favorite). Tornike shatters the mournful mood, screaming at Abel in horror: "How can you go on lying forever? . . . You'd swear the innocent were guilty; the sane, insane." He runs to his room. With guests arriving to celebrate Keti's conviction, "Sunny" blaring loudly on the stereo, and Guliko pounding at the door, Tornike shoots himself with the gun his grandfather gave him, the same rifle he had used to shoot Keti.

Abel can no longer avoid his fate. Weeping piteously over his son's coffin,[31] he cries out "Why were you born, you fiend, Abel Aravidze?" (*not* Varlam Aravidze). He feverishly digs up his father and throws the corpse over the cliff to the ravens.

The meaning of this is all very clear: classic tragedy (if overwrought by Western standards). Then Abuladze pulls his most inexplicable and maddening stunt. The film is not over, as it should be. We return to the bakery, and see—the woman who may be Keti, not in prison or the asylum but as she was at the beginning of the movie, in the company of the man in the uniform, surrounded by her fanciful cakes, reading Varlam's death notice in the newspaper. An elderly woman carrying a suitcase taps at the window: "Does this road lead to the church?" Keti looks at her sadly: "This is Varlam Street. It will not take you to a church." The old woman responds, "Then what's the use of it? What good is a road if it doesn't lead you to a church?" As the camera backs away, Keti watches her walking slowly down the narrow alley. And *this* is the end of the film.

What are we to believe? Was it all a dream?

Keti functions in this film as Abuladze's surrogate; she is *Repentance*'s historian. Her account of events has been reconstructed, but no more (or less) so than any historian's account of any historical situation. She is driven throughout by the historian's fundamental imperative: not only to remember the story but to *tell* it, in such a way as to ensure that it will not be forgotten. Varlam, too, respects history: he exploits it for political purposes (when he manufactures the putative blood tie between Sandro and himself as descendants of the same ancient hero) and fears it (hence his dynamiting of the church). Varlam manipulates the past for his own ends and destroys the past when it suits him, but by so doing he implicitly pays tribute to the past by acknowledging history's power over the present.

Abel, on the other hand, is history's true enemy, counterhistorian to Keti's historian. Abel is simply silent, the ultimate subversive act. His silence is worse than a lie, and it is for this that he must repent, not for any blood debt the Aravidzes owe the Baratelis. Tornike kills himself because of what Abel has *not* done, not for what Varlam did. Abel knows this, hence his heart-wrenching cry "Why were you born, you fiend, Abel Aravidze?" and his decision, finally, to resurrect the past by unearthing Varlam's corpse.

So how should we construe the ambiguous ending? It seems to me that the key lies in the identity of the elderly woman who makes her way to Keti's window. As is true of so much in *Repentance*, she is not what she appears to be. She is not just "any" old woman but Veriko Andzhaparidze, one of the most beloved actresses of Georgian cinema in her final role. Andzhaparidze's career, which began in 1923, spanned the entirety of Georgian cinema; she *is* Georgian film history—personified.[32] "Then what's the use of it?" she asks Keti when she is told that there is no church on Varlam Street. She walks off without expecting an answer, because the answer is obvious.

What's the good of a street without a church? Of a people without their culture? Of a nation without its past? Of art "tongue-tied by authority"? Keti will tell her story, Abel will unearth Varlam, the Soviet people will remember—and Tengiz Abuladze will make movies, openly and honestly.[33]

As William Faulkner said (and as *Repentance* forcefully demonstrates): "The past is never dead. It's not even past."[34]

10

Hitler: A Film from Germany

CINEMA, HISTORY, AND STRUCTURES OF FEELING

RUDY KOSHAR

ASIDE FROM the French Revolution, no phenomenon of modern European history has been written about or discussed more widely by scholars than the dictatorship of Adolf Hitler. More than other historical subjects, however, this academic cottage industry, supplier of luxury goods to a small group of privileged consumers, has been overwhelmed by mass-market literature, electronic media, and other popular cultural products. Visual imagery, especially that of cinema and television, has been particularly prominent in this industrial revolution of historical imagination. One can think of many examples: the TV comedy series "Hogan's Heroes," the ubiquitous reruns of the "World at War" documentary, the made-for-television film *Holocaust*, and many feature films. There is a surplus of mass-produced Nazi imagery in the wider society, a surplus that makes Nazism not only a product of the past but more directly than most other historical phenomena a product of the videogenic present. This surplus suggests, among other things, how marginal academic history is to public constructions of the past in North America.

Assuming there are scholars who worry about this marginality and would like to do something about it, I would argue that one useful response to the situation is to take film seriously as a way of meaningfully constructing the history of Nazism, to consider *historiophoty*, a term I discuss below, as a legitimate mode of making historical narratives. Historians most often consider film as an adjunct to historical scholarship or a document that can be read in the same way archival material is read. These are legitimate uses, but to make them the only or the most important ones is to narrow the potential of film as a way of constructing pasts. Encouraged by the work of scholars such as Robert A. Rosenstone, I want to consider film as a vehicle of historical representation in its own right, equal in status (though not in form) to the other monuments of historical scholarship: the monograph, the historical synthesis, the journal article, the conference paper, and the classroom lecture. This statement could apply to any field of historical inquiry, but it is of special relevance in studies of Nazism, partly for reasons I have already mentioned but partly also because Nazism's public image was in a most significant way manufactured through cinema and newsreel footage. I will take as my example Hans-Jürgen Syberberg's *Hitler: A Film from Germany*, which I argue is not only challenging cinema but also interesting history. *Hitler* is not popular culture, to be sure, but some of the arguments I want to make here apply to popular film as easily as they do to so-called art cinema.

Few movies have been more controversial than Syberberg's *Hitler*. Produced in 1977, the seven-hour film has been harshly criticized by Saul Friedländer, who argues that it is an aestheticization of history akin to fascist cultural forms. It has been praised by no less than Susan Sontag, who has called it a "magistral rendering of the Symbolist potentialities of cinema" and a "masterpiece." The film scholar Anton Kaes has linked *Hitler* with current discourse on the Holocaust and postmodern aesthetics. The Germanist Eric Santner and many others have discussed Syberbergian themes of mourning and memory. And Thomas Elsaesser has focused on Syberberg's use of myth.[1] In addition to these perspectives, there have been numerous reviews and commentaries on both sides of the Atlantic that have attacked or praised the movie. The reception of Syberberg has taken a new twist since the unification of Germany thanks to Syberberg's controversial neoconservative argument that a "Jewish-left aesthetics" has had a corrosive effect on postwar German culture.[2]

The reception of *Hitler* has been (and will continue to be) fragmented and contentious, but most commentators agree on one thing: the film is not about the historical Hitler that unleashed the furies of World War II and the "Final Solution." Some reviewers see this as a positive feature of the work, while others respond negatively. Sontag writes that the film offers "very few ideas about Hitler." Kaes argues it rejects narrative discourse, turns history into spectacle, adopts a multiplicity of perspectives, and posits the "end of history." Elsaesser writes that "nothing in Syberberg inscribes itself in a facile teleology of cause-and-effect"—as if this is what most historical narrative "inscribes itself in." Vincent Canby, taking the whole thing literally, predictably found the film's distortions of history to be unpardonable.[3] Syberberg himself argues that his film is only marginally concerned with the Hitler of Nazi Germany, being a representation of the "Hitlers" that appear in different historical contexts; it is a film from Germany, not about it.[4] Historians have voted with their feet; or rather, one should say they have let their fingers do their walking: their word processors have been virtually silent about the film as historical representation. The structure of *Hitler* would seem to support such readings: the film uses a minimum of documentary footage, deploys no actual interviews or location shots, and intersperses actual sound recordings without regard for accepted chronologies.

Given such responses, it may seem either provocative or naive, or both, to suggest that the film may be read not only as significant cinema but also as history. Although *Hitler* laboriously rejects the sort of realist-narrative relationship with the past that a historical monograph, documentary, or Hollywood film establishes, it invites speculation on what use the historian can make of it. If Syberberg subverts realism or frustrates the search for "historical truth," as many reviewers argue he does, then it is perhaps only fitting to take the spirit of the work to heart and subvert the subverter. This is what I propose to do in this essay. I am not interested in looking for a unilinear narrative or unambiguous causal chains, which so many reviewers of the film incorrectly assume to be the stock in trade of all historical analysis when they compare Syberberg's approach to some hypothetical foil. Rather, I intend to ask if it is at all possible to use—or misuse—the film for understanding the history of Nazi Germany and its relationship to contemporary history, that is, for understanding both the historical and "our" Hitler.

Hayden White has used the term *historiophoty* to refer to "the representation of history and our thought about it in visual images and filmic discourse."[5] Most commentators concentrate on the cinematic-theoretical dimensions of *Hitler*, but to the limited extent they consider historiophotic questions, they deal mainly with the second part of the definition rather than the first. The best exception I have seen (and it is only a partial exception) is the already-mentioned book by Saul Friedländer, who argues that Syberberg aestheticizes the past and thereby distorts the actual historical representation of Nazism. Friedländer's goal is not to discuss the history of National Socialism in detail; the full nature and scope of the distortion he pinpoints must remain unspecified. Nonetheless, his perspective is helpful because it draws attention to connections between the two elements of White's definition, although it does not agree with the argument I want to develop in this essay. I am more interested in what might be called the narrative possibilities of Syberberg's metahistorical distortions than in the distortions of the accepted historical record that Friedländer pinpoints. If it is accepted that there is a very thin line between the two parts, if we accept that "our thought about" historical representation implies a shifting "real" representation (whose full relationship with actual historical events is arguable but unrecoverable), then both historiophotic features, their ways of contradicting and reinforcing one another, merit much more consideration in the discussion of *Hitler* than they have had so far.

In this article I want to consider two broad problems. The first deals with methodological issues, though as the preceding suggests these can never be neatly separated from questions of historical content. Do techniques such as the film's apparent rejection of linear narrative, its use of a multiple, seemingly equally legitimate perspectives, and its associative use of sources give us new ways of critically discussing not only the representation of Nazism in particular but also the problem of filmic representation of history in general? Second, does the film make a contribution to the representation of the history of Nazism of a kind that would interest most professional historians? There are of course many possible questions to be asked here. For instance, does the film have anything useful to say to historians about the context of Nazism? Can the film be used to construct an argument about the way in which the Nazi party mobilized support, seized power, and maintained a brutal dictatorship? Can it tell us more about the "ambience" of Nazism than written or other filmic documents do? Does the film offer an explanation for the rise of the "Final Solution"? Does the film suggest any good explanations for the continuation in the postwar world of certain cultural and psychological conditions that benefited National Socialist rule? Can historians use the film to engage long-standing debates over the notion of Germany's *Sonderweg*, or special path, in modern history? It is impossible to address all these questions in a short article. But in the last section below I will suggest that *Hitler*, and perhaps filmic history in general, is much less able to give useful answers about specific problems such as the composition of Nazi party support or policy steps that led to mass extermination than it is able to give a rather distant visual representation to such things as the "structure of feeling" in which Nazism developed and to which it gave political shape.[6]

Considering the film in this way calls for reading parts of it against the grain. But it is important to stress that my goal will not be to reduce *Hitler* to a single story about German fascism or simply to compare it to previous filmic and written narratives (although this will be necessary at various points). Instead, by misusing the film as a work that is not only about doing (and undoing) representation but about historical representation specifically, I want to tease out a range of historiophotic issues that may be of use to historians who are willing to consider film as a viable form of historical imagining. Throughout the essay, the point will be not to appropriate Syberberg as a historian but to say that to pretend he is one is worth the irony as well as the intellectual effort. My approach will be that of a nonspecialist as far as cinema history goes. One could argue that *Hitler* must be seen in the context of the development of New German cinema in general and of Syberberg's artistic evolution in particular. This

is true from the point of view of the film historian, but it is a less conse-
quential truth for this author and for the contributors to this volume.
Indeed, from the point of view of the historian or theoretician of film, we
are all misusing film in what we hope are productive and imaginative
ways.

Getting the Stories Crooked

Syberberg's *Hitler* is divided into four parts whose titles suggest its texture: "Hitler: A Film from Germany (From the World Ash Tree to the
Goethe Oak of Buchenwald)"; "A German Dream (. . . Until the End of
the World)"; "The End of a Winter's Tale (And the Final Victory of Progress)"; and "We Children of Hell (Recall the Age of the Grail)." It begins
and ends with scenes of outer space, a gesture that could be attacked
because it allegedly trivializes historical events, reducing the entire past,
even its most hideous moments, to irrelevance.[7] Of course, this criticism
overlooks the fact that the director spends nearly seven hours discussing
its historical subject, the filmic equivalent of a multivolume project in
written history and a testament to the film's seriousness about the human
past. It overlooks the fact that Syberberg may be satirizing a common
cinematic device of placing film within a cosmic context, as exemplified in
the opening to every Universal Pictures feature film.[8] And it ignores
Syberberg's use of such cosmic blackness as a backdrop to the crumbling
block letters "the Grail," which Sontag has convincingly portrayed as a
symbol of the director's belief in the ultimate impossibility of redemption—certainly a key moment in a film about Wagner, Hitler, and myth.[9]

Within this frame of intergalactic endlessness, Syberberg digresses and
backtracks, creating a mournful atmosphere punctuated by bizarre and
seemingly grudging humor that only accentuates the darkness. He eschews standard historical narrative, uses documentary footage in unorthodox ways, deploys no interviews or location shots, makes provocative
juxtapositions (Nazi judges, the heads of major Hollywood studios, and
the Russian director Sergei Eisenstein's enemies, for example), and inter-
weaves recordings of historic German radio broadcasts with Wagner,
Mozart, and popular music. The film is not without structure, but its
winding, nonlinear, and associative technique gives it several beginnings,
middles, and ends. Its sheer excess, stemming partly from Syberberg's
goal of creating a cinematic "total work of art,"[10] is more likely to engender fatigue than critical reflection. All the action, if that is what it can be
called, occurs on a stage where actors perform monologues as they project themselves onto Hitler, "the German Napoleon of the twentieth cen-

tury" who is "more of a nonperson," as the circus master of ceremonies played by Heinz Schubert says early in part 1.[11] Hitler is an empty center, a cinematic and historical absence that various actors, portraying historical as well as fictional characters, fill with their own memories, fantasies, and anxieties. Schubert speaks the key lines: "Let's give him his chance, let's give ourselves our chance" (p. 41).

What follows is a multilayered intertext of Richard Wagner and Bertolt Brecht, kitsch and colportage, pornographic and Hollywood imagery, fragments of Hitler's recorded speeches and other German radio broadcasts, commentaries on absurd historical trash ("gouged-out eyes of SS men" and the replica of a canister of Hitler's sperm "on the model of the original sperm bank in Hollywood" [p. 105]), background projections of famous paintings and newsreel footage, and much classical music—all interwoven with the actors' monologues. These monologues are sometimes spoken to or through puppets of Ludwig II, Hitler (complete with bloody bullet hole in his head), Eva Braun, and Nazi officials Joseph Goebbels, Hermann Goering, Heinrich Himmler, and Albert Speer. There are many disturbing scenes: an SA man (played by Peter Kern) reciting the murderer's final monologue from "M"; Hitler (Schubert) wearing a Roman toga while arising from Richard Wagner's grave as Wagner's "Rienzi" plays in the background; and Himmler (Schubert again) revealing his innermost thoughts to his masseuse while actors playing SS men recount tales of extermination.

The foregoing should make it clear that *Hitler* is a filmic text different from written history as well as from other filmic texts, popular or avant-garde. It is intentionally complex, difficult, apparently nonnarrative, and calculated to create distance rather than audience involvement and emotional investment. But more than this, it challenges not only the historic representations that scholars have used to analyze Nazism but also the popular-filmic ones associated with Hollywood feature films, documentaries, and television. It is a representation of these varying representations, an attempt to juxtapose, at oblique angles, the multitude of ways Nazism has been constructed historically. It is as if the film has created a photomontage not of actual historical images but of other montages of those images. If it were a scholarly book, it would be one in which primary sources were reduced to providing a kind of sophisticated atmospherics and previous narratives of Nazism were laced together in almost random fashion. But randomness would not be the goal. These narratives would be placed next to one another on the basis of seemingly inconsequential details in order to be ridiculed unceasingly for their complicity with the subject they were designed to analyze.

Viewing *Hitler* creates a discursive space in which the filmmaker can experiment and "get the story crooked," to use the phrase Hans Kellner has provided as the subtitle of his book on historical representation. "Getting the story crooked," writes Kellner,

> is a way of reading. It means looking at the historical text in such a way as to make more apparent the problems and decisions that shape its strategies, however hidden or disguised they may be. It is a way of looking honestly at the other sources of history, found not in archives or computer databases, but in discourse and rhetoric.[12]

This captures a significant part of what could be seen as Syberberg's project, although in this case the filmmaker has put pressure on the cinematic and visual language of a whole battery of stories.

Leaving aside for the moment the contents of the stories that are being made crooked, it is useful to argue that the "constructedness" of the film, its placement in a studio "reality" far away from the historical reality to which it only gestures, could be used by historians as a springboard for considering the strategies, advantages, and shortcomings not of the film but of previous historical narratives, filmic and written. Most historians of Nazism will not want to go as far as Syberberg does in distancing himself so ostentatiously from any realistic mode of history or in distorting historical accounts, to say the least, but they will find in *Hitler* an upper limit for constructing a self-referential account of their own strategies of representation, the mirrors they use to construct the past. At the very least, then, *Hitler* leads to more introspection about how we produce the history of Nazism, and it encourages the historian to get the story crooked in order to get it "straighter"—more compelling, more interesting, more capable of creating a consensus among scholars who have done their homework, more self-conscious—in the long run.

This is controversial. Asking historians to consider getting the history of Nazism "crooked" strikes at the heart of what many scholars consider to be a story that must always be gotten straight because of the unprecedented evil it depicts. If some historians would accept the necessity to be more introspective about strategies of representation on a theoretical level, they would feel uneasy about it in the case of Nazism for moral reasons. If some historians would accept the need for a more self-conscious, playful, and experimental approach to their work on one level, they would step back from undertaking such an approach once they entered the difficult terrain of the history of Nazism. This is one of the reasons why many historians of twentieth-century Germany react negatively or indifferently to postmodernist discourse's relentless self-referentiality and multiple narratives. Yet in my opinion there are good moral as well as analytical grounds for the kinds of distortions I am referring to here. In explicating this more fully, I want to consider precisely what methods Syberberg uses to get the stories crooked.

Narratives from Germany

David Carr has argued that one of the functions of narrative is the

> drawing together [of] any temporally extended sequence, whether of action, experience, or even a whole life, when such a sequence has gone astray or lost its coherence. Discovering or rediscovering the story, picking up the thread, reminding ourselves where we stand, where we have been and where we are going—these are typical narrative-practical modes of discourse.[13]

Almost all critics of the film agree that Syberberg has rejected an overall narrative structure. On a first viewing, this indeed seems to be the case. From particular vantage points, however, one senses a certain progression, a "drawing together of a temporally extended sequence," perhaps not in the sense of having moved through a clearly demarcated beginning, middle, and end but a moving forward nonetheless. Or perhaps it is more accurate to say there is a tension between the sense of moving from point *A* to point *B* and the sense that one has vacillated between them without ever having settled on one or the other. For instance, by the time Andre Heller engages the Hitler puppet in a dialogue near the end of the fourth part of the film, the viewer has a sense that a certain narrative of triumph and unprecedented destruction—a rise and fall, "the story of the death of light, from the Holy Grail to the destruction of the West" (p. 240)—has been traveled. When Heller says he wants to talk "about lost life" (p. 241) and tells the puppet, "You took away our sunsets, sunsets by Caspar David Friedrich. You are to blame that we can no longer look at a field of grain without thinking of you" (p. 242), one senses the finality with which Hitler's destructive politics has driven a deep wedge in the mental world of the "we" for whom Heller speaks.

Yet it is this finality that also serves as a springboard for the lack of progression in the narrative. Immediately preceding these lines, Heller has spoken of Hitler's ultimate victory, which is described as a postwar "freedom without a human face" and which is evidenced not only in the loss of Friedrichian sunsets but in fast-food restaurants, loss of pride, and inability to use words such as *honor* or *Fatherland* without remembering Hitler's corruption of them. Hitler is the "new old philistine." "The common thing is everlasting yesterday, said Wallenstein, which always was and always comes again, and counts tomorrow because it counted today, for man is made of commonness, and he calls habit his wet nurse" (p. 242). This sense of circularity and return undercuts any sense of movement from one historical epoch to another, a circularity to which the already-mentioned scenes of interstellar blackness at the beginning and end of the film give melodramatic reinforcement, as does the passage of the young-old child (Canby argues that she is Democracy, whereas Sontag claims that she evokes Alice in Wonderland, the spirit of cinema, and the symbolism of melancholy[14]) at the beginning and end of each of the four parts.

This tension between a weak linearity and a strong circularity highlights the actual narrative elements of the film. Narrative is the basis for the act of destruction that gives the film much of its power and appeal. Even though Syberberg intends to fragment conventional stories of the Nazi period, his cinematic destructiveness is based on rather substantial understanding of and reliance on the accounts that have made Hitler and National Socialism cohere as a representation of social experience. He must stand on the shoulders of the historians, filmmakers, and journalists he criticizes so vehemently.

Popular historical accounts have produced many different ways of talking about Nazism. Similarly, historical scholarship on Nazism has consisted not of a single story but of competing accounts of the rise of the Nazi party, the relationship of politics and economics in the Nazi state, Hitler's foreign policy, the Holocaust, and the broader impact of the Nazi period on German society.[15] *Hitler* does not treat the academic models that were available to the director in the late 1970s in any systematic fashion. This was not the film's goal. But the film may be used to ask how competing narratives find their way into Syberberg's discourse and what the result of this process is. *Hitler* includes many of those stories in one cinematic experience, interweaving them in a blur of imagery that seems to make no decision about their "rightness" or "wrongness." For instance, as Kaes has pointed out, Syberberg uses well-known popular imagery of Hitler as Charlie Chaplin from "The Great Dictator," as a house painter, as a maniac, and as the compulsive sex killer from Fritz Lang's famous "M." Kaes writes:

> It is left to the viewer what exactly to make of the connection between the paranoid child murderer from Lang's 1931 film and the Hitler of 1939, between the criminal's blubbering about innocence and the intoxicated masses whose collective madness expresses itself in their enthusiastic "Sieg Heil!" The hysteria of the people and the shocking wretchedness of the captured criminal are related to each other in a montage, but for what purpose? Is Hitler to be exculpated as a victim of his drives? Are we to place the blame on the masses who shouted for a "Führer"? Or is the hysteria of this scene supposed to evoke the atmosphere of the era?[16]

Just as many historians would disavow the project of getting the history of National Socialism crooked, they would also decry such open-endedness, saying that at best it obscures the subject or at worst is immoral. But this response is based on measuring film against the yardstick

"I gave them what they put into me."

of the kind of written history that demands unequivocal choices between competing models and arguments as well as a filmic history that demands resolution, closure, and conformity to what are presumed to be the audience's expectations. Such approaches overlook the fact that synoptic accounts and value judgments can be made only after considering the sources of knowledge and all the competing explanations that have been constructed on the basis of that knowledge. A relentless scrutiny of all narratives and sources—as well as one's investment in them—is after all part of the moral responsibility of the scholar. I would argue that precisely because cinema can array jarring, immediate, specific, and compelling narratives, it is a useful site for the presentation of multiple and often contradictory interpretations. This of course does not mean that written historical scholarship cannot be more experimental in its consideration of competing narratives; it can and should be. But cinema allows for more starkly drawn juxtapositions.

Moreover, because the cinematic spectator is usually regarded as a passive consumer, Syberberg's demands on his audience and his apparent lack of choice challenge the spectator finally to take action and make a choice. This is particularly true if one takes *Hitler* as it was originally intended to be taken—in small doses (it has twenty-two "chapters") and on television. One could imagine using shorter segments of the film in the classroom, challenging students to reconstruct the many narratives of the film—Hitler as madman, Hitler as demonic force, Hitler as a tool of the masses—and then asking them to consider the utility of each approach. When Heinz Schubert emerges as Hitler from Wagner's grave and claims, "I gave them what they put into me" (p. 128), does this scene suggest that Nazism should be understood within a long-term narrative of the rise of modern political community as "collective personality" in the nineteenth and twentieth centuries, as discussed in Richard Sennett's classic study?[17] Or is it more useful to take a narrower "functionalist" view and consider Hitler as a "weak dictator" whose policies stemmed primarily from the social conflicts underlying the notionally smooth surface of the Nazi state?[18] The point is not that the film offers answers but rather that it is a site in which the questions can be asked in dramatic, complex, and compelling ways. At the same time, the representation of competing narratives leads to a classical question of historical analysis: what was left out? Why, for instance, do we not see a representation of Hitler as tool of the capitalist "ruling classes"? This is not to say that this narrative is more useful than the others; but if Syberberg is convinced there must be more than one story to tell, then why not all the stories all the time, or at least all the ones we know, even the discredited ones? Such specific criticisms notwithstanding, I find the existence of multiple narratives to be a useful heuristic tool not only for a generation that is already videogenic but for one that wants to become more so.

If one of *Hitler*'s techniques is to make no choice, at other points it seems to condemn all available choices. Near the beginning of the film the actor Heinz Schubert plays a circus barker who announces what this "show of shows" will be about. Overlaid with a radio broadcast from 30 June 1933 and against the backdrop of images from Berlin and Vienna in the early Third Reich, designs for Berlin's future by Speer and Hitler, and scenes from Wagner's operas, Schubert pointedly stresses what the film will not be:

> Anyone who wants to see Stalingrad again or the Twentieth of July plot or the lone wolf's last days in the bunker or Riefenstahl's Nuremberg will be disappointed. We are not showing the unrepeatable reality, nor the feelings of the victims with their stories, nor the non-fiction of the authors, nor the big business of trading on morality and horror, on fear and death and atonement and arrogance and righteous wrath. . . . So nothing of the leftist concentration-camp pornographers and celluloid spectators. (Pp. 43–44)

This rant expresses Syberberg's assault on the entire filmic record of the history of Nazism, from Riefenstahl to cinematic oral history and documentaries. It is an attack on the very sources that filmmakers, historians, and the wider public have used to create their own understanding of the Hitler period. Here "Riefenstahl" stands for the imagery the Nazis themselves produced to sell the Third Reich. The historical record of Nazism has been substantially shaped by such imagery, partly because the Nazis used filmic resources more than previous political regimes had, giving us endless scenes of fluttering banners, marching SA units, and mesmerized audiences to convince Germans as well as non-Germans of the power, solidarity, and invulnerability of the National Socialist behemoth.[19] One could say that although Nazism lost its political-military war it won the cinematic one; the images it produced still dominate popular as well as scholarly imaginings of its history.

But it is also an assault on independent imagery that, in Syberberg's view, has exploited legitimate feelings of moral horror and disgust to sell the history of Nazism on the visual marketplace of modern capitalism. For Syberberg, leftist "concentration-camp pornographers" are just as suspect in this marketing game as Riefenstahl and the Nazis were; all trade on genocide, death, and destruction. The complicity of such images has been considered from different angles and with varying success by scholars, including historians of the Holocaust, film theorists, and historians of the National Socialist dictatorship.[20]

Significantly, this perspective had functional equivalents in an area that Syberberg would decry, the popular and commercial culture of the late 1970s. Although the actual intentions of the punk rock group the Sex Pistols' controversial record "Holidays in the Sun," released in England in 1977, remains hidden not only to audiences but probably to the group itself, its lyrics suggest a stance similar to that of Syberberg's. The song's frightening opening call for "cheap vacations in other people's misery," the lines "I don't want a holiday in the sun / I want to go to the new Belsen," and the bizarre imagery of the lead singer, Johnny Rotten, at the Berlin Wall ("I'm lookin' over the wall an' they're lookin' at me"), condemned forms of spectatorship that selfishly fed off other people's tragedies.[21]

But no one has dealt with the issue of complicity in quite the way Syberberg has. Syberberg "misuses" newsreel footage and other historical materials in order to critique the images that have fed off precisely such tragedies. He seems to argue that the origins and manipulation of these images by the mass media make conventional scholarly use of them impossible if not illicit. His "Hitler" is a passionate counterdiscourse to the "Hitler" that has become "a film."

Once again, historians should not let the extreme nature or (to some) moral offensiveness of certain of Syberberg's claims dissuade them from asking what the utility of such broad criticisms are. Historians can use this critique as a reminder of the need to consider the "worklike" as well as documentary aspects of "authentic" historical images they often take for granted.[22] If today so much of Nazism is a picture supplemented by words, and if that picture is viewed not as an unproblematic document but as a result of the perpetrators' self-presentation as well as the designs of those who seek financial, moral-political, or scholarly gain by depicting "other people's miseries," then historians ought to be as careful in their use of these sources as Syberberg is ruthless in manipulating and condemning them. In short, the very images that often fascinate scholars, students, and the general public should be used to create distance and skepticism. Should the scenes of public adulation of Hitler in German newsreel footage (to say nothing of Riefenstahl's *Triumph of the Will*) be taken as documents of Nazism's success in mass mobilization—which is, I would argue, still the dominant usage—or should they be read as the most manipulative and effective crowd scenes ever shot in the history of political cinema? And is the continued recycling of those images the result of a critical-heuristic need or of the desire to perpetuate their impact for academic-careerist, ideological, moral, and commercial uses? I have stated these issues as either/or propositions, but I realize there are no either/or answers to them. And I have stated them knowing that all these uses have their legitimate place in public and academic discourse as long as their specific investments in the subject are open to the widest possible scrutiny.

Syberberg's associative technique is also of considerable interest here. It is part of his postmodern pastiche: he takes various historical images, decontextualizes them, and recombines them in a variety of ways. I have already referred to the scene from "M." There are many others derived from classical and popular music, radio broadcasts, images from film, theater, and opera. Often, these juxtapositions are hackneyed: who is surprised, for example, by the constant linking of Wagnerian music and Germanic myth with Hitler and the rise of Nazism? At other times the pastiche is more effective and challenging. Near the end of part 1 Syberberg combines voice-overs of the roll call of 9 November martyrs (the Nazi party members killed in Hitler's abortive coup attempt in 1923) and a radio broadcast of the 5 May 1933 book-burning by the Nazified German Student Association on the Opernplatz on Unter den Linden in Berlin with the Hitler eagle, the logo of UFA (Universum Film AG, the biggest interwar German film company), the courtyard of the Reich chancellery, a blackboard with the names of East German critics who condemned the work of the political singer Wolf Biermann, and then another "blackboard in the hell all around us" in front of which there are bizarre, pornographic papier-mâché figures ("their flies are open and

huge cocks stick out, red and smoking" [p. 80]), representing various film
critics and cultural brokers in West Germany. Offscreen the actor Andre
Heller says:

> And a few Young Ones dismally allied with the Old Ones, who say: the main
> thing is that the box office is in order, and after us the deluge, and the best
> movie is the one that does best. The nasty ethos of the wheeler-dealer. Young
> Ones closely allied with those who claim the German cinema can do without
> culture. Realizing in their own way the bitter legacy of the Nazi, the legacy of
> the statement: "Whenever I hear the word 'culture,' I reach for my pistol."
> Hitler's heirs in Germany's West, film department. Young and old. Blood and
> balls of the German entertainment movie. The human countenance in Germany
> after Hitler. Inhuman with a genuine plastic face. Something for the Human
> Rights Commission at the Last Judgement, for the torture of the human soul.
> Blood-covered and with the greasy hand on the branch they're sitting on. All
> pants down. (Pp. 80–81)

Many historians of course would find this a treachery, or at least a
hopeless elision of developments that require separate treatment and discussion. They are right. But they are also wrong from the point of view of
the kind of cinematic "creative lying" that occurs here.[23]

This lying claims insight into a reality without being realistic, an approach that Nietzsche considered to be the true value of new and original
art. The director's unhinging of images from their proper historical contexts can lead to new ways of recontextualizing sources also, to new ways
of making historical connections. These are not necessarily causal connections but something else. The juxtaposition of Nazism's attack on
"culture," book-burning, Hollywood, East German repression of cultural expression, and West German commercialism in the film industry
raises the issue of what Nazism shares with the whole "structure of feeling" in the contemporary West, an issue I want to take up momentarily.

It is important to stress that such techniques are possibilities not only
for cinema but for written historiography as well. In *Lipstick Traces*, for
example, Greil Marcus gives the reader a melange of images beginning
with the Sex Pistols' release of "Anarchy in the U.K." late in 1976 and
moving to various moments in the history of popular and rock music, the
Situationist International and 1968 in France, surrealism, the Dada
movement, Karl Marx, Saint-Just, various medieval heretics, and the
Knights of the Round Table. The connections are made not to tell a single, coherent story or to write a "history of" anything but to "suggest that
the entanglement of now and then is fundamentally a mystery."[24] In *Lipstick Traces*, Marcus skillfully demonstrates how a kind of genealogical
discussion can highlight the mystery of the past's relationship with the
present. Syberberg's *Hitler* can be read in a similar way: as a mystery that

may be used to suggest new ways of talking about the horrific cross-fertilization of Nazism and contemporary life.

It could be argued, of course, that all the competing popular and academic narratives mentioned here, all the arrayed sources, and all the techniques that have been used to put the sources in some meaningful order are housed under one theoretical edifice—that of the rationalist discourse of Western modernity. This discourse reduces analysis of Nazism to binary oppositions between good and evil, rational and irrational, in which of course Nazism must always be the ultimate and homogeneous evil, the outcropping of a seamless, subterranean irrationality that always threatens Western pursuit of the good, the essential, and the universal. *Hitler* attacks this discursive rationality, the entire house in which the other narratives have found rooms, and then praises the forces of irrationality that undermined the house in Nazism. But to illustrate this point, it is necessary to consider somewhat more closely the content of Syberberg's jostled narratives.

Structure of Feeling

It is easy to dispense with a film such as *Hitler* from the point of view of analytical history because Syberberg appears to have no specific answers to classic questions of historiography such as why Hitler achieved power, how he was able to mobilize support and from whom he received it, how the dictatorship worked, how the extermination camps came about, and so forth. Or rather, he insists that such questions and their answers are finally irrelevant given the cosmic and apocalyptic background against which he sets his "posthistorical" stories. Nonetheless, the film is not without answers on some of these issues. For example, a significant part of Syberberg's account of why there was mass receptivity for Hitler's message can be found in the opening moments of the film. After the credits, the viewer sees Syberberg's daughter in a black, hooded cape of the kind older women wore. After playing with several dolls, including one of the Bavarian king Ludwig, the little girl walks through several scenes in which a Hitler doll hangs from a gallows and figures of the immensely popular pulp novelist Karl May appear, all accompanied by music from *Götterdämmerung* and the prelude to *Parsifal*. Offscreen the actor Andre Heller says in a monotone voice:

> It was in the good old days of the democratic twentieth century when all children were urged to do well in school, learned about progress, learned how to become big and make it, learned how to make money, to become rich and famous, as always in all our fairy tales. And learned that it was sweet to die for one's country.

Or:

I am not worthy to have you under my roof.

Or:

The Party is always right, or one for all and all for one.

And they learned how to make any sacrifice in the name of progress. And the politicians did not see how unhappy people became. (Pp. 36–37)

The effect of these words, in combination with the eerie scenes of the young-old girl walking through the stagescape of German history, is first of all to dehistoricize Hitler and the rise of Nazism completely by placing it in a "once upon a time" of the "good old days." Yet the fairy tale is not quite beyond history. It is described with words that return the viewer to the general historical context of democracy, "the Party," materialism, progress, the power of money, and the nationalist message of the sweetness of dying for one's country. Moreover, Syberberg refers directly to the unhappiness fostered by the idea that any sacrifice was worthy if it was done "in the name of progress." The historical moment of Nazism—and, by extension, of the "our Hitler"—is the disillusionment with the promises of modernity and the "democratic twentieth century." Democracy is in turn linked not with a specific form of government but with the "masses"—with all the pejorative connotations of the term Syberberg can give it throughout the film—as the primary referent of all contemporary politics and culture.

The disillusionment brought forth a man who was willing to give "blood sacrifices," who understood that people were still moved by "the old feelings." In short, the disillusionment brought forth a person who was able to break through the rationalist discourses of twentieth-century life and unleash ancient (though constantly renewed) irrational longings for something better, something perfect, something as removed from history as death itself. Heller continues:

And then a man came who knew that the greater the sacrifice, the greater the god. And he knew that blood sacrifices were required of the sacrosanct goods of art and morality on the altar of faith. And they were still moved by the old feelings and by the way he told that he who sacrifices is chosen. A chosen people. And then that man from the legendary nullity of nothingness, from the landscape and forests of that people, gained access to undreamed-of energies, carried by all, by that majority, the quality of this century, beloved like no man before him and mystically redeemed, a redeemed Redeemer. A true miracle. (P. 37)

Now, this representation is not that far removed from written academic narratives that posit, in Weberian fashion, the eruption of the irrational and charismatic into the bureaucratic rationality that shapes everyday life in the West.[25] It is also not that far removed from countless arguments that have seen Nazism as part of a longer lineage of German irrationality and uncanniness, an argument that has been taken up not only by scholars but by native ideologues, the proponents of a Sonderweg for the "chosen people." And some of its specific elisions—for example, equating East and West in the age of the masses, the party, and democracy—remind one not so much of sloppy historical analysis (although there is much of this) as of the countless academic careers that were made by the exploitation of totalitarianism theory, which equated Hitler and Stalin, National Socialism and Bolshevism.

Of course, for some the shocking aspect of Syberberg's discourse here is that he revives this irrationality as a positive force in contemporary political culture.[26] Or, to be more accurate, he refers directly and positively to the myth of German uncanniness and mourns its inapplicability to contemporary life. This is one of the sources of the elegiac strains of the movie. In his introduction to the film book, he writes:

> It would be wrong and mistaken to deny the necessity of myth—myth as a response to a reality that cannot be recovered. The will to myth means escaping the knowledge of reference books. It would be a disastrous error to reduce a nation's needs to flaunt itself, its will to sacrifice itself—reduce them to money principles and spare-time rescheduling or the annual union negotiations as fulfilling the promised happiness of freedom's revolutions. Whole eras of European civilization were nourished by the fact that cathedrals, temples, palaces, monuments and castles, and parks and cities were coming into being, usable by few, but identifiable as representative objects for all, until an era that did not understand itself and wiped itself out through revolutions, putsches, and wars. (Pp. 7–8)

It is this positive, if mournful, stance toward myth that makes the Syberbergian project in *Hitler* so controversial for generations of thinkers who have built their careers on pinpointing such myths as the origin of Nazism.

Yet it must be stressed that *Hitler* would be far less effective *as cinema* if Syberberg rejected irrationality and mythic themes in the way that the majority of professional historians writing about the phenomenon do. Regardless of how one judges his historical analysis in relation either to other more popular filmic narratives or to written academic history and documentaries, *Hitler* creates a sense of the power of broken and corrupted myth in a way that newsreel footage, Hollywood-style realist narrative, or the academic monograph never could.

The Syberbergian world is one in which linear, rational academic history has no place. And yet, in a surprising and very uncomfortable way, *Hitler* succeeds in doing something that academic history, rooted in nineteenth-century historicist imaginings, has always wanted to do. Historical discourse in Western modernity has been based in large part on empathetic reconstructions of the past. Despite the many specific philosophical, theoretical, and social-scientific filters through which academic history in the West has been put since the nineteenth century, this effort to reconstruct the "real" in history remains a part of the professional and amateur historian's agenda. In the case of Nazism, the project of empathetic reconstruction has always faced its most difficult task. How could the historian reconstruct the utter horror of an age of extermination and world war? Was not the printed word an immediate displacement and therefore a kind of erasure of that horror? And how could the historian identify with all the historical actors, not just the victims but the perpetrators as well? If empathetic understanding was the goal, then who could—and who would want to—think one's way into the mind of a mass murderer?

Syberberg has not given satisfying answers to any of these questions. But I would argue that in pinpointing the centrality of a desire for myth he moves us closer to the "structure of feeling" that nurtured Nazism, gave it its popular resonance, and ensured its mass support until very late in World War II. Raymond Williams has argued that a structure of feeling is a "particular quality of social experience and relationship, historically distinct from other particular qualities, which gives the sense of a generation or of a period."[27] Although Syberberg's action takes place within the confines of a darkened studio, it achieves a certain postmodern identification with its historical subject, partly because it grieves for the myths that Hitler and the entire twentieth century are said to have dashed, and partly because it creates an ambience that, from the distance of the late twentieth century, seems to be invested with something of the longing, the ingredients of the structure of feeling, that produced Nazism in the first place.[28] Syberberg's longing is not for the Third Reich, which the director sees as a crude misappropriation not only of the longing for myth but of the political, commercial, and cultural forces that produced the desire for something beyond the "good old days" of twentieth-century democracy. Instead, the ambience of longing created by Syberberg is one that seeks a purer identity untainted by "the knowledge of reference books" or the specific goals of political regimes. For Syberberg it is perhaps only in the world of art that such an identity can be imagined; yet as the broken block letters of "the Grail" at the beginning and end of the film suggest, this identity is now (and always?) beyond reach. Nonetheless, the entire film cannot fail to remind us that this search for an identity beyond all identities does assume particular and historically specific forms not only in politics but in commercial culture as well.

If Syberberg's project leads him to distort the "truths" of academic scholarship—as Friedländer and others rightly insist it does—then it must be stressed that the result of that distortion is another "truth," a cinematic one, that remains closed off to written history. Indeed, in assessing *Hitler* the film as history, one should reverse the terms of the discussion: the question is not whether the film willfully distorts the historical record so painstakingly and skillfully built up by academic scholars (including this one) but whether that academic record, based on rationalist discourse, inevitably distorts the "truth" to which Syberberg's cinematic representation of the mythic and irrational lays claim.

11

From the Pole to the Equator

A VISION OF A WORDLESS PAST

DAN SIPE

FOR WESTERN civilization, the practice of history has been inextricably linked with the written word. Professional historians assume that writing is both the best form of evidence and the most effective way to present an interpretation. Now, in a fundamental shift, moving images are beginning to offer the first serious challenge to the hegemony of the written word, particularly as the medium for the popular dissemination of history.

To date, few historians have confronted this momentous shift and the complex issues it raises. Conversely, a growing number of films that seriously address history have been produced, yet their makers rarely systematically analyze the relationship between moving images and history. Fortunately, a few films and videos confront historical themes with such originality that one can glimpse some of the larger possibilities of a history using moving images.

One such work is *From the Pole to the Equator*, a purely wordless work that radically stretches the parameters of film. An ingenious reworking of the silent footage of a pioneering filmmaker of travelogues, this film focuses wholly on documentary moving images of the past, eschewing narration, titles, or words in any form. It is a film structured to make us reconsider film, a minor masterpiece of reflexive moviemaking that can rightfully be called a "metafilm," which it stretches our sense of the boundaries of the medium and impels us toward a reconsideration of our basic assumptions. The filmmakers, Yervant Gianikian and Angela Ricci Lucchi, have dared to create a film without two of the most elemental components of the medium: words and "real time"—that is, images moving at the same pace as real life. The absence of these two elements reveals more about them than their presence ever did; the viewer becomes conscious of their roles and their relationships to other constituent elements.

Just as important, the structural opening created by the deletion of words and real time is filled by a compelling examination of ways that purely visual documentary images can serve as direct evidence and connect us with the past. By relying entirely on soundless documentary film for its evidence, *From The Pole to the Equator* raises essential issues for historians as they face film becoming a medium for doing history. A compelling case for the capacity of film and video to present serious interpretations of history has been made by historians such as Robert A. Rosenstone, Natalie Zemon Davis, Daniel Walkowitz, and Robert Brent Toplin.[1] Yet if moving images are to be accepted as a mode for presenting history, the debate must be extended to include more particular questions such as that of film's and video's potential to serve as primary documentary evidence—the raw material of history.

Documentary moving images as evidence, the role of real time, and the functions of words in film are pivotal issues that historians need to address as the role of film and video in interpreting and presenting history to the public expands almost exponentially. *From the Pole to the Equator* does not resolve any of these questions; instead it verifies their significance and indicates how little they have been explored. In its shredding of the typical film categories, this motion picture reminds us both of the profound potential of moving images and of the routinized and limited nature of most of today's film and video.

The gush of televised images and feature films offered to us reflects a very limited number of standardized forms. In the United States, even our best historical documentaries tend to be packaged in a standard format that includes narration, documentary images of some sort, and talking experts combined into a smooth flow. While a few filmmakers in this country are moving beyond that form, a much wider range of experimentation has been taking place around the world, most notably in Africa, Latin America, and Germany.[2] *From the Pole to the Equator* stands out even among these experiments as a singular attempt to revision the past because it elegantly reworks old forms to offer a new perspective on the potential of moving images to do history.

The Film

The background of the film is crucial to understanding its significance. *From the Pole to the Equator* is composed of documentary footage shot primarily between 1900 and 1920 by Luca Comerio, a pioneering Italian silent documentary filmmaker who specialized in travelogues.[3] Archivists and filmmakers Yervant Gianikian and Angela Ricci Lucchi acquired his archives, which included both his silent films and, most critically, all his unused footage. They masterfully reedited footage from both the films and the outtakes to create an entirely new work that fulfills a film editor's fantasy: the director is long dead and the scriptwriter never existed.

But the filming was controlled by Comerio, and the form and content

of the footage reflect his consciousness. Without even knowing that Comerio was a supporter of Mussolini, we perceive that he was unabashedly
Eurocentric, celebrating the power and dominance of European civilization over nature and more "primitive" peoples. Gianikian's and Lucchi's
reediting is a relentless critique of Comerio's—and most of the West's—
view of the world. In a certain sense, Comerio is still the director, but the
editors have seized control. The palpable tension between Gianikian's
and Lucchi's views and Comerio's vision pervades the film and provides
a revealing reflexive dimension. Always lurking beneath this film are the
ghosts—the doppelgängers—of films that Comerio made, including one
that was in fact entitled *From the Pole to the Equator*.

Intellectually, one knows there are many ways to edit a film, yet one
rarely experiences a reediting that is so radical and yet retains a connection with the original. With a profound respect for the integrity of the
images, Gianikian and Lucchi have intently and even lovingly studied this
old footage. They made this film in passionate response to these found
images instead of using them to illustrate some prior thesis. In essence, the
film itself *is* their response to Comerio's footage. Thus, *From the Pole to
the Equator* lucidly presents the construction of radically different meanings out of the same footage. By embodying two conflicting interpretations—Comerio's and Gianikian's/Lucchi's—the film directly reminds us
that even more interpretations and multiple reeditings are possible.

The "unwording" of Comerio's work is the most daring aspect of the
film. The archivist-filmmakers use only short introductory titles; not a
single word is ever spoken. The only sound is a low-key, rather monoto-
nous synthesizer drone that sets a slightly eerie and dolorous tone but
does not comment on the specific images. This unwording embodies the
filmmakers' devotion to the integrity of the footage. No documentary
sound has been eliminated, only the imposed titles—the explicit narration. After a lifetime of immersion in worded films, we are liberated from
the directing, constantly indicating role of words. In this film, images are
the only focus.

The title *From the Pole to the Equator* suggests ideas of travel, motion,
and an overview of the world. That the revised edition begins and ends in
Europe is appropriate because Comerio was so wholly and representa-
tively Eurocentric. We begin in motion on a train snaking picturesquely
through what seems to be the Alps. Placing the usually immobile camera
on the train allows it to move; we actually experience travel. Moreover,
the train neatly embodies the industrial might of Europe—its measured
and controlled but relentless advance. Deprived of words, we begin to
focus on the image. The camera continues to move along the track but at
a slightly slower-than-life pace; sometimes there is a red tint to the black
and white footage. We watch more intently, yet "nothing" happens. No

A dreamlike state in which images supersede words, in which interpretation can be suspended, in which the unconscious can awaken.

people come into focus as we roll through the mountains. Gliding into a tunnel and hurtling down a long grade are highlights. The droning music, the images, and the pace combine to creating a lulling effect, pushing one into a semidreamlike state. Dreaming is a state in which images supersede words, in which interpretation can be suspended, and in which the unconscious can awaken. The dream begins to evaporate as we finally see a town with a spire and finally move toward a familiar ending to a trip—a train station. However, just before we reach the station, an abrupt cut confronts us with a ship assaulted by snow as it slices through Arctic waters. The signal is clear: there will be no familiar endings, few customary guideposts. This will be a different kind of journey.

The jump to the ship in the Arctic is also a leap to some sort of narrative, fragmented and open-ended but encompassing only parts of stories. The tension between Comerio's work and this version comes into high relief in this segment, which focuses on hunting walruses and polar bears. We know that Comerio shot the footage, but we do not know how he edited it or what other scenes he filmed. We watch a herd of panicked walruses flee from an ice floe, leaving behind one who was shot. We look over the side of the ship as a struggling young polar bear hangs in the water by a rope around its neck and its mother lunges at the ship trying to protect her cub. Abruptly, we see them swimming free but with the ship bearing down on them. The mother bear defiantly turns to defend her offspring. Next, a grievously bleeding polar bear is hauled by a crane from the sea, still alive and hanging almost as if crucified. We have no way of knowing whether this is the mother polar bear, but the intended story is clear—and is unlikely to have been anything like Comerio's. The advantage of alternative stories is not so much the option of choosing one as the way it spurs the watcher to view both critically and to conceive of other possibilities.

The film then jumps to a totally different scene printed as a negative reversal. We watch as a line of men who might be soldiers march across what appears to be a field of snow, but now white is black. Before we can even fully grasp the puzzling scene, we are catapulted to a totally unrelated place. This enigmatic intrusion of negative footage presages the final segment of the film, when we return to Europe to witness scenes of World War I. Placing the war footage at the end, including extensive scenes in negative reversal, helps create one of the few clear narrative structures in the movie. The "story" or master narrative of *From the Pole to the Equator* could be reduced to "Watch European men dominate nature and native peoples. See them kill animals and watch the exotic 'other' perform." The war sequences add, "Then watch European men kill one another." Like many other techniques in this film, such as tinting and the use of damaged film, the use of negative film refocuses our attention on the images. The negative film also casts an aura of eerie foreboding, which signals that we are watching a sequence unlike most of the film. Unsubtly but appropriately, the reversed images embody the reversal of the Europeans' status brought about by the war.

The spectral footage also demarcates the boundary between the relatively clear story of the polar bears and the beginning of a swirl of tantalizing sequences that swing through Europe, Africa, and Asia. We see places and people, but rarely are we presented with anything approaching a story. The travel film as a surrogate for real travel is an old convention,[4] but it is as if we are on a trip to places where we do not speak the language and have no tour guide. Instead we glimpse intriguing moments that we must quickly process and interpret, or simply watch.

After the disorienting negative reversal fragment, the film leaps to scenes of what may be Russia, setting the stage for a meeting between what may be Cossacks and Tsarist generals. A crowd of Cossacks rides in front of us. A man and a woman do a little dance for the officials and the camera. The ceremony bores us as much as it might have bored the participants, but we can visually wander into the crowd and observe the people staring at the camera. We wonder why some smile and some seem sullen. The lack of words, the slow pace, and the banality of the action allow us to focus on aspects of the images that we would otherwise not notice. We are searching for cues, watching intently, but in the process we are seeing details and alternative meanings. We have the time to wonder, "What did these people think about this ceremony? How did they feel about the camera? How did they live? What were their stories?" We find new agendas, new questions; and we are encouraged to approach the footage as analysts, as active questioners, rather than as passive viewers.

One begins to realize how passively we have watched moving images and particularly documentary footage. We have allowed narration and dialogue to direct and dull our vision. In motion pictures depicting reality, the cameraperson has control of the camera but not of the situation. An unpredictable moment and an uncooperative person can disrupt a plan and even sneak into an edited version of a film. A subject of the filming can stare or glare at the camera rather than perform or be picturesque. There is almost always more to be seen. How often do we see it?

The opportunities offered by *From the Pole to the Equator* for multiple interpretations do not spring from a stance of neutrality on the part of Gianikian and Lucchi. On the contrary, their hostile reediting of Comerio's footage ruthlessly critiques European domination in a very direct manner. What is most fascinating, however, is the way that the structure and the strategy of the film allow other interpretations to emerge. The acknowledgment of the possibility of multiple approaches structures questioning into a work. Even more intriguingly, a reliance on images alone makes it more difficult for the creator to impose meanings. The longer the film goes on, the more the viewer's consciousness can take over and construct his or her own interpretations. It is as though the filmmakers have ceded much of their power to the audience and in so doing deepen their critique of the Western compulsion for control by extending it to include the filmmakers' usually tight domination over their films.

As an audience, we are conditioned to having a story presented to us. Bereft of the typical narratives, we are impelled to decipher what we see before us—where we are, whom we are watching and what they are doing. The broad themes of *From the Pole to the Equator* are apparent, but there is none of the "Here's what you're watching and this is why it's important" narration to which we are accustomed. As a result, we scramble for answers that are usually just given to us. We begin to have an inkling that maybe there are other questions to ask or, perhaps, that questions do not even need to be asked. We can look with new eyes.

The Cossack sequence is followed by a series of vignettes, most of which are tantalizingly incomplete by the standards of conventional film. This pastiche of short sequences spins around Asia and Africa: glimpses of what seem to be North African, Thai, Indian, and Chinese cities; twice, short sequences of three ragged little girls sitting together and grooming one another's hair; a line of monks marching in front of a young boy as he fills their bowls with rice. In what is probably Thailand we watch a young monk being wrapped in a robe. Although it is interesting to see how this is done, it leads nowhere. Once wrapped, he disappears; we leap to another exotic locale. A nun dressed in white teaches African children to pray and cross themselves. It is as though Gianikian and Lucchi selected the footage that most interested them and simply inserted it. We are sampling the world.

And we wonder. As we watch a young African woman look directly into the camera, she demonstrates brushing her teeth with a twig while a baby sleeps on her hip. That is all she does; she never appears before or afterward. Yet these images can be mesmerizing. For example, one can slip into meditating on what this woman was thinking as she brushed her teeth, what she thought of the camera, what her life was like, how the original audience perceived this if Comerio actually used it in any of his films. While most films directly answer questions or point the viewer toward certain answers, *From the Pole to the Equator* stimulates questions, most of which it does not even pretend to answer.

A few sequences are more structured and have apparent significance. In a wonderfully reflexive moment, the filmmakers expose Comerio and confront us with the potential of documentary film for manipulation. In an awkwardly staged skirmish in a village square that well might be in Eritrea, natives run about brandishing spears and being appropriately fierce while a white man stands in the middle and calmly fires his rifle. With the camera positioned in such an exposed position that the fighting cannot be real, one immediately notes that no one looks at the camera, much less charges it. This staged battle is then followed by a shot of a caravan of exotic animals, including ostriches and zebras, being marched through the same square. The theme of performance for Europeans is repeated with many variations, whether as an Indian parade watched from a balcony by a group of European women or as a staged performance for Comerio's audience.

In its later stages, the film turns to a grim focus on big game hunting in Africa. We witness the aftermath of slaughter, ranging from piles of carcasses to the butchering of a slain rhinoceros to a grinning hunter holding a wounded, struggling antelope by its horns and turning and petting it. Another successful hunter displays his trophy and then, wiping his hands, turns the animal over to the natives. This slaughter prepares us for the return to Europe and a string of sequences of the Italian participation in World War I.

The early teasing, presaging segment of soldiers marching across a valley is repeated at greater length still in negative reversal, but now with magenta tinting at times—garish but riveting. Field exercises are mixed with wonderfully bizarre moments, such as a group of soldiers chipping a huge cross out of ice. The war portion ends with shots of what appears to be actual combat, with soldiers attacking and falling dead or wounded. The film then cuts to a flock of sheep on a hillside, who are herded to form the only words in the entire film, "Vive il Rey." The irony of those words and the absurdity of their setting is followed by the closing shot, in which a group of women in a garden laugh as a mustached man baits a pack of dogs with a terrified rabbit. The image rolls up and down as though the film has slipped out of alignment with the projector. After beginning with the smooth, almost soporific forward motion of a powerful train, the film ends out of joint and on this note of petty sadism.

History and Moving Images

By uncompromisingly flouting our expectations about motion pictures, *From the Pole to the Equator* can help viewers reconsider some deeply held presumptions about moving images as a medium for doing history. Two areas need to be developed in order to begin creating a conceptual framework for understanding moving images as a medium for history. First, because the practice of history ultimately depends on evidence, the potential of film and video as evidence needs to be evaluated. Such an examination will require a more general historical investigation of the relationship between modes of communication and evidence, and then of the role of images of reality in history. Second, the role of the image separate from words must be be discussed, emphasizing the special psychological dimension of "real" images, the role of real time in moving images, and the differences between images and words as signs. With its undiluted focus on documentary footage—images that mechanically reproduce reality—*From the Pole to the Equator* provides a powerful example from which to begin these discussions. Only after these broader contexts are set can we return to the specifics of *From the Pole to the Equator* and more fully grasp the originality and significance of this film.

The starting point is that every medium of communication generates historical evidence of varying quality through the very act of communication. The dominant role of writing in the practice of history is based both on its power as a form of communication and on its utility as evidence. A useful counterexample is the telephone, a potent medium for communication but an abysmal form of evidence. Conversely, writing has been so central to history precisely because it nearly always creates a document. Moving images also tend automatically to create a document, but a radically different type of document with its own evidentiary value.

The greatest limit on the utility of motion pictures as direct evidence for historians is the youth of the medium. For most historians no moving images exist for the eras that they study. Although many anthropologists have extensively used film and video for documentation, the majority of historians do not have that option. Surely, learning a complex new method of communicating has much less appeal if it has no relationship to the heart of one's work and, in fact, requires translating one's evidence from one mode of communication to another. Moreover, even for the substantial minority of historians who study the recent past, substantial film evidence exists but only as part of the already overwhelming flood of data in our century. Given the complexities of working with moving images and the lack of training, support, or rewards from the profession, understandably few historians who could use moving pictures as evidence have taken up the challenge.

Historians are also put off by the nature of much of the existing filmed evidence. Documents vary in their intended use, be it entertainment, direct communication of information, or record keeping. Clearly, the usual intentions behind the production of these written and filmed documents are very different. The roots of writing are in record keeping, situations in which some degree of accuracy, governed by some internal standard, is necessary. Records such as tax rolls or censuses must reflect reality in some form, the logic of which is usually possible to divine. Historians thrive on such records and have honed their analytic skills on them for centuries. Similarly, historians value correspondence from the past and are adept at interpreting the intentions. To date, moving images have not been typically used for either records or direct communication.

Instead, the roots of moving images are primarily in entertainment. Much of the surviving footage from the past and most of the modern work we see today are fictionalized entertainments created for profit. These fictional films are primary evidence only for the history of film; as secondary evidence, they are grist for general intellectual, social, and cultural history—the *mentalité* of an era. Thus, feature films have distinctly limited utility as evidence.

Given so many factors limiting the appeal of film and video as evidence, historians' preference for the written word up to now has been eminently sensible. However, changes in technology can transform the role of a medium, as most clearly demonstrated by the impact of printing upon the written word. The technologies of moving images are so dynamic that yesterday's good judgment could be tomorrow's folly. Documentary moving images have only recently begun to come into their own as evidence.

Two technological innovations—television and video—have already irrevocably raised the status of moving images as evidence. Television led to television news, and journalism has always had value as evidence. Because a large number of historians are practiced in working with print journalism, the segue to film and video journalism is less daunting. Moreover, the vast majority of individuals in industrialized nations have been conditioned to accept, if not expect, moving images as the primary source of news, thus creating an audience accustomed to moving images as evidence. Simultaneously, the spread of inexpensive home video cameras used primarily to document reality is generating an overwhelming mass of evidence for which writing provides no analogy. The videotaping of Rodney King's beating is only the tip of this evidentiary iceberg. Further advances in moving image technologies—such as smaller, cheaper videocams, videodisks and CD-ROM linked to computers, and video editing capabilities on personal computers—will open up even more intriguing possibilities for video as evidence. Unfortunately, already-existing technologies are used in such a routinized, commercialized manner that their potential is largely obscured, so that pessimism about the creative use of new technologies would seem reasonable. Ironically, *From the Pole to the Equator* is an innovative film not because it utilizes any technological development but because it innovatively uses a long-discarded technology—silent film.

This potential of moving images as evidence has been demonstrated in several areas. For example, film and video are arguably the best media to record oral history. By capturing the affect of the speaker, the context of the interview and the dynamic of the relationship between the interviewer and interviewee, moving images can provide superior evidence for many types of oral history interviews.[5] Moreover, because they capture such minute detail and can be examined in so many ways, moving images have provided vital scientific evidence on natural processes such as the movement of stars, the eruption of volcanoes, and the flow of glaciers.

While documentary moving images have clear utility as evidence and will grow in quantity, quality, and significance, *From the Pole to the Equator* suggests that they have the potential to express a psychological dimension that is qualitatively different from written documents. Granted, these images were shot, sometimes even orchestrated, then edited and reedited by conscious human beings, and thus have a constructed, highly subjective aspect. At the same time, however, they also record actual people, places, and things with a verisimilitude that no other medium can match; there is some irreducible and residual "realness" to them that we recognize. Call them actuality footage, images of reality, or "real" images, but they are a special type of evidence with a particular power.

The psychological impact of the image alone is not usually discussed, perhaps because documentary moving images appear so seldom without words. These kinds of images have an unusually high degree of credibility despite all the possibilities of manipulation. The viewer's faith springs only partly from the knowledge that moving images are produced by machines with predictable processes; a more important influence is individuals' direct experience with "real" images. The original "real" image is the mirror.[6] Mirrors reverse and may even distort images, yet people rely on them because they have certain dependable properties: consider our trust in rear-view mirrors. More intriguingly, myths and fairy tales from many cultures abound with examples of the magical power of mirrors, which were, for millennia, the only way to reproduce reality directly. "Real" images embody a human fascination with the power of reproducing an object or reflecting its reality. Although the impact of mirrors is limited in time and space, they allow individuals to regularly experience personal control over the production of images of reality that they can monitor.

Photography was the most important advance in "real" images after the mirror, and it quickly gained acceptance as a way to record personal life. Oliver Wendell Holmes put it succinctly in 1859 when he hailed photography as a "mirror with a memory."[7] Photography changed the nature of visual memory. Even today, most photographs are taken to capture images of people and places that individuals want to remember. In this way, photographs represent a limited but very personal mastery over time and space.

Originally, an individual could choose the photographer, the time, and the plan of the image; soon afterward, the individual could control the actual production of photographic images. This personal control and the universality of photographs in Western cultures conditions most people to believe in the fundamental "reality" of photographic images, even mass-produced ones. Almost everyone has at least one photograph with an almost talismanic or totemic significance—an image that takes us across time and space and triggers memories, thoughts, and emotions. After all, totems are images or symbols of a blood connection, and many photographs are exactly that. Therefore, we are familiar with many wordless images of reality for which we provide the context and the belief in their "realness."

Photography laid a base of trust in moving pictures. However, while moving images are even more "real" than photos, they have not as typically been used for personal purposes, primarily because of the expense involved in doing so. Moreover, they have almost always been used in conjunction with words, so the palpable power of "real" images has always been alloyed with language. The role of language, writing, and narrative in structuring presentations of history has been closely analyzed by a handful of historians led by Hayden White.[8] As part of his analysis of the "content of the form" of history, White has suggested that moving images of history can be examined in a similar fashion, even coining the term *historiophoty* for "the representation of history and our thought about it in visual images and filmic discourse."[9] In his use of the phrase "filmic discourse," White implicitly recognizes that film and video are mixed forms of media. Any thorough analysis of the content of this form requires an examination of the constituent parts as well as of their interactions. Because of its total focus on unworded documentary images from the past, *From the Pole to the Equator* provides a superlative opportunity to cleanly sever word from image.

One useful way to contrast words and moving images is to consider them as signs in the semiotic sense. Charles S. Peirce's semiotic categories of iconic, indexical, and symbolic signs provide a vocabulary and a conceptual framework that illuminate crucial differences between moving images and words.[10] An iconic sign directly resembles its object in some way. The simplest iconic form is an image, whereas a diagram such as a graph embodies a more complex portrayal by analogy. Indexical signs differ in that they generate concepts in the mind of the viewer yet are not entirely abstract or arbitrary. A weather vane or a hand pointing in a direction are good examples of indexical signs. One might say that they indicate rather than reproduce. In Peirce's analysis, symbolic signs are the most complex form. Symbols are arbitrary signs for conceptual objects and must be learned. Language is a prime example of symbolic signs.

Most signs, however, encompass more than one category. Words are rooted in the symbolic yet can at the same time be indexical. Moving images are iconic, but editing, camera work, and lighting provide an indexical dimension. Clearly, the combination of all three categories of signs in mixed media such as film and video makes complex signification possible. While any systematic comparison of the strongly iconic locus of moving images with the essentially symbolic roots of language is beyond the scope of this essay, *From the Pole to the Equator* provides a lucid example of the functioning of largely iconic signs. The iconic nature of documentary moving images makes them evidence with an immediacy and specificity beyond any written form.

These signs are deeply iconic because they are reproductions of real objects through a mechanical process. The match between object and sign is very close. Rooted in visual specificity rather than abstraction, these images embody John Berger's statement that "seeing comes before words. The child looks and recognizes before it can speak. . . . It is seeing which establishes our place in the surrounding world: we explain that world with words, but words can never undo the fact that we are surrounded by it."[11]

With a slowed pace and without words giving direction, these highly specific "real" images are *the* focus for ninety-six minutes. Indexical and symbolic aspects do not disappear, but the center of gravity shifts. The brutally explicit master narrative excoriates the Europeans' abuse of nature, the exotic other, and themselves, but, at all levels beneath the master narrative, any putative narrative is incomplete or inchoate. More than structuring our understanding, these fragments tantalize us and remind us of the absence of narratives. With the diminution of the indexical and symbolic aspects, the viewer scrambles to create narratives, ransacking his or her consciousness for the context that will "explain" what is happening. What, literally, is the story?

The story is whatever meaning one can create out of these iconic images, which depends on the viewer's context and conceptual frameworks, as well as on the willingness to think. While these iconic images are mesmerizing evidence, they stupefy a passive viewer conditioned to having meanings indicated and overindicated. The film provides limpid evidence for multiple, fascinating historical narratives and other forms of interpretation, but the watcher must take an active or even leading role to create the abstractions called narratives. Whereas the primary thrust of moving images in our society is to engender a numbing passivity, *From the Pole to the Equator* impels the viewer towards an exhilarating creativity.

The film snaps another preconceived notion about film through its unorthodox pacing. Almost all the films and videos that we see move at the same speed as real time, yet because they are highly edited, the viewer sees them as more concentrated, more intense than reality itself—almost hyperreal. As Oliver Wendell Holmes foresaw in 1859, the image would "become more important than the object itself."[12] Moreover, this rapid pace leaves little time for careful looking or intelligent questioning, much less formulating alternative interpretations. As Walter Benjamin put it, "The film takes control of time."[13]

The unusually slow pace of *From the Pole to the Equator* reminds us that real time is merely a convention, and when footage is edited real time is an illusion. In a sense, the film's pacing is more realistic than real time because it makes clear that we are under the filmmakers' control. Time is manipulated in a transparent manner that acknowledges that it is a construction, but because the pace is both slowed and constant, it allows a focus on the actual images. Gianikian and Lucchi cede much of the directive power of pacing to the viewer, just as they surrender the capacity of both words and sound to control meaning. As a result, they privilege the images while also empowering the viewer. At the same time, the absence of words and real time reveals our usual dependence on them. The trip on which Gianikian and Lucchi are leading us is not a package tour and certainly not a cruise. It is more like an archeological dig in an unmapped area where no one speaks our language.

Conceiving of this film as a trip is more than just a metaphor. *From the Pole to the Equator* records travel, looks like a journey, and is structured like a trip. The origin of these documentary images in travelogues provides a slender unifying thread. The film feels similar to situations in an actual journey when a tourist, while passing by, observes fragments of lives. Unlike a journey, however, there is no interpreter or travel guide on board, and the vehicle never stops. This journey is more exploration than tourism. In response, the viewer may bolt for home or gamely attempt to find or create meaning. Alternatively, one may choose finally to surrender meaning and simply watch.

In this trip without signposts, the viewer's mind has space to wander and time to raise questions ranging from "Why am I still sitting here?" to "Where has all this gone?" to "What was that person thinking?" French linguist Emile Benveniste has articulated the useful concept of an unconscious or latent discourse that lurks beneath every conscious discourse.[14] By leaving huge narrative gaps in a field of specific images of the "real," *From the Pole to the Equator* creates a severely truncated conscious discourse—a discourse without words—which allows the unconscious to filter up. Although some viewers may feel as if they have entered into a dream state of some sort, it may be only the residual effect of being pushed out of familiar frameworks and cozy categories.

From the Pole to the Equator could be seen as an exemplar of what might be called reflexive realism, an attitude that spurns illusions of reality to dissect the realities of illusion. By acknowledging the constructed nature of history, including the artifice of narrative and "real time," and by using a transparent methodology that makes assumptions and intentions explicit, historians can begin to reveal the content of their forms. *From the Pole to the Equator* rips apart our preconceptions about the film form, shifting the focus from our presumptions to the actual evidence. The viewer becomes empowered, both by creating interpretation and by glimpsing the processes of generating historical meaning.

12

Walker and *Mississippi Burning*

POSTMODERNISM VERSUS ILLUSIONIST
NARRATIVE

SUMIKO HIGASHI

Is HISTORY dead? In 1989 *Newsweek, Time,* and the *New York Times Magazine* featured articles about Francis Fukuyama, a state department official who heralded "the end of history" as communist regimes went bankrupt, even before Pepsi-Cola and AT&T commercials co-opted the dismantling of the Berlin Wall. Fukuyama's postmortem about the triumph of Western capitalism has since become the subject of academic discourse.[1] Charting the postmodern, Fredric Jameson informs us that since "the waning of the great high-modernist thematics of time and temporality, the elegiac mysteries of durée and memory . . . we now inhabit the synchronic rather than the diachronic . . . , our daily life . . . dominated by categories of space rather than by categories of time."[2] Albeit from opposite ends of the political spectrum, both Fukuyama and Jameson associate the eclipse of history with the triumph of late capitalism and Western-style consumerism. Jameson is particularly concerned about the way in which the rapid processing of information by the news media results in "a series of perpetual presents" and induces "historical amnesia."[3] But is not history being prematurely interred? Critics like Fredric Jameson and David Harvey, who comment on the waning of historicity in postmodernist society, do so from a modernist perspective that includes linear time and periodization, as opposed to spatial and atemporal concepts such as Foucauldian genealogy. Jameson, for example, postulates three stages of capitalistic growth—market capitalism, imperialism, and multinationalism—that correspond to cultural forms labeled realism, modernism, and postmodernism, a schematic evolution of infrastructure in relation to superstructure. Analyzing twentieth-century

I wish to thank Ronald Gottesman, Robert Rosen, Vivian Sobchack, and Charles Wolfe for comments on previous drafts read at the Society for Cinema Studies conference in Los Angeles in 1991 and at the American Studies annual meeting in Costa Mesa in 1992.

capitalism as a progression from assembly-line Fordism to flexible accumulation or global financial systems transcending nation-states, Harvey
asserts the relevance of Marx, who "restored historical time."[4] As evidenced by the linear perspective of the very critics who are alarmed by the
disappearance of the historical referent in late capitalist society, traditional concepts of history still persist. In fact, a close scrutiny of *Walker*
(1987) and *Mississippi Burning* (1988), two very different films about
historical events, reveals that history is still sacrosanct and that efforts to
reconceptualize it provoke fractious debate.

A brief survey of recent historiographical developments, which include
discourse on film as history, reveals that the historical profession is indeed
very much divided.[5] Although traditional history rooted in nineteenth-
century German historiography could be labeled a modernist (and thus
outmoded) discipline, controversy among historians demonstrates that
the field has been reconceptualized so that political history about nation-
states now coexists with the "New History," a catch-all category including the social history of groups excluded from access to traditional forms
of power, the new economic history or cliometrics, and the new cultural
and intellectual history informed by poststructuralism.[6] Primary in the
canon constituting the "New History" is the work of Fernand Braudel
(1902–85), the most influential historian of the *Annales* school in Paris
and a colleague of structuralist Claude Lévi-Strauss. Contrary to claims
that the accelerating displacement of time by space in postmodernist consumer society means the end of history, Braudel boldly reconceptualized
historical time in three tiers so that it was spatial and visual. Parallel to
rapidly developing political events are social and economic patterns
evolving at a slower pace and almost immobile geographical factors that
can only be observed over the *longue durée*.[7] Significantly, Braudel used
the language of film montage to describe how time could be manipulated
and cautioned that history would "not lend itself so easily to . . . juggling
with the synchronic and diachronic."[8]

Precisely the juxtaposition of synchronic and diachronic aspects of
time that is so difficult to achieve in the writing of history is possible in
postmodernist as opposed to illusionist representations of history in film.
A consideration of *Walker* (1987), a parody about a nineteenth-century
American adventurer who became president of Nicaragua, and *Mississippi Burning* (1988), an account of the events of Freedom Summer in
1964, will be the focus of this essay. As a postmodernist narrative,
Walker is self-reflexive, ironical, and absurdist in contrast to *Mississippi
Burning*, a social problem and male bonding film constructed according
to genre conventions. Unfortunately, the powerful reality effect of the
civil rights drama, which will be discussed later, limited public discourse
on historicity to questions of the authenticity of its representation. By

contrast, *Walker* cleverly exploits the cinematic apparatus that results in time compression to provoke thought about the meaning of the past and how it is constructed. Specifically, the film's representation of events is chronological and linear, but the present is superimposed on the past so that American foreign policy in Central America is informed by events of the Vietnam War and, more recently, Desert Shield and Desert Storm. In effect, the juxtaposition of contemporary military exploits with previous ones illustrates Braudel's concept of the spatialization of time that yields perspective on history viewed from a distance.[9] *Walker*, in other words, engages in a continuous dialogue about the ways in which past and present are constructed in relation to each other. Further, the synchronic and diachronic dimensions of historical experience are made visible so that the emphasis is upon continuity as well as change. Consequently, the film does not represent an endorsement of modernization as progress in a linear unfolding of time. As scriptwriter Rudy Wurlitzer concluded, "I've learned . . . about . . . the currents and cycles of history, how history is really not linear, and that it comes around with its own laws."[10]

Given Jameson's observation about the disappearance of the historical referent in late capitalist society, why does *Walker* succeed as history? As a representation of past events, the film exploits a series of contradictions, not the least of which is the concept of postmodernist cinema as history. Director Alex Cox and Wurlitzer consciously engage in a self-reflexive exercise that frustrates audience expectations with respect to genres traditionally associated with dramatizing historical events, namely, documentary, docudrama, and biopic. As a matter of fact, they eschew any attempt at illusionist narrative, play fast and loose with the facts, and collapse past and present tense by telescoping events. Further, they effect a satirical tone through a disjunction between image and sound in which voice-over narration, dialogue, and nondiegetic music are contradicted by the mise-en-scène. As Charles Jencks observes, a distanced and ironical view of the past, in which innocence is no longer possible, is the essence of postmodernist thought about time.[11] What emerges in *Walker* is thus a sense of history that runs counter to a nostalgic and romanticized construction of past events equivalent to forgetfulness. The film functions instead as a hilarious commentary on the psychosexual character of American Puritans who subordinated women and peoples of color, on the role of capital in the pursuit of Manifest Destiny, and on the relentlessness of modernization, including a commodified media culture.

A montage of events past and present that sharpens our perspective about both, *Walker* is a representation of American spread-eagle diplomacy that ascribes capitalist exploitation of Third World peoples to institutionalized racism and sexism. Although their meeting in the film is apocryphal, industrial magnate Cornelius Vanderbilt (Peter Boyle) summons William Walker (Ed Harris), the filibusterer who was once a household word in this country and is ironically remembered today only in Nicaragua.[12] Arriving on horseback at the site of railroad construction where Chinese workers are laying tracks, a symbolic scene with reference to Manifest Destiny, Walker meets Vanderbilt underling Ephraim Squier (Richard Masur). As Squier conducts him through a series of passenger cars—a scene that is privileged as a transitional moment in the film because two men emerge outdoors where they began—Walker listens to his guide salivate about imperialistic conquest. "Central America," exclaims Squier, is "land . . . for the taking . . . [with] bare-breasted beauties under trees laden with fruit—seven to every man." A cartoonish figure seated in the midst of railroad construction, Commodore Vanderbilt echoes the business executives coded as villains in black and white as opposed to color photography in California Newsreel's *Controlling Interest* (1978). Pointing to a map of Nicaragua, dismissed as "a fucked-up little country somewhere south of here," the industrialist exclaims, "What I need is for some man to go down there and take over. I want that country stable." When Vanderbilt fails to appeal to the ambition of his guest, who affects the dress of a clergyman, he is cunning enough to exploit his self-righteous and fanatical belief in the country's ideals. "Do you prize democracy, universal suffrage, the principles of our founding fathers? . . . Nicaragua needs democracy." Affectless throughout most of the film's tumultuous events, Walker is devastated by the sudden death of his fiancée, Ellen Martin (Marlee Matlin), decides to accept Vanderbilt's challenge, and sets sail for Nicaragua with his "Immortals." Chief among his followers is a fictional black fighter who accompanied him on an earlier filibuster in Mexico.[13] According to a convention of historical epics, documentaries, and educational film, a map is superimposed over a sailing ship as voice-over narration first announces a "new era for Nicaragua and all Central America" and then, as Walker is shot in the foreground with a cross, switches to first-person commentary inflected with ironical reference to Vietnam: "We paused at the small, unregenerated hamlet of Realejo."

Walker's complexity as a postmodernist historical film includes its representation of the politics of the "Other" as oppressed but nevertheless heterogeneous groups of people. In fact, Walker emerges victorious in Nicaragua after a disastrous series of setbacks because the country is divided by civil war between Conservative and Liberal factions. Although the Nicaraguan masses have no voice in the film, the members of the ruling class define their interests in economic rather than nationalist terms and are thus easily co-opted. Witnessing an American setback at Rivas, a Nicaraguan sympathizer rails against his countrymen's opposition: "Our American brothers came here to bring Peace, Democracy, and Liberty. . . . To improve our civilization. And strengthen our economy." Walker stumbles onto victory by accident rather than design and forms an alliance with Doña Yrena (Blanca Guerra), a Nicaraguan aristocrat who would rather sleep with an American imperialist than embrace democratic reform. Also divided are American blacks in Walker's ragtag army, the Immortals. After staging an election to declare himself president of Nicaragua, Walker decrees slavery in order to end a labor shortage and court an alliance with the antebellum South. When he announces his intention during a zany performance of *Julius Caesar*, his black followers angrily leave the theater, but their political reactions differ. Walker's most trusted black lieutenant contests his argument that Nicaraguan Indians, like negroes, are suited for slavery by reason of their "fidelity and docility and . . . capacity for labor," but he remains a steadfast supporter. Another African-American fighter, however, contemptuously tosses his medal in the dirt and rides out of town. As his wife, who accompanied him to Nicaragua, had predicted in contemporary lingo, "Next thing you know they'll reinstitute slavery. It's the same racist, macho, sexist shit we turned our backs on." Since these events are part of a historical continuum that includes ongoing oppression of African-Americans in the United States and recent Nicaraguan struggle between Sandinistas and Contras, the elusiveness of political and socioeconomic change is underscored.

Aside from its sophisticated vision of the politics of the developing world and of ethnic minorities, *Walker* reverberates with echoes of feminist discourse on the filmic representation of women. The heroines who are romantically or sexually linked with Walker are, not coincidentally, unable to communicate in English and thus represented as constructs of different forms of language. Unfortunately, not much is known about Walker's brief relationship with Ellen Martin, a hearing-impaired Southern woman who succumbed to yellow fever.[14] Condemning Manifest Destiny as "a cover-up for slavery," she quickly emerges as the moral center of the film. Despite her inability to speak and hear, Ellen reduces Walker to despair during a quarrel sparked by his refusal to convey her political sentiments to Squier, a smug expansionist. She signs to him, "You never represent me. You're always paraphrasing everything I say. Censoring me. . . . I don't trust you." Walker is photographed against a painting of a fertile landscape and next to a model of a sailing ship when he swears, "I'll never leave again." Since the film's cinematography and editing contradict the sound track, Ellen's hearing impairment questions speech or utterance as symbolic of the diachronic in favor of mise-en-scène as visual evidence of the synchronic. When Ellen suddenly dies of yellow fever, Walker accepts Vanderbilt's offer to invade Nicaragua, only to succumb to the influence of yet another strong-willed woman, Doña Yrena.

Unlike Ellen, the Nicaraguan aristocrat is a completely fictional construct but a necessary one in that sexual politics is symbolic of colonialist expansion. Again, sexual difference, complicated in this instance by cultural difference, is conveyed by the woman's lack of access to the language spoken by male imperialists. Doña Yrena disguises her ability to speak English, decreed the official language of Nicaragua, so that her Spanish dialogue is subtitled on the screen. Although Walker is repeatedly photographed in foreground and at low angle, Doña Yrena, who is sexually aggressive, observes his slight physical stature and reassures him that his performance in bed is "not great, but for a gringo good enough." Walker's decision to execute General Ponciano Corral, the legitimist leader, and to torch the centuries-old city of Granada are vindictive reactions to Doña Yrena's defiance. She contemptuously dismisses him as "a dog's asshole." The representation of territorial conquest as sexual imperative is nothing new, but the film's sex role reversals and irreverent tone provide more than a little amusement.

Perhaps most telling in *Walker*'s juxtaposition of past and present to emphasize the continuity of capitalist exploitation is the use of twentieth-century icons in the narrative of a nineteenth-century adventurer. When Doña Yrena escapes from Granada with two Nicaraguan legitimists, her companions are reading *People* and *Newsweek,* both featuring cover stories about Walker, self-styled "Gray-Eyed Man of [Manifest] Destiny." As they discuss the politics of "those crazy gringos" in a horse-drawn carriage, a Mercedes overtakes them on the dirt road. During an interview with a news reporter, Walker asserts that the ends, which he has admittedly forgotten, justify the means. As the two men walk down a stretch of beach in an extreme long shot, in the foreground are icons of multinational corporate dominance, an American with a Coca-Cola bottle and a pack of Marlboros. Undoubtedly most disturbing in the film's anachronistic mise-en-scène is the presence of a computer terminal signifying the information age and Foucauldian panoptic surveillance in Vanderbilt's quarters. At the conclusion, when Walker and his men retreat during the burning of Granada, World War II air raid sirens are heard on the sound track and a helicopter, the quintessential symbol of the Vietnam War, descends in front of the Palacio Nacional to rescue men who can produce American passports. Finally, as the credits roll, a video monitor on screen right shows President Ronald Reagan reassuring the public, "Let me say to those who invoke the men of Vietnam . . . there is no thought of sending American combat troops to Central America." But the newsreel footage shows American men involved in maneuvers and lifeless bodies of Nicaraguan victims. An instance of yet another juxtaposition between past and present tense to achieve historical consciousness, the transition from film to television as a medium for reporting news events, especially military intervention abroad, is particularly apt in representing an era dominated by the small screen.

Despite "the evaporation of any sense of historical continuity and memory" attributed to the postmodern condition by critics like David Harvey, *Walker* demonstrates that postmodernist cinema can indeed be compelling as history. Clarification of this argument requires a focus on the narrower issue of modernization because critics are by no means in agreement about definitions of postmodernism versus modernism, or the extent to which these are overlapping and continuous cultural practices. Andreas Huyssen, for example, argues that poststructuralism is "primarily a discourse of and about modernism," whereas Brook Thomas aligns such discourse with the postmodern and thus construes it as existing in tension with the new historicism. Complicating critical discourse even further, T. J. Jackson Lears points out that literary critics and historians do not agree on definitions of modernism, a phenomenon that he labels antimodernism for the purposes of his argument. In addition, critics have expressed disagreement regarding the issue of postmodernism in relation to history. Marshall Berman, for example, critiques both structuralism and postmodernism, which in some instances he equates with modernism, as essentially ahistorical. Linda Hutcheon argues, on the other hand, that contrary to Jameson's observation about the waning of historicity, postmodernist writing characterized by self-reflexivity and parody is indeed rooted in the historical world. Given these disagreements, I focus on the more limited subject of *Walker* as discourse on the issue of modernization as a significant aspect of modernity. Although Berman indicts social scientists for splintering discussions of modernity into compartmentalized subjects such as industrialization, market formation, urbanization, and nation-states, these issues are significant precisely because historians, not all of whom claim to be social scientists, have traditionally studied processes of political, economic, and social change.[15]

As a historical film *Walker* is an interesting amalgam because it calls for a critique of American economic domination, in both its imperialistic and multinational corporate phases, and of modernization, albeit in an innovative postmodernist form. Are we then to assume that the film as postmodernist narrative reconceptualizes history? *Walker* does constitute a departure in that it exemplifies Linda Hutcheon's discussion of "historiographic metafiction" as writing that foregrounds both history and fiction as constructs and employs this awareness to rework the "forms and contents of the past." Yet despite the privileging of multiple voices in response to American hegemony, *Walker* is ultimately limited in rethinking history because it focuses on such traditional issues as nationhood, diplomacy, and military conquest. *Annales* historians, it should be remembered, shifted the terms of debate about modernization and rejected as peculiarly Western the notion that the experience of a modern industrialized society should serve as a yardstick by which to measure the history of the rest of the world.[16] Given this perspective, *Walker* remains tradi-

In a satirical and absurdist world, tradition remains—white men are still in the saddle, and history remains a story of military conquest. Copyright © by Universal City Studios, Inc. Reproduced courtesy of MCA Publishing Rights, a Division of MCA Inc.

tionalist in its subject matter despite elements of satire, irony, and absurdist humor. Suppose the history of Walker's exploits had been represented instead as Doña Yrena's autobiography or memoir, a Nicaraguan perspective that contradicts and overlaps with American accounts including those written by the filibusterer.[17] Such a representational strategy would produce disjunction resulting from differences in terms not only of culture but of gender.

Walker, to be sure, remains an interesting departure, but reconceptualizing history provokes resistance, as an analysis of its reception demonstrates, because traditional concepts based on empiricism, objective truth, and linear progress are still dominant in bourgeois culture. As historical reenactment, *Walker* does not conform to the legacy of public images of history validated by realistic representation in mainstream cinema. A film that begins with voice-over narration associated with documentararies and a title proclaiming "THIS IS A TRUE STORY"—only to show battle scenes recalling Sam Peckinpah westerns to the tune of festive Latin rhythms—does not qualify as history. Filmgoers stayed away from the box office, and film critics focused on questions of authenticity and unconventional form. *Newsweek*'s David Ansen, for example, listed several factual errors in the film and concluded, "Wurlitzer's script offers a tinny, underground-commix view of history. What a waste. The real story of

Walker . . . would make a great epic." As a matter of fact, *Walker* questions the adequacy of the historical epic as a representation of the past in
its parodic staging of *Julius Caesar*. *Variety*'s critic objected that *Walker*
was "completely unconvincing in its presentation of events" and faulted
"surrealist anachronisms that have been woven into the visual fabric . . .
to emphasize the modern parallels." The *Wall Street Journal* described
Walker as a "convoluted—and generally silly—spoof" like "Saturday
Night Live." Apparently without humor, Michael Wilmington warned in
the *Los Angeles Times* that some audiences "may conclude the movie
makers have gotten confused about what century they're in."[18]

Walker did receive more appreciative notices from Richard Schickel in
Time, David Sterritt in the *Christian Science Monitor*, and Stanley
Kauffmann in the *New Republic*. Vincent Canby of the *New York Times*
liked its "hip, cool, political satire" and observed that its "neo-Brechtian
believe-it-or-not inventory of character and events . . . must strike most
Americans as outlandishly unbelievable, while many Central Americans
may simply nod their heads in recognition." In fact, the *Los Angeles
Times* reported that contrary to its reception in the United States, *Walker*
played to packed houses in Managua, Nicaragua, despite the fact that the
price of a ticket exceeded the daily earnings of an average worker. Although Nicaraguan reviewers, like their American counterparts, tallied
up factual errors in the film and did not always appreciate farcical humor,
filmgoers in Managua reportedly broke into laughter over the juxtaposition of past and present events.[19] Apparently, postmodernist film as history does speak to the "Other" in multiple voices.

The fact that most reviewers objected to *Walker*'s collapsed temporality, presentism, and ironical sense of time, not to mention its absurdist
humor, is instructive regarding the public's definition of historical film. A
consideration of critical as well as audience reception, in other words,
demonstrates that postmodernist reading strategies are in effect addressed
to insiders willing to consider a historiographic representation in which
constructing history as opposed to subject matter becomes the focus. Director Alex Cox evidently misread moviegoers because his intention was
"to steer the film away from a drab 'Masterpiece Theater' presentation"
and to "reach a broader audience, not just the people who go to the art
houses." On the contrary, *Walker* is the sort of release that would be
exhibited in art film theaters rather than in shopping malls. The negative
reception of film critics demonstrates that postmodernist historical narrative is unacceptable to a public still invested in realistic representations of
the past as opposed to discourse on the nature of those very representations. Consequently, the commercial and critical success of *Mississippi
Burning* is quite revealing because its powerful realism focused debate on
questions of authenticity, as did the postmodernist approach of *Walker*,

but not on the issue of history itself as a construct. Coincidentally, director Alan Parker, like his British countryman Cox, also denigrated public television broadcasting because he wanted to reach a mass audience. Unlike Cox, he succeeded.[20]

In contrast to *Walker, Mississippi Burning* is an illusionist narrative constructed according to the conventions of the social problem film as well as of the detective and male buddy genres. One reviewer dubbed it "Dirty Harry beats dirty laundry."[21] The precredit and credit sequences establish the film's concern with racial injustice: as black spiritual music wails on the sound track, a white man and a black boy drink from separate water fountains, and a building torched by the Ku Klux Klan goes up in flames. Civil rights workers modeled on Andrew Goodman, Michael Schwerner, and James Cheney are stopped at night on a lonely country road and murdered by white southern rednecks. Assigned to head investigation of the crime are two FBI agents, Alan Ward (Willem Dafoe), a punctilious eastern bureaucrat who is ineffectual, and Rupert Anderson (Gene Hackman), a rumpled but savvy southerner who eventually convinces his sidekick to resort to KKK tactics. Aside from ignoring procedure and playing rough, Anderson shrewdly observes the local citizenry and exploits Mrs. Pell (Frances McDormand), the lonely and sensitive young wife of the deputy sheriff. At the beginning of the film, Ward and Anderson sit in their car and observe a small town shortly after their arrival in Mississippi. What appear to be casual street scenes photographed in extreme long shot and in soft focus reveal potential sources of information to the southern agent. A symbol of white conscience, Mrs. Pell eventually betrays her husband and discloses to Anderson where the civil rights workers are buried. In fact, the location of the burial site was revealed by an informant who collected a thirty-thousand-dollar reward.[22]

Switching into high gear, the two FBI agents lead a team, including an African-American agent, who trick and terrorize the guilty. Accelerating events lead to a montage of men being arrested and subsequently leaving a courthouse with black and white still shots that identify each convicted man by name and jail sentence. Unfortunately, this last tactic, as well as the documentary-style interviews of local denizens voicing their opinions about race relations, tends to historicize events and fuel controversy about the film. At the conclusion, a tracking shot of a cemetery stops to focus on the vandalized tombstone of the black civil rights worker. But this image of persistent racism is undercut by the film's characterization of black men as essentially passive and impotent, a representation that attests to white paranoia expressed in the myth of the black stud and a history of lynching. Consistent with the precredit sequence in which both an African-American boy and a white adult man drink water from segregated fountains, the only fearless black male in the film is a child. A significant aspect of the narrative strategy of *Mississippi Burning* as a buddy film is to displace irreconcilable racial division onto categories of males, both black and white civil rights workers and FBI agents, who are characterized as either macho or impotent. Further, the appeal to male camaraderie provides a means of resolving a particularly heinous crime in the civil rights era. To put it another way, the film achieves narrative closure by encoding a pattern of social organization based on male bonding that cuts across class and racial lines. Such camaraderie, however, is in reality restricted to rituals like professional athletics because macho codes are not only elitist but also sexist. Anderson is able to exploit Mrs. Pell, for example, because she is socially isolated; as a consequence of her betrayal, she is savagely beaten by her husband in the presence of Klansmen.

The reception of *Mississippi Burning*, a release that received far more attention than *Walker*, provides evidence of what the public construes as a legitimate historical film. Distributed in December 1988 according to a phased release schedule involving only nine screens nationwide, the film required strong reviews, especially in New York, for a successful run. As the result of a *Time* cover story, several *New York Times* articles, and a "CBS This Morning" report, *Mississippi Burning* became the subject of controversy that led to brisk box-office business and primed the audience for a wide release in January and a video release in July.[23] Despite a disclaimer that the film was a fictionalized account based on true events, its strong reality effect influenced reviewers to react in terms of conventional views about history. Put simply, such views equate history with objectivity and truth. *Variety*'s critic wrote, "Approach is fictional, but . . . [the] script captures much of the truth in its telling of the impact of a 1964 FBI probe into the murders of three civil rights workers." But several reviewers objected to two gross distortions in the film: the blatant repression of black activism in the civil rights movement and the glorification of FBI agents who had in actuality thwarted rights workers. Pauline Kael, sounding a note of disagreement among New York critics, claimed, "Alan Parker is essentially putting blacks at the back [of the bus] again." Similarly, Abbie Hoffman responded to Stuart Klawans's positive review in The *Nation*, by asserting that "the idea that the FBI brought an end to a segregated South is about as ludicrous as saying that noble elements inside the Joint Chiefs of Staff were essentially responsible for ending the war in Vietnam."[24]

Clearly, controversy about the historical authenticity of this film was based on concern that filmgoers, unable to differentiate between fact and fiction, would accept Parker's representation of the civil rights struggle. Claims to historical truth are vigorously debated because competing visions of the past are invoked to influence social attitudes and to shape public policy. At least since the controversial premiere of *The Birth of a Nation* (1915), film as history has been subject to debate because it is based on realistic representation. As Jack E. White asserted in the *Time* cover story, "Many viewers, whose ability to discern a whopper . . . has been obliterated by an age of TV docudramas, . . . leave the theater believing a version of history so distorted that it amounts to a cinematic lynching of the truth." Signficantly, reviewers who defended the film resorted to the strategy of downplaying the importance of historical accuracy. Vincent Canby, for example, asserted that social issues were best represented in documentaries but claimed that "nothing . . . seriously damages the film's validity as a melodrama or as an evocation of recent history." Canby later argued in a convoluted defense of his views that *Mississippi Burning* was such a powerful indictment of racism that it could only be undermined by "finding reasons not to believe the film." Attempting to minimize objections to the film on the grounds of its lack of credibility, he questioned the value of objectivity and was not above firing salvos at *We Are Not Afraid*, Seth Cagin's and Philip Dray's monograph about the Freedom Summer murders.[25]

Discourse on *Mississippi Burning* was not restricted to newspapers, magazines, and trade journals but also appeared in scholarly publications. Robert Toplin gave a detailed summary of factual errors in the film in *Perspectives*, the newsletter of the American Historical Association. Why did academics not simply dismiss *Mississippi Burning* as just another movie? Sundiata K. Cha-Jua argued in *Radical History Review* that for most moviegoers, especially youth who were not old enough to recall the civil rights movement, the film might be their only source of information and, moreover, obscured a public television series such as "Eyes on the Prize." Similarly, Thomas Doherty expressed concern about the impact of the film on teenaged audiences in *Cineaste*, a journal whose editors condemned Parker's "egregious inversion of historical facts." Ultimately, the argument provoked by the film in the popular press, if not in scholarly publications, probably cost it Academy Awards—though not nominations. Despite a formidable campaign launched by distributor Orion to counteract negative publicity, the film won an Oscar in only one of seven categories, editing. Nevertheless, *Mississippi Burning* earned respectable figures at the box office even though it could not compete with star-studded blockbusters like *Rain Man* (1988) or *Twins* (1989), also released during the Christmas season. When the film last appeared on *Variety*'s charts, its cumulative gross receipts during a period of 178 days totaled more than thirty-four million dollars. Additionally, when *Mississippi Burning* was released in video format, it remained on the list of top-ten rentals for more than two months and was more popular than *Twins*.[26]

Controversy about *Mississippi Burning* demonstrates that traditional conceptualizations of history are still widely held, not only among professional historians but among film reviewers and their readership. Peter Novick defines the concept of historical objectivity as follows: "The assumptions on which it rests include a commitment to the reality of the past, and to truth as correspondence to that reality; a sharp separation between knower and known, between fact and value, and, above all, between history and fiction." Although most filmgoers are obviously not trained as historians, they would most likely agree with this formulation because it dovetails with their educational experience and ideological beliefs. As Fukuyama stresses, history deteriorates into antiquarianism unless it is enlisted in a larger cause.[27] Despite his belief that the triumph of Western capitalism signaled the end of history, discourse on historical representation in film, most recently the contentious reception of *JFK* (1991), demonstrates that the public is still invested in traditional concepts about the past. As for the historical profession, Lawrence Stone has observed that despite serious challenges mounted by the "new history," political history based on empiricist research is still dominant in the discipline.[28] Critics' proclamation of a new postmodernist age notwithstanding, traditional history remains as one of the bulwarks of modernist thought in which the individual is still constituted as an autonomous subject, however beleaguered, as opposed to being reduced to a textual construct. The epistemological divide between critical theorists and historians, in other words, is underscored to a significant extent by debate on the issue of human agency as opposed to the privileging of reified texts.[29] Whether repeated calls for the historicizing of texts, on the one hand, and greater attention to history as a construct, on the other, will lead to more frequent cross-disciplinary dialogue that will affect future historiography remains a matter of speculation.

A final word about the argument provoked by *Mississippi Burning* is in order. Ultimately, public discourse on the film's authenticity reinforced belief in linearity, progress, and the ability of Americans to accomplish social engineering. The very fact that the film had been made was cited as a sign of improved race relations despite statistics to the contrary.[30] Controversy, however, did not move beyond questions of veracity to include a consideration of either history itself or the ideological function of history. *Walker*, on the other hand, provokes thought about the relationship between past and present through its lack of verisimilitude and its spatialization of time so that the result is cyclical rather than teleological. Progress is not equated with linear development in a patriotic celebration of American civic virtues, as is the case in *Mississippi Burning*. Despite its limitations, *Walker* does provoke thought about the nature of historical representation as a construct that often validates nationalism and patriotism. As such, it succeeds, whereas *Mississippi Burning* does not. But it was the latter film that found favor with most critics, made millions of dollars at the box office and video rental shops, and garnered Golden Globe awards and Oscar nominations. The lesson is that not only is postmodernist historical representation unacceptable for a public still invested in traditional notions about history; so too are the sweeping generalizations of critics about the waning of historicity itself.

13

Walker

THE DRAMATIC FILM AS (POSTMODERN) HISTORY

ROBERT A. ROSENSTONE

> The job of the historian . . . is not to reduplicate
> the lost world of the past but to ask questions
> and answer them.
> —*Louis Mink*[1]

AMONG ACADEMIC HISTORIANS there is a general, if largely unarticulated, feeling that historical works conveyed through film, particularly dramatized history, can never be as worthwhile or as "true" as historical works conveyed through the printed page. Such a notion seems to arise from a sense that words are able to provide a serious and complex past reality that film, with its supposed need to entertain people, can never hope to match. To show that such a view of the possibilities of history on film is both shortsighted and wrong, I want to discuss the ways in which a single film—*Walker*—creates a past that is at once serious, complex, challenging, and "true" in its ability to render the meanings rather than the literal reality of past events. I also want to show that a good part of the film's truth stems from its unusual narrative strategies—strategies that challenge the "realism" of both written history and the standard dramatic or documentary historical film and that expand the vocabulary in which history can speak. Strategies that, were we interested in labels, we might wish to name *postmodern*.

Directed by British-born Alex Cox and released by an American distributor, *Walker* (1987) plays with and against many of the canons of both traditional history and the standard historical drama.[2] As a work of history, it successfully does the following three things: 1) performs a variety of traditional historical tasks; 2) goes beyond these tasks to create new ways of visualizing our relationship to the past; and 3) provides a "truth" that can stand beside all the written versions of William Walker's story that have appeared over the last 135 years. Like any good historical work, *Walker* recounts, explains, and interprets events in the past and then attempts to justify the way it has undertaken these tasks. Like any work of history, the film situates itself within a tradition of historical questions, which means the answers provided by its story comment upon all the previous versions of the subject that have appeared. The film handles data and makes its argument within the format of a drama that utilizes five particular strategies: *omission* and *condensation* (both common to written history), *alteration* and *invention* (common to all works of history on film) and *anachronism* (rare in any sort of history, except— postmodern history).

The Story of Walker

Like any historical tale, that of William Walker may be told in a few words or in many. Both have been done. The longest work on Walker runs to 397 pages. Short, general histories of the pre–Civil War period dismiss him in a sentence or two. Let me provide a mere outline of his life here: Walker was a Nashville-born (1824) physician, attorney (New Orleans), and newspaperman (San Francisco) who, in what may be considered an extended gesture of Manifest Destiny, led a small band of adventurers into the state of Sonora, Mexico, in 1854 with the aim of creating a "free" country. Defeated by terrain, weather, native troops, and lack of support from home, Walker returned to the United States. A year later, he entered Nicaragua at the head of an army of fifty-eight men—dubbed "the Immortals" by the press—supposedly to help the Liberal party in an ongoing civil war. By October 1855 he was commanding general of the Nicaraguan army, and by July 1856 president of the republic. During his time in office, Walker was an activist president who, among other things, instituted negro slavery in Nicaragua and annulled the lucrative charter of Cornelius Vanderbilt's Accessory Transit Company, which controlled the chief route from the East Coast of the United States to California. Ten months later, after suffering severe military defeats at the hands of armies from all over Central America, and after being cut off from fresh recruits and military supplies from the U.S., Walker torched the capital city of Granada, surrendered through the offices of a U.S. Naval Captain, and returned home, a hero to a goodly number of Americans. Twice more in the next three years he attempted to land in or near Nicaragua at the head of a military force. In September 1860, he was captured and shot by the Honduran army. To his captors, he identified himself as "William Walker, president of Nicaragua."

Walker's story has been told and retold many times in both English and Spanish. The first account, written by his friend William V. Wells, appeared in 1856, shortly before Walker became president. The second, by

Walker himself, was published four years later, just before his death. Since then, Walker's life and exploits have been the subject of at least six book-length historical works in the United States and several in Latin America; he has also been treated in a number of scholarly articles and in chapters of several other works devoted either to U.S. diplomacy or to offbeat American adventurers and imperialists.[3]

To assess *Walker*, the film, it is important to underscore the following: virtually all the essential details that we know about Walker in Nicaragua today appear in the earliest accounts, including the books by Walker and Wells—which is to say, all the studies of Walker utilize the same facts and recount essentially the same details concerning the who, how, where, and what that occurred when the Americans invaded Nicaragua. This is true for Walker's own actions and for the broader political-economic-social context in which he acted, the complicated economic and diplomatic maneuverings of both private interests and the governments of the United States, Great Britain, and various Central American countries. Yet if the details are clear, evaluations of the causes and the meanings of Walker's actions—for Walker, or for his supporters, or America, or the world— have shifted and changed over the decades. In short: for 140 years there has been no dispute over the facts of Walker's actions or the dimensions of both his successes and his failures. The only real differences between historians surround such questions as, Why did he do what he did? What were his personal and political aims? Did his actions help or hurt the cause of America, or of "civilization"?

Stages of Interpretation

During his own time and throughout the late nineteenth century, books on William Walker in Nicaragua generally took him on his own terms as an unqualified hero, a stalwart patriot who strove to spread the benefits of American civilization to those who suffered from Catholicism and bad government, a selfless man who wished to regenerate Central America, a man thwarted by shortsighted American politicians who refused to extend economic aid or diplomatic recognition to his fledgling regime. This approach lasted into the twentieth century. In 1913, E. Alexander Powell included a chapter on Walker in *Gentlemen Rovers* (1913), a work written as a tribute to forgotten heroes, men who were important in expansion of United States as they "stoutly upheld American prestige and traditions in many far corners of the world."[4]

Criticisms of Walker began in the second decade of this century, no doubt reflecting the liberalizing attitudes toward neighboring countries that were part of the Progressive era. The earliest work to fault him found problems less with the mission than with the man. In *Filibusters and Fi-*

nanciers (1916), William O. Scroggs depicted a Walker whose shortcomings of character and inability to understand human nature ruined a good chance to help spread the benefits of American civilization southward (newspapers and American music are in particular singled out as "civilizing" agents). The book depicted Walker's followers as heroes, fine pioneers who had developed the "supreme civilization in California."[5] By misleading them, Walker destroyed a splendid opportunity to regenerate Central America.

In the 1930s, with dictatorships flexing their muscles all across Europe, writing on Walker took on a decidedly antifascist turn. William Green's *The Filibuster: The Career of William Walker* (1937), reeks with suspicion of Walker as a "ruthless dictator," a little man who aimed solely at power, and it describes his men not as heroes but as vagrants who came to fight, seduce, plunder, and kill.[6] These sentiments were not matched with any parallel concern for the rights of Central Americans. Overtly contemptuous of all Latins, the author describes them in terms of traditional stereotypes—as a passionate, fickle, and treacherous people who love you one day and hate you the next.

More recent treatments of Walker provide an equally contemporary gloss on the man and his times. Albert Carr's *The World and William Walker* (1963) takes an approach that suits the decade in which it was written—the sixties. At once anti-imperialist and psychoanalytic, the book portrays Walker as a harbinger of twentieth-century American relations with the world. The personal part of the volume focuses on Walker's sexuality, or lack of it, emphasizing his puritan upbringing, his early interest in Walter Scott and the romantic tradition; indeed, the work suggests that sublimated sexuality accounts for the man's will to dominate as well as for his career in Nicaragua. The public part of the book details the larger sphere in which Walker moved—the antislavery controversy that was to tear the United States apart; the detailed competition between American and British diplomats and military men. Here, Walker the ideologue of Manifest Destiny is portrayed as a semiwitting stalking horse for larger strategic and economic interests.

The most recent work on Walker, Frederic Rosengarten's *Freebooters Must Die* (1976), takes what one might call the multicultural interpretation. Making much of that fact that Walker is remembered in Central America as "a devil," the book claims that though he was interested in power it was not for power's sake alone. He was a man with a mission, but it was a deeply flawed one. His mission to regenerate Central America would have instead created a slave empire, one that would have built and controlled a strategic canal from the Atlantic to the Pacific. If he had succeeded, Walker would have destroyed the precious Spanish-American cultural heritage and replaced it with a ruthless Anglo-Saxon autocracy.

Despite these widely different interpretations, all the books present a similar picture of the historical context in which Walker acted. All point to the Gold Rush, the Mexican-American War, the increasing acrimony between North and South over the extension of slavery, and the acquisition of California as factors that helped to fuel the expansionist mind-set that took Walker (and other Americans) to Central America. All name that mind-set "Manifest Destiny" and see it as not just a simple rationale for economic interests but a peculiar national task, an odd sort of democratic imperialism, a sense that it was America's god-given mission to regenerate a benighted mankind. All detail the doings of Walker's economic counterpart, Cornelius Vanderbilt, whose mission is more simply understood—to promote and protect his monopoly over the lucrative sea-and-land route through Nicaragua.

The picture of Walker the man—or at least of his personal characteristics and habits—is also remarkably consistent across the decades. All books agree that he was fearless, heroic, and financially incorruptible, a leader who was absolutely worshiped by his men. All show him as a stickler for discipline, a man who treated his own troops as harshly as natives over infractions. All portray Walker as a Puritan ascetic who did not drink or smoke, who ate moderately, and almost never laughed. Concerning his sexual proclivities and activities, there are some sharp differences of interpretation. Some see Walker as asexual, some hint at possible homosexuality, and some suggest he had a discreet affair with a Nicaraguan woman of noble birth—and it is a great virtue of the film that it is able to suggest all three interpretations without insisting on any one of them. About Walker and sex one thing is clear: his sexual practices, whatever they were, disturbed contemporaries and have continued to disturb most historians, except for Carr, the only author to link sex and the drive for power.

As with larger historical issues, the only disagreements over Walker the man come largely over the sorts of matters that an appeal to data cannot solve: why did he develop from a democrat into a dictator? Where did he really stand with regard to slavery? Why was he first so successful in Nicaragua, and then, afterward, why did he fail so miserably? Why did he burn down the capital city?

Walker and the Tasks of History

Anyone who has seen the film will already be familiar with many of these details of William Walker's foray into Nicaragua. But the question of *Walker* as a piece of history—that is, of the film as a way of making the life and career of the man meaningful to us in the present—must be answered not merely by pointing to the existence of data but by assessing the way the data is utilized to create a historical world. My contention is that *Walker* takes the data familiar to all who have worked on the topic and, using a sense of historical awareness (shall we call it quasi-Marxist?) and aesthetic sensibility (postmodern) common to the late twentieth century, creates a William Walker suited to a contemporary historical consciousness. Certainly the mode of the film may be seen as a kind of black farce (closer at times to Monty Python than to Eric Hobsbawm). But the film's humor and blatant absurdities are crucial to its multidimensional portrait of Walker and his undertakings. Instead of detracting from the seriousness of the film, they are very much involved with the way the movie frames the past and fulfills four traditional tasks of any historical work—recounting, explaining, and interpreting the events of the past, and then justifying its fulfillment of those tasks.

Recounting. The William Walker whose story is recounted in the film is a figure whose complications mirror larger issues in the American character, then and now. He is portrayed as the emblem of Manifest Destiny—self-centered (especially after the death of his fiancée), single-minded, cold, fearless, and absolutely convinced of the righteousness of his personal vision and actions. Unlike all written accounts, which seem unable to explain his increasingly ruthless actions, the actor who plays Walker (Ed Harris) presents us with a character whose mystical and sincere, if demagogic, democratic vision is corrupted by the taste of power (an eroticized power) he increasingly acquires in Nicaragua. The broader context of the "history" is provided by scenes that depict the way in which Walker's democratic imperialism clashes with the overtly economic imperialism of Cornelius Vanderbilt, an imperialism whose ideology is static—as if capital is capital and always acts in its own interest. Walker in the film is, at least at the outset, an idealist—one whose ideals lead to fanaticism. Vanderbilt is a cynic, whose ruthlessness leads to profit.

Explaining and interpreting. The film shows both economic and democratic imperialism as being borne out of the boundlessness of nineteenth-century America. It is the land itself, one feels, that has created both Walker and Vanderbilt. One image says it all: when the two men meet face-to-face and one of the commodore's minions insists on the vast amounts of land available in Nicaragua, the men are all located in a Southwestern U.S. landscape virtually devoid of humanity as far as the eye can see. At that meeting, Walker overtly refuses to work with the unsavory Vanderbilt, but his own sense of mission lands him on the same side of the Nicaragua question. His form of imperialism, the film suggests, is older, more traditional than that of Vanderbilt. Clearly, the film wants to show that capital utilizes the democratic impulse as an ideology to cover whatever illegal or immoral actions it uses to make profits; it also depicts William Walker's personal corruption as of another sort—less economic than moral, an inevitable corrosion of the spirit when it is exposed to too much power, a corruption bound to wreak havoc and cause tragedy.

Justifying. Because motion pictures lack scholarly apparatus (footnotes, bibliography, appeal to authorities), this is always the most difficult aspect of historical practice for a film to undertake. *Walker* makes its attempt in part by appealing to the historical Walker's real writings, used as voice-overs. This is, of course, a strategy pursued by many historical films. Much more important in *Walker* is a brilliant (postmodern) turn by which it uses a most unorthodox way of justifying its portrait—I refer to the film's overt appeal to the audience's knowledge (or sense) of how America has repeatedly intervened in Latin America (or elsewhere in the world—parallels to Vietnam haunt the imagery of the film) and was clearly doing so in 1987, as the film was being made. The point is driven home by the many anachronisms that speak directly of contemporary America: Walker's troops utilize Zippo lighters, drink Cokes, and smoke Marlboros. Walker appears on the covers of *Time* and *Newsweek*. Walker, in a parting statement to the Nicaraguans, insists: "We have a right to rule you. We will never leave you alone." The notion of historical repetition and continuity is emphasized by TV images below the final credits—President Reagan talking about Sandinistas; American troops on maneuvers in the Honduras; dead and wounded Nicaraguan peasants who have been caught in attacks by Contra rebels.

Strategies of Representation

To create a Walker for our time, the film utilizes, as I have already noted, a number of strategies for rendering history: omission and condensation, alteration, invention, and anachronism. The first two are integral to all forms of history, written, oral, or filmed, for regardless of how detailed any portrait of the past may be, the data included is always only a highly selected and condensed sample of what could be included on a given topic. *Walker* tells us nothing of its subject's childhood, family, or schooling (save that he is a doctor and a lawyer); only hints at his medical and newspaper career in New Orleans and California; omits anything about the Mexican War or the complicated international diplomatic maneuverings between Great Britain, the U.S., and the Central American countries over regional issues; barely touches the North-South slavery debate; and never specifies Walker's beliefs beyond the simplest level of exposition: "I hate slavery," or "I'm a social democrat" (a remark that also belongs under the rubric of anachronism).

The strategies of alteration and invention are alike in that both depart from the norms of written history; indeed, both "create" historical fact (or incident) as a way of summarizing historical data that either cannot be expressed through visual images or whose expression in such images would be so inefficient that the (dramatic) structure of the work would be impaired. The two differ in that alteration changes documentable historical fact by relocating or restructuring incidents or events (altering time, place, participants), whereas invention freely creates characters and incidents. (What I refer to here are major sorts of inventions, for, as I have argued elsewhere, the most "accurate" works of dramatic history on film will always contains huge doses of what we might call small invention, acts of creation that historians who work in words will call "fiction." Because the camera demands more specificity than historians can ever know, all historical settings are what might be called "proximate" fictions. Similarly, costume, dialogue, gesture, action, the very use of dramatic structure—all these are full of small fictions used, at best, to create larger historical "truths," truths that can be judged only by examining the extent to which they engage the arguments and "truths" of our existing historical knowledge on any given topic.)[7]

All the major alterations in *Walker* can be seen and justified as ways of expressing metaphoric or symbolic historical truths. For example: by opening the film with a battle in Mexico and misplacing (or re-placing) his fiancée's death after that battle, the film makes us focus immediately on the relationship between Manifest Destiny and violence that are its very historical core and portrays Walker (as do written works) as a man once torn between the personal and the political until her death turned him into a wholly public man. By having Walker march forward on foot dressed in a (historically documentable) black suit during horrendously violent battles rather than riding (as he did) a horse, the film provides an indelible image of the man's fearlessness and unshrinking determination described in all contemporary accounts. By collapsing two Nicaraguan political figures into a single leader, whom Walker first sets up as a puppet president and later executes, the film underscores the irrelevancy of actual Nicaraguans to Walker's ventures and policies. The same point is further emphasized when Walker has trouble remembering the names of the Nicaraguan leaders or when his soldiers complain that there seems to be no difference between Liberal Nicaraguans, for whom they fight, and the Conservatives, their enemies. (Again, Vietnam and other recent interventions abroad are clearly implied.)

The inventions of the film also work as apposite, symbolic historical assertions. For example: by making Walker's chief lieutenant a black American (the historical record shows no such individual, though some blacks did serve with Walker), the film points up his original antislavery

Walker striding through the Battle of Rivas—an indelible image of fearlessness and unshrinking determination. Copyright ©by Universal City Studios, Inc. Reproduced courtesy of MCA Publishing Rights, a Division of MCA Inc.

beliefs and shows that his later introduction of slavery into Nicaragua was neither easy nor foreordained but rather the result of the perceived necessity to obtain both a labor pool and the support of southern American states. By showing his affair with the aristocratic Doña Yrena, the film suggests how easily the democratic Walker climbed into bed with the Nicaragua's upper classes. Her subsequent attack on him with a pistol becomes an apt rendering of how quickly and angrily this unnatural alliance fell apart. Through the skilled acting of Ed Harris, the film is able to suggest multiple interpretations of Walker's sexuality; the affair with Doña Yrena shows him as sexually inexperienced; scenes with the soldier named Timothy suggest homoerotic attachments; still other scenes suggest masochism or the sublimation of sexuality into the quest for power. Such visual hints, which may be seen as a claim that multiple interpretations *are all true*, let the film achieve an interpretive complexity that would be less likely in a written text; certainly no historian to date has suggested that Walker might be multisexual.

No doubt the most important of the inventions is the encounter between Walker and Vanderbilt. Historically, the two men never met face to face, yet their angry dispute in an obviously mythic space—alongside a railroad track in Arizona, decades before trains came to the West—is crucial to the meaning of the film. In this clash between powerful individuals, the two sorts of American imperialisms—economic and demo-cratic—stake out the terms of their debate with each other and with the larger world. The exchange reveals the clash of greed and self-interest, the fervent if misplaced idealism, and the hidden complicities that have fueled American expansionism for 150 years. To portray this same conflict, the historian who works in words would have created this encounter on the page, by outlining the ideology or mind-set of each man. That ideas com-pete in neat paragraphs is no less a "fiction" than the on-screen meeting between Walker and Vanderbilt. The difference is that this sort of written "fiction" has become an unquestioned convention of history. Needing an image, film works in a different way. Yet each technique of rendering this quarrel merely utilizes a suitable way of using a particular medium to talk about the past.

To make this assertion is to run against the common but mistaken (public) notion that the historical film somehow provides an accurate window onto the world of the past. Elsewhere I have argued that film can never do this, for it is always a construction that points to the world of the past by providing proximate images of vanished realities.[8] *Walker* makes certain that it cannot possibly be taken for a window onto history by the overt and creative strategy of anachronism. The Zippo lighters, Coke bot-tles, and Marlboros of Walker's troops, the *Time* and *Newsweek* maga-zines with his picture on the cover, the hip contemporary language, the glimpse of a Mercedes roaring by a carriage, the computer terminals in Vanderbilt's office, and the final evacuation of the Americans from Granada in helicopters—all these images point to the inevitable interpen-etration of past and present. Beyond destroying the surface "realism" of the film, they work to demystify the pretensions of professional history, cast into doubt notions of historical distance and objectivity, and insist that the questions we take to the past always arise from our current con-cerns—that, in fact, it is impossible for us to see the world of Walker, or any historical realm, without images of automobiles, helicopters, and computer terminals (or a sense of their absence) in our minds.

Walker's use of alteration and invention is shared—less consciously, to be sure—by all historical films. Anachronism, too, is not an original de-vice, but no other historical film has ever used it so overtly and often in an effort to keep us aware of the continuity of historical questions and issues. Perhaps the most important part of the film's creative strategy comes in the way it uses the sound track against the image to render historical complexities not easily obtainable by the written word. *Walker* opens with upbeat Latin music that is wholly at odds with the images of violent death and destruction during a battle in Sonora, Mexico. For the rest of the film, sound continues to play against image to provide a double vision of historical reality. Or is it a multiple vision? Joyous music at odds with destruction provides a critique both of war itself and of the long tradition of historical films that utilize music to make battle glamorous and heroic. Another contradiction between sound and image comes in the voice-over narration, taken in part from Walker's memoirs. Here the leader's lofty, idealized descriptions of the expeditionary force are repeatedly undercut by actions on screen. The voice speaks of cultural reforms, and we see natives being flogged; it speaks of regenerating a nation, and we see American soldiers drinking, fighting, stealing from natives, and assaulting females of more than one species ("The colonel says it's a democracy," shouts one soldier, as he climbs into a sheep pen and lowers his pants).

The doubled vision presented by playing sound against image, and the humor involved in odd juxtapositions, seem to work in a variety of ways. Distanced from Walker and his men, we can study their behavior without the normal tugs of sentiment or patriotism. The doubling also hints at the perennial gap between history and behavior, official rhetoric and experience, the language utilized by the distant observer or the scholar and the realities it purports to encompass. By highlighting such contradictions, *Walker* directs us to the problems of all historical representation and understanding. Quite consciously, the film delivers a story at once invented, postmodern, and, I would argue, true—a story that comments on our past and present and never lets us forget that the two always interpenetrate.

In breaking with the normal conventions of the historical motion picture, *Walker* highlights the limits of Hollywood's favorite way of constructing a world on the screen—illusionist realism. Working against the far edges of the historical genre, its sometimes farcical, layered history suggests a complexity to historical knowledge that a traditional single-line narrative could never handle. The film's argument is certainly clear enough: intervention abroad based upon Manifest Destiny—democratic or economic, past or present—is bound to corrupt and wreak havoc on both Americans and those they wish either to help or to exploit. Yet for all the single-minded strength of this moral stance, the overtly innovative strategies and black humor of the film point toward the contested nature of historical knowledge.

To put it simply: from the opening moments, *Walker* outrageously problematizes its own assertions—and also teaches us how to "read" the history we are about to see. It begins with a battle scene in which ragtag Mexican soldiers run across a field to the sound of upbeat Latin music. The screen goes black, and then we see in bold red letters "THIS IS A TRUE STORY," followed by images of American troopers exploding out of a farmhouse in a kind of slow-motion death ballet while the joyous music continues. Here at the outset we are shown that whatever the "truth" of the story may be, it is not a literal truth. The screen cannot be a window onto the past—and not just because the window has been blown away but because we know that in the real world men do not die in slow motion to the sound of dance music. *Walker* warns us at the outset that the history it delivers is not to be taken as reality and suggests that the literal reconstruction of the past is not at stake in this (or perhaps in any other) project of historical understanding. What should matter, the film suggests, is the seriousness with which we ask and answer, in whatever form of address or medium, questions about the meaning of the past.

Notes

Introduction

1. Collections on history and film include the following: K.R.M. Short, ed., *Feature Films as History* (Knoxville: University of Tennessee Press, 1981); John E. O'Connor and Martin A. Jackson, eds., *American History/American Film* (New York: Frederick Ungar, 1979); and Peter C. Rollins, ed., *Hollywood as Historian* (Lexington: University of Kentucky Press, 1983). Volumes by single authors include Pierre Sorlin, *The Film in History* (Totowa, N.J.: Barnes and Noble, 1980); and Marc Ferro, *Cinéma et Histoire* (Paris: Denoel, 1977), translated as *Cinema and History* (Detroit: Wayne State University Press, 1988). A five-article forum devoted to cinema and history appeared in the *American Historical Review* 30 (December 1988): 1173–1227.

2. For more on African, Latin American, and German historical film see my essay "Revisioning History: Contemporary Filmmakers and the Construction of the Past," *Comparative Studies in Society and History* 32 ((1990): 822–37.

3. Fred Weinstein, *History and Theory after the Fall* (Chicago: University of Chicago Press, 1990), p. 31. See also Allan Megill, "'Grand Narrative' and the Discipline of History," in Frank Ankersmit and Hans Kellner, eds., *The New Philosophy of History* (London: Reaktion Books, 1994).

4. See my essay "Like Writing History with Lightning: Historical Film/Historical Truth," *Contention* 2 (Spring 1993): 191–204.

Chapter One
Distant Voices, Still Lives

1. For the thoughts in this essay I am indebted to a number of friends, whether for their work, for their conversation, or for their film intelligence, including Becky Conekin, Nick Dirks, Karl Pohrt, Sherry Ortner, and Ron Suny. Lauren Berlant played a crucial role in how the essay came to be written, particularly its framing and the thinking-through of the conclusion. She gave me some of its best ideas and helped me see more clearly what I wanted to say. Last, I would like to thank Carolyn Steedman for a number of specific suggestions. More important, without her writings the essay would not exist.

2. A massive and complex history is simplified into this paragraph. The best general introduction to the foundational experience is still Angus Calder, *The People's War: Britain, 1939–1945* (New York: Pantheon, 1969). For the filmic context, see Marcia Landy, *British Genres: Cinema and Society, 1930–1960* (Princeton: Princeton University Press, 1991). For Orwell, see Raymond Williams, *Orwell* (London: Fontana, 1971); and Christopher Norris, ed., *Inside the Myth: Orwell—Views from the Left* (London: Lawrence and Wishart, 1984). For Priestley, see D. L. LeMahieu, *A Culture for Democracy: Mass Communication and the Cultivated Mind in Britain between the Wars* (Oxford: Oxford University

Press, 1988), pp. 317–33. More generally, see also Anthony Barnett, *Iron Britannia* (London: Allison and Busby, 1982).

3. The phrases are taken from Landy, *British Genres*, p. 370 (said of Ealing); and LeMahieu, *A Culture for Democracy*, p. 318 (said of Priestley). This populist cleaving to the values of ordinariness and decency had enormous power in the 1940s and 1950s. In one emblematic representation of British social life of the time, the two films *Holiday Camp* (1947) and *Here Come the Huggetts* (1948) and the radio and television spin-offs, the social referent is definitely a particular construction of the lower middle class, into which a sanitized, complaisant, and completely depoliticized ideal of working-class respectability is subsumed. In another central document of the period, the television drama staple *Dixon of Dock Green* (lasting from 1954 to the end of the 1960s), with its origin in the Ealing drama *The Blue Lamp* (1950), an everyday chronicle of urban community life, the solid and reassuring voice of moral authority is that of the policeman on the beat, George Dixon, in sociological terms no doubt ambiguously located, but in the social discourse of this indestructible series, ineluctably lower middle-class. The same actor, Jack Warner as Mr. Huggett and Dixon, was the avuncular face of this unthreatening, unclassed normality. See Geoffrey Gorer, "Modification of National Character: The Role of the Police in England," *Journal of Social Issues* 11, no. 2 (1955).

4. Peter Wollen, in a recent and enjoyably disrespectful polemic, disputes this cinema's status as a British New Wave comparable to those of France, Italy, and Germany, as it meets none of the main criteria for the latter, namely, auteurism or "the project of directorial 'authorship'," "putting film first and not subordinating it to literature or theater," and the aesthetic preference for "modernism" as against the British addiction to "realism." Instead, he ascribes the final appearance of a New Wave in Britain to the "delayed modernism" and anti-Thatcherist oppositional film culture of the 1980s, constructing an alternative lineage for the latter that runs through a variety of lost moments of British film history, beginning with the London Film Society and the journal *Close Up* in the 1930s, a variety of individual influences either marginalized or lost to North America (like Alfred Hitchcock or John Grierson), the "New Romanticism" of the later 1940s and its brief nationally protected moment of British film production, and a postwar avant-garde tradition inaugurated by the Independent Group of artists, architects, and critics in the *This Is Tomorrow* exhibition at the Whitechapel Gallery, which opened (appropriately enough) a few months after *Look Back in Anger* at the Royal Court (8 August 1956, as opposed to 8 May). The real conditions of possibility for a British New Wave, Wollen argues, were generated by the "sixties transformation of British culture" and the commercially oriented aesthetics of pop, which were precisely what made the Angry Young Men filmmakers most nervous. This argument, which speaks from Wollen's own thirty-year career as Britain's most interesting film intellectual, is persuasive. See Peter Wollen, "The Last New Wave: Modernism in the British Films of the Thatcher Era," in Lester Friedman, ed., *Fires Were Started: British Cinema and Thatcherism* (Minneapolis: University of Minnesota Press, 1993), especially pp. 35–43. More generally, see Wollen's essays, *Raiding the Icebox: Reflections on Twentieth-Century Cul-*

ture (London: Verso, 1993), and his *Singin' in the Rain* (London: BFI Publishing, 1992), a wonderful exemplification of his credo.

5. After this essay was completed, Carolyn Steedman drew my attention to Terry Lovell's excellent discussion of this intellectual moment of the 1960s, which, reassuringly, abstracts similar themes to my own, but with much greater richness in relation to the so-called New Wave films themselves. In particular, using *A Taste of Honey* (which was adapted from Shelagh Delaney's play of the same name) she shows how "looking back in gender" can allow readings that "the masculine address of this whole group of New Wave films, the masculine identity of their visual enunciation," tends to obscure. See Terry Lovell, "Landscapes and Stories in 1960s British realism," *Screen* 31, no. 4 (Winter 1990): 357–76. The quotation is taken from p. 376.

6. Isabel Quigly in the *Spectator*, cited by Robert Hewison, *In Anger: British Culture in the Cold War, 1945–60* (Oxford: Oxford University Press, 1981), p. 155.

7. John Hill, *Sex, Class, and Realism: British Cinema, 1956–1963* (London: BFI Publishing, 1986), p. 150.

8. In *Films and Filming*, May 1963, p. 10; cited by Hill, *Sex, Class, and Realism*, p. 218.

9. Ibid., p. 156.

10. For Lovell's dissonant reading of the woman's position in *A Taste of Honey*, which explores the interesting gaps between Delaney's play and the structure of feeling onto which it became sutured in Richardson's film, see "Landscapes and Stories," pp. 367ff.

11. Richard Hoggart, *The Uses of Literacy: Aspects of Working-Class Life with Special Reference to Publications and Entertainment* (New York: Oxford University Press, 1957); Raymond Williams, *Culture and Society, 1780–1950* (New York: Harper and Row, 1958); and Edward Thompson, *The Making of the English Working Class* (London: Victor Gollancz, 1963). The affluent worker study was an emblematic research project of the 1960s testing the so-called embourgeoisement thesis of the impact of improving living standards on working-class values, conducted on car workers in Luton: see J. H. Goldthorpe and D. Lockwood, *The Affluent Worker*, 3 vols. (Cambridge: Cambridge University Press, 1968–69). The reference to the New Left specifically invokes Perry Anderson's essay "Components of the National Culture," *New Left Review* 50 (July–August 1968): 3–57, now reprinted in Anderson, *English Questions* (London: Verso, 1992), pp. 48–104; but more generally it refers to debates and ideas developed in the 1960s in *New Left Review*. For the phrase "rituals and rebellion," see Stuart Hall and Tony Jefferson, eds., *Resistance through Rituals: Youth Subcultures in Post-War Britain* (London: Hutchinson, in association with the Center for Contemporary Cultural Studies, University of Birmingham, 1976); the Birmingham Center was founded by Hoggart, who was later succeeded by Hall. See also Stuart Hall and Paddy Whannel, *The Popular Arts* (London: Hutchinson, 1964), and Denys Thompson, ed., *Discrimination and Popular Culture* (Harmondsworth: Penguin, 1964). There is now a considerable literature around these intellectual histories. Among the most useful are: Hewison, *In Anger*, and its suc-

cessor volume, Robert Hewison, *Too Much: Art and Society in the Sixties, 1960–75* (Oxford: Oxford University Press, 1986); Alan Sinfield, *Literature, Politics, and Culture in Postwar Britain* (Berkeley and Los Angeles: University of California Press, 1989); Julia Swindells and Lisa Jardine, *What's Left? Women in Culture and the Labour Movement* (London: Routledge, 1990); John Clarke, Chas Critcher, and Richard Johnson, eds., *Working-Class Culture: Studies in History and Theory* (London: Hutchinson, in association with the Center for Contemporary Cultural Studies, University of Birmingham, 1979); Richard Johnson, Gregor McLennan, Bill Schwarz, and David Sutton, eds., *Making Histories: Studies in History-Writing and Politics* (London: Hutchinson, in association with the Center for Contemporary Cultural Studies, University of Birmingham, 1982).

12. Eric Hobsbawm, "The Making of the Working Class, 1870–1914," in *Workers: Worlds of Labor* (New York: Pantheon, 1984), p. 194.

13. See Martin Jacques and Francis Mulhearn, eds., *The Forward March of Labour Halted?* (London: Verso, in association with Marxism Today, 1981); Stuart Hall and Martin Jacques, eds., *New Times: The Changing Face of Politics in the 1990s* (London: Lawrence and Wishart, in association with Marxism Today, 1989).

14. For a brilliant reflection, in a different period and context, on the thematics of "national fantasy," from which I continue to learn, see Lauren Berlant, *The Anatomy of National Fantasy: Hawthorne, Utopia, and Everyday Life* (Chicago: University of Chicago Press, 1991).

15. The screenwriter of *Chariots of Fire*, Colin Welland, has an interesting career. Beginning as an actor on the pioneering social realist BBC drama series *Z Cars* (1962–65), a radical alternative to *Dixon of Dock Green*, he then worked for the left-wing grouping around Tony Garnett (producer) and Ken Loach (director), first in television and then in the cinema with the film *Kes* (Ken Loach, 1969). The Garnett-Loach team specialized in a frank documentary realism, focusing on social issues (as in the remarkable success of the BBC play *Cathy Come Home* of November 1966, an indictment of homelessness and the housing problem) or overtly political events in labor history, including *The Big Flame* of 1969 (on an imaginery workers' occupation of the Liverpool docks), and *Days of Hope* of 1975 (a four-play cycle culminating in the 1926 General Strike). Welland then began writing scripts and screenplays, *Chariots of Fire* becoming his major success. The avowedly socialist credentials of its screenwriter casts the film's patriotism in a particular light. The title, of course, is taken from William Blake's *Jerusalem*, a favorite hymn of the British labor movement. For a useful analysis, see Sheila Johnston, "Charioteers and Ploughmen," in Martyn Auty and Nick Roddick, eds., *British Cinema Now* (London: BFI Publishing, 1985), pp. 99–110.

16. Judith Williamson, "Do You Want to Know a Secret?" *New Statesman*, 29 May 1987, pp. 27f., now reprinted in Judith Williamson, *Deadline at Dawn: Film Criticism, 1980–1990* (London: Marion Boyers, 1993), pp. 158–61.

17. The film and screenplay of *Mona Lisa*, and the other films of Neil Jordan (especially *Angel* [American title: *Danny Boy*], 1982; *The Company of Wolves*, 1984; and *The Crying Game*, 1992), repay careful analysis. The richness of *Mona*

Lisa is unfortunately compromised by the bluntness of its sexual politics. Thus the young prostitutes are reduced entirely to their bodies (through their drug dependencies and their servicing of male sexual demands), while Mortwell's weakness for white floppy-eared rabbits is probably a facile marker of homosexuality (in the clichéd combination of effeteness and violence). A related critique could be developed of the film's treatment of race, again as played through the reactions of George to the changes in his world (where the black presence works mainly as a sign for urban disorder and decay), and concentrated in the figure of Simone. See Lola Young, "A Nasty Piece of Work: A Psychoanalytic Study of Sexual and Racial Difference in 'Mona Lisa'," in Jonathan Rutherford, ed., *Identity: Community, Culture, Difference* (London: Lawrence and Wishart, 1990), pp. 188–206.

18. Anne Billson, reviewing Terence Davies's *The Long Day Closes* (1992), *New Statesman and Society*, 22 May 1992, p. 36.

19. Davies's accompanying note to the screenplay of *Distant Voices, Still Lives*, in Terence Davies, *A Modest Pageant: Six Screenplays with an Introduction* (London: Faber and Faber, 1992), p. 74. The second phrase is in quotation marks in the original, but Davies gives no source.

20. I owe my thinking about the place of song in the film to Lauren Berlant.

21. From the screenplay, Davies, *A Modest Pageant*, p. 78.

22. Accompanying note to the screenplay, ibid., p. 103

23. See the description of the production process in Pat Kirkham and Mike O'Shaughnessy, "Designing Desire," *Sight and Sound*, May 1992, pp. 13–15. While this article is concerned with the later film, *The Long Day Closes*, in principle it applies as well to *Distant Voices, Still Lives*. The quoted phrase is from ibid., p. 14.

24. "The reason I began making films came from a deep *need* to do so in order to come to terms with my family's history and suffering, to make sense of the past and to explore my own personal terrors, both mental and spiritual, and to examine the destructive nature of Catholicism. Film as an expression of guilt, film as confession (psychotherapy would be much cheaper but a lot less fun." See Davies's introduction to *A Modest Pageant*, p. ix.

25. Ibid., p. xi.

26. Kirkham and O'Shaughnessy, "Designing Desire," p. 13. See also Carolyn Steedman, "History and Autobiography: Different Pasts," in *Past Tenses: Essays on Writing, Autobiography and History* (London: Rivers Oram Press, 1992), pp. 45ff.

27. John Caughie, "Halfway to Paradise," *Sight and Sound*, May 1992, p. 12.

28. Roger Bromley, *Lost Narratives: Popular Fictions, Politics, and Recent History* (London: Routledge, 1988), pp. 7f. The past as another country originates with L. P. Hartley's novel *The Go Between* (1953), made into a film of the same name by Joseph Losey (1970). A further film was made by Marek Kanievska, *Another Country* (1984), this time an exploration of the formation of ruling-class attitudes in the public-school culture of the 1930s. See also David Lowenthal, *The Past Is a Foreign Country* (Cambridge: Cambridge University Press, 1985); and Patrick Wright, *On Living in an Old Country: The National*

Past in Contemporary Britain (London: Verso, 1985). The exact original is the first sentence of the Hartley novel: "The Past is a foreign country: they do things differently there." See the Scarborough House edition (Chelsea, Mich., 1980), p. 3.

29. Bromley, *Lost Narratives*, pp. 5, 13, 7, 9, 3, 189. Of course, I have not discussed at all another version of filmic memory making, namely, the nostalgia for an earlier twentieth-century aristocratic and upper-class Britain, invariably attached to the empire. See Andrew Higson, "Re-Presenting the National Past: Nostalgia and Pastiche in the Heritage Film," in Friedman, ed., *Fires Were Started*, pp. 109–29.

30. Caughie, "Halfway to Paradise," p. 12.

31. Ibid., p. 13.

32. This exclusion of all background references to political/public events of the time is all the more striking given the importance of the radio to the texture of Davies's film, because the use of radio news has otherwise become such a familiar element of the mise en scene of British period cinema. Moreover, the absence of politics is worth comparing with the method of another recent film concerned with the embedded drama of a difficult everyday life, Mike Leigh's *Life Is Sweet* (1990). The setting of the latter is contemporary, and the sensibility quite different. The main text—the importance of maintaining a good-humored sense of possibility, however impractical and symbolic, and the need not to give up—is not given explicitly political shape. But politics is nonetheless inserted as a reminder via the vituperative feminism and leftism of the bulimic daughter's incoherent rage. Thus Leigh succeeds in telling a story of working-class family life, which focuses on the hurts and pains of everyday struggles, and avoids the fiction that working people are revolutionaries in disguise, but without relinquishing political reference and possibility.

33. Alessandro Portelli, "Uchronic Dreams: Working-Class Memory and Possible Worlds," in Raphael Samuel and Paul Thompson, eds., *The Myths We Live By* (London: Routledge, 1990), p. 145.

34. Carolyn Kay Steedman, *Landscape for a Good Woman: A Story of Two Lives* (New Brunswick, N.J.: Rutgers University Press, 1987), p. 10.

35. Jeremy Seabrook, *Working-Class Childhood* (London: Gollancz, 1982), pp. 202, 147, cited by Steedman, *Landscape*, p. 108.

36. Ibid., pp. 11, 16, 8.

37. The lines quoted in this paragraph are taken from the screenplay, Davies, *A Modest Pageant*, pp. 117, 122, 98.

38. Tony is wearing his soldier's uniform. After smashing the windows and symbolically "breaking in" to his own home, he pleads in a controlled manner for his father to join him for a drink, holding two beer bottles in his now bloodied hands. His father, sitting by the fireside, refuses. Then Tony takes two old pennies from his pocket and throws them on the fire: "Tuppence—that's all I've got. But I wouldn't give *you* daylight." In response, the father deliberately pokes the coins deeper into the fire. The scene shows a stark refusal of feeling, an angry resistance to communication. The situation ends with Tony's arrest by the military police. His attempt at violent confrontation is completely nugatory: it lacks any effect on

his father, damages only his own body, and lands him in jail (after forceful eviction from the house). See ibid., pp. 78f.

39. The quoted phrase is from Davies's accompanying note to the screenplay, ibid., p. 74.

40. Carolyn Steedman, "Class of Heroes," *New Statesman and Society*, 14 April 1989, p. 27.

41. Ibid., p. 28.

42. The films of Peter Medak are a good example. At one level, *The Krays* tells a story of strong mothers and weak fathers, who somehow produce violent sons; while Derek Bentley's father in *Let Him Have It* is the epitome of ineffectual, accepting, fatalistic respectability. For a sympathetic reading of *The Krays*, see Mary Desjardins, "Free From the Apron Strings: Representations of Mothers in the Maternal British State," in Friedman, ed., *Fires Were Started*, pp. 130–44. For the difference that "looking back in gender" now makes, see Lovell, "Landscapes and Stories," and for a cognate discussion of theater, Michelene Wandor, *Look Back in Gender: Sexuality and the Family in Post-War British Drama* (London: Methuen, 1987).

43. Caughie, "Halfway to Paradise," p. 13. Davies, *A Modest Pageant*, p. xi. Again, it is worth comparing *Distant Voices, Still Lives* with Mike Leigh's filmmaking in this regard. In *High Hopes* (1988), *Life is Sweet*'s equally wonderful predecessor, the aging working-class mother is presented with a minimum of conventional sentimentality and achieves an understated dignity that is harnessed for the film's general humanist purposes rather than for the more familiar mythologizing of "our mam."

44. There is a major issue that this essay has not treated, and that is Davies's Catholicism, which in this film (as opposed to the earlier trilogy) is more latent but nonetheless implicates another familiar text of Catholicism, Irishness, brutish fathers, and martyred mothers, drawing us to the seldom-discussed Protestantism of contemporary English culture and the difficulties of cultural analysis in facing this field of national-religious difference within the working class. If "Irishness" is the Other of "Englishness," in other words, particularly in Liverpool and the Northwest, then the postwar emplacement of the working class in the national fantasy would need to be explored in its racialist and imperialist dimensions, too—a task I have not attempted here. As in so many other ways, Neil Jordan's recent *The Crying Game* (1992) would provide a rich beginning for such a discussion. I am grateful to Carolyn Steedman for reminding me of this missing dimension.

45. Steedman, *Landscape*, pp. 21f.

46. One fascinating juxtaposition, which would open a space for the additional essay I describe, would set, say, *Distant Voices, Still Lives* and the militant gayness of Derek Jarman's remarkable retelling of *Edward II* (1991) against Neil Jordan's *Mona Lisa* and *The Crying Game*. See the "New Queer Cinema" symposium in *Sight and Sound*, September 1992, pp. 30–39, including statements by Derek Jarman, Pratibha Parmar, Isaac Julien, and Constantin Giannaris. My thinking has benefited from Eve Kosofsky Sedgwick, *Epistemology of the Closet* (Berkeley and Los Angeles: University of California Press, 1990); Michael

Warner's introduction to his edited volume, *Fear of a Queer Planet: Queer Politics and Social Theory* (Minneapolis: University of Minnesota Press, 1993), pp. vii–xxxi; and especially Lauren Berlant and Elizabeth Freeman, "Queer Nationality," *boundary 2* 19 (1992): 149–80, now reprinted in Warner, ed., *Fear of a Queer Planet*, pp. 193–229. For the British context, see a number of the essays in Rutherford, ed., *Identity*, including Jonathan Rutherford, "A Place Called Home: Identity and the Cultural Politics of Difference," pp. 9–27; Kobena Mercer, "Welcome to the Jungle: Identity and Diversity in Postmodern Politics," pp. 43–71; and Simon Watney, "Practices of Freedom: 'Citizenship' and the Politics of Identity in the Age of AIDS," pp. 157–87. I have also benefited from reading a forthcoming essay by Frank Mort, "Essentialism Revisited? Identity Politics and Late Twentieth-Century Discourses of Homosexuality." For a reading of *Distant Voices, Still Lives* that incorporates Davies's gayness in a somewhat literalized pyschoanalytic way, see Tony Williams, "The Masochistic Fix: Gender Oppression in the Films of Terence Davies," in Friedman, ed., *Fires Were Started*, pp. 237–54.

47. I take the category of the postpatriarchal from Lauren Berlant.

48. Again, see here Lovell's discussion of the "mass culture/traditional culture paradigm," in "Landscapes and Stories," pp. 372ff.

Chapter Two
The Home and the World

1. Sumit Sarkar, *The Swadeshi Movement in Bengal, 1903–1908* (New Delhi: People's Publishing House, 1973), p. 53

2. Ibid., p. 54.

3. Ibid., pp. 56–57.

4. Ibid., p. 83.

5. *Ghare Baire*; first published in English in 1919 by Macmillan (London).

6. Ibid., p. 99.

7. Ibid., p. 101.

8. Ibid., p. 185.

9. Ibid., p. 264.

10. Ibid., p. 43.

11. Ibid., p. 44.

12. Ibid., p. 122.

13. Ibid., p. 292.

14. Ibid., p. 324.

15. Nicholas B. Dirks, "Castes of Mind," *Representations* (Winter 1992): 56–78.

16. Lata Mani, "Contentious Traditions: The Debate on Sati in Colonial India," in Kumkum Sangari and Sudesh Vaid, eds., *Recasting Women: Essays in Colonial History* (New Delhi: Kali for Women, 1989).

17. Partha Chatterjee, "Colonialism, Nationalism, and Colonized Women: The Contest in India," *American Ethnologist* 16, no. 4 (1989): 625.

18. Meredith Borthwick, *The Changing Role of Women in Bengal, 1849–1905* (Princeton: Princeton University Press, 1984), pp. 60–108.

19. See Chatterjee's complete argument in *The Nation and Its Fragments: Studies in Colonial and Post-Colonial Histories* (Princeton: Princeton University Press, 1993).

20. I single Nandy out in this context not only because of the controversy attending his recent writing but also because he is one of the most sophisticated, though frequently misunderstood, cultural critics of modernity in contemporary India. See *The Intimate Enemy: Loss and Recovery of Self under Colonialism* (Delhi: Oxford University Press, 1983); *At the Edge of Psychology: Essays in Politics and Culture* (Delhi: Oxford University Press, 1990); *Science, Hegemony, and Violence: Requiem for Modernity* (Delhi: Oxford University Press, 1990); "The Politics of Secularism," in Veena Das, ed., *Mirrors of Violence: Communities, Riots, and Survivors in South Asia* (Delhi: Oxford University Press, 1990); and "Secularism," *Seminar* 394 (June 1992): 88–126.

21. Nandy, *The Intimate Enemy*, p. x.

22. Ibid., p. xviii.

23. Nandy, "Secularism," p. 29.

24. Nandy, "The Politics of Secularism," p. 90.

25. In marked contrast to the heralded Bengali writings of Bankim Chandra Chatterjee. See, for example, Partha Chatterjee, *Nationalist Thought and the Contemporary World* (London: Zed Books, 1986).

26. For a useful biographical and filmographical account of Ray, see Andrew Robinson, *Satyajit Ray: The Inner Eye* (London: Andre Deutsch, 1989).

27. Though one could suggest that colonialism was in fact fundamental to the historical development and philosophical foundations of modernity. See my argument in the introduction to Nicholas B. Dirks, ed., *Colonialism and Culture* (Ann Arbor: University of Michigan Press, 1992).

28. See, in this context, the extraordinarily intriguing critique of the binarisms of some literature in colonial discourse studies by Sara Suleri, *The Rhetoric of English India* (Chicago: University of Chicago Press, 1992).

Chapter Three
Eijanaika

1. Michel Foucault, *Language, Counter-Memory, Practice*, trans. Donald F. Bouchard and Sherry Simon (Ithaca, N.Y.: Cornell University Press, 1977), p. 160.

2. Some of the terms competing to characterize the restoration are discussed in George M. Wilson, *Patriots and Redeemers in Japan: Motives in the Meiji Restoration* (Chicago: University of Chicago Press, 1992), pp. 5–6.

3. A woodblock print by Hiroshige II commemorates the entrance of a "Great Elephant from India" into the Ryōgoku pleasure quarters in 1863. Imamura postpones the elephant's arrival from 1863 to 1866, but otherwise faithfully records the scene. See H. M. Kaempfer, ed. *Ukiyoe Studies and Pleasures* (The Hague: Society for Japanese Arts and Crafts, 1978), p. 54.

4. Pierre Sorlin, *The Film in History: Restaging the Past* (Totowa, N.J.: Barnes and Noble, 1980), pp. 20–21.

5. There is now a lengthy literature on *eijanaika*. Useful surveys include Yano

Yoshiko, "'Okagemairi' to 'eijanaika,'" in *Ikki*, vol. 4: *Seikatsu, bunka, shisō*, ed. Aoki Michio et al. (Tokyo: Tokyo Daigaku Shuppankai, 1981); Takagi Shunsuke, *Eijanaika* (Tokyo: Kyōikusha, 1979); and Tamura Sadao, *Eijanaika hajimaru* (Tokyo: Aoki Shoten, 1987). In English, only George Wilson offers any extended analysis of the riots: *Patriots and Redeemers*, pp. 77–131.

6. This is how Wilson characterizes the Restoration (*Patriots and Redeemers*, p. 130).

7. We use *carnival* in the sense made famous in Mikhail Bakhtin, *Rabelais and His World*, trans. Hélène Iswolsky (Bloomington: Indiana University Press, 1984). Peter Stallybrass and Allon White provide an extremely useful and suggestive exploration of Bakhtin's thought in *The Politics and Poetics of Transgression* (Ithaca, N.Y.: Cornell University Press, 1986), esp. chap. 1.

8. This is how Roland Barthes characterizes the novel in "Writing and the Novel," in *Writing Degree Zero*, trans. Annette Lavers and Colin Smith (New York: Hill and Wang, 1968), p. 39. The similarities between historical and novelistic discourse are well established; Barthes' analysis, at any rate, encompasses both.

9. For a concise discussion of *minshūshi* historiography, see Carol Gluck, "The People in History: Recent Trends in Japanese Historiography," *Journal of Asian Studies* 38, no. 1 (1978): 25–50. Most of the work of people's historians is available only in Japanese, although Irokawa Daikichi's *Meiji no bunka* (Tokyo: Iwanami Shoten, 1970) has been translated: *The Culture of the Meiji Period*, trans. Marius Jansen et al. (Princeton: Princeton University Press, 1985).

10. These definitions are offered by Saitō Hiroshi and Haga Noboru, respectively. See Saitō, *Minshūshi no kōzō—Nihon kindaika no kitei kara* (Tokyo: Shinhyōronsha, 1975), p. 13; and Haga, *Minshūshi no sōzō* (Tokyo: NHK Books, 1974), p. 24.

11. Gluck, "The People in History," p. 34; she paraphrases Morita Shirō, *Chiisai buraku* (Tokyo: Asahi Shinbunsha, 1973), pp. 3–9.

12. Irokawa Daikichi's objections to official accounts of the Chichibu uprising of 1884 seem to mine the same vein. The Meiji government blamed "hoodlums" for this revolt by thousands of impoverished peasants. Irokawa's reasons for rejecting this explanation are revealing: "Could "hoodlums" lead and direct people? My answer is, obviously not. Gangsters and gamblers infringed on the *tsūzoku dōtoku* (conventional morality) from which the Japanese masses derived their energy for self-discipline . . . Hoodlums transgressed this ethic . . . they were good-for-nothing scoundrels who found it impossible to live up to the masses' moral code of hard work, frugality, honesty, harmony, modesty, and filial piety, and instead sank into wickedness, idleness, dissipation, extravagance, truculence, arrogance, and unfilial behavior" (*The Culture of the Meiji Period*, pp. 172–73).

One of the clearest examples of Irokawa's tendency to generalize from the particular is the case of Chiba Takusaburō, which is referenced repeatedly in his writing. Descendant of rural samurai and something of a scholar, Chiba and his class allies formed a political study group and in 1880 drafted a constitution. Irokawa unearthed this document in the Chiba family's storehouse in 1968. Although the document is one of a kind and the product of a particular class fraction, Irokawa characteristically insists on reading it as the collective product of the people (he calls it a "people's constitution"). See Irokawa, *The Culture of the Meiji Period*, pp. 44–50, 76–122.

13. Masao Miyoshi, *Off Center: Power and Culture Relations between Japan and the United States* (Cambridge: Harvard University Press, 1991), p. 88. Miyoshi, it must be stressed, does not believe that Japan is alone in this style of thinking; America is for him similarly preoccupied with its "Americanness."

14. See Kristin Thompson, "The Concept of Cinematic Excess," anthologized in Philip Rosen, ed., *Narrative, Apparatus, Ideology: A Film Theory Reader* (New York.: Columbia University Press, 1986), pp. 130–42; Roland Barthes, "The Third Meaning," in *Image/Music/Text*, trans. Stephen Heath (New York: Farrar, Straus, Giroux, 1977), pp. 52–68.

15. "The notion of central subjects is crucial to the logical structure of historical narrative. Assuming for the moment that history could be analyzed completely into a single set of atomistic elements, there are indefinitely many ways in which these elements can be organized into historical sequence. The role of the central subject is to form the main strand around which the historical narrative is woven": David Hull, "Central Subjects and Historical Narrative," *History and Theory* 14 (1975), cited in Dana Polan, *Power and Paranoia: History, Narrative, and the American Cinema, 1940–1950* (New York: Columbia University Press, 1986), p. 66.

16. The quotation is from Georg Lukács, *The Historical Novel*, trans. Stanley and Hannah Mitchell (Lincoln: University of Nebraska Press, 1983), p. 19. For a discussion of Hollywood historical film that makes interesting references to the Lukacsian aesthetic of the "typical character," see Philip Rosen, "Securing the Historical: Historiography and the Classical Cinema," in Patricia Mellencamp and Philip Rosen, eds., *Cinema Histories/Cinema Practices* (Los Angeles: American Film Institute Publications, 1984), pp. 24–27. See also Sorlin, *The Film in History*, pp. 21, 164.

17. Riverside areas like Ryōgoku were suspect sites in Japan's geographical imagination—thanks perhaps to their association in the medieval era with tanners, butchers, and undertakers, whose defiling occupations violated Shinto and Buddhist taboos. They were also sites consigned to pleasure.

18. Imamura's *Vengeance Is Mine* (1979), which dramatizes a police search for a serial killer and interrogates the state's right to take away the murderer's life in revenge for his killings, also raises interesting questions about authentic traditions and ethnicities, national belonging, and the rituals of citizenship in contemporary Japan. Two women working in an allotment garden quite literally overlook the corpse of the murderer's first victim, because, blinded by their racist assumptions, they see a drunken Korean: "He's not drunk, he's dead. . . . He's not Korean, he's Japanese." The murderer is himself a native of the southern island of Gotō who was penalized during his wartime childhood for his family's Catholicism: he escapes the police by assuming the identity of a "professor of microanalysis at Kyoto University"—by, that is, transmuting his ethnic marginality into cultural capital and ideological centrality.

19. Homi Bhabha, "Of Mimicry and Man: The Ambivalence of Colonial Discourse," *October* 28 (1984): 126–28.

20. Norma Field discusses the continuing economic and ideological colonization of the Ryukyu islands in chap. 1 of *In the Realm of a Dying Emperor* (New York: Pantheon, 1991).

21. E.g., David Desser, *Eros plus Massacre: An Introduction to the Japanese New Wave Cinema* (Bloomington: Indiana University Press, 1988), pp. 122–27.

22. For instance, a juxtaposition of historical change and timeless feminine suffering organizes both Imamura's *Insect Woman* (1963) and his *History of Postwar Japan as Told by a Bar Hostess* (1970). Instead of following critical consensus and construing the prevalence of this trope as evidence of Imamura's status as a *feminisuto* director or of "his politicized view of women" (Desser, *Eros plus Massacre*, p. 109), one might note the difference between recognizing women's oppression and conceptualizing it as a condition that can be changed, a condition susceptible to alteration by politics as such. (For a similar criticism of the definitions of "feminism" that prevail in Japanese film studies, see Scott Nygren, "Reconsidering Modernism: Japanese Film and the Postmodern Context," *Wide Angle* 11, no. 3 [1989]: 12.) If—and this is debatable—Imamura makes feminist films, the feminism is more likely to adhere in a challenge to this conventional association of the feminine and the archetypical than in its reinforcement. Tellingly, in making *Eijanaika*, Imamura evidently chose *not* to work with materials that document women's leadership of the new millenarian sects of the 1850s and 1860s.

23. It is worth recalling that one of Imamura's best-known films in the West is *The Pornographers: An Introduction to Anthropology* (1966). One might apply Robert Stam's insights into the connections between cinematic eroticism and the grotesque body of Bakhtinian theory to both *The Pornographers* and *Eijanaika*: "It is useful to regard porn . . . as an 'ersatz' or 'degraded' carnival, one that capitalizes on the repressed desire for carnival-style eroticism by serving up the simulacrum of its utopian promise. Commercial porn, in this sense, can be envisaged as a torn shred of carnival, the detritus of a once robust and irreverent tradition" (*Subversive Pleasures: Bakhtin, Cultural Criticism, and Film* [Baltimore, Md.: Johns Hopkins University Press, 1989], p. 169).

24. Alan Liu, "The Power of Formalism: The New Historicism," *ELH* 54 (1989): 735.

25. The phrase originates in Alfred de Vigny's nineteenth-century writings on the French Revolution, but one can easily imagine it, emblazoned calligraphically, supplying the starting point for a Hollywood historical epic.

26. Bakhtin, *Rabelais and His World*, p. 418.

27. The most innovative work on historical agency occurs, significantly, not in Western historiography but in the debates constituting postcolonial theory, debates alert to the dualistic traps of ethnocentrism and reverse ethnocentrism: see Bhabha, "Of Mimicry and Man," and Gayatri Chakravorty Spivak, "Subaltern Studies: Deconstructing Historiography," in *In Other Worlds: Essays in Cultural Politics* (New York: Routledge, 1988), pp. 197–221. For a guide to questions about historical agency in this work see Robert Young, *White Mythologies: Writing History and the West* (London: Routledge, 1990).

28. Stephen Heath, "Narrative Space," in *Questions of Cinema* (Bloomington: Indiana University Press, 1981), p. 38.

29. The samurai character who carries out the political assassination in Kyoto provides, together with his geisha lover, the most lurid example of such repetitions. Near the conclusion of the film the two commit suicide together, repeating a suicide attempt in the past: with his sword, Furukawa retraces the scars that the first attempt left on his lover's body.

30. Indeed, the shot of the dog running toward us with a charm around its neck replicates a famous sequence in Akira Kurosawa's samurai film–*cum*–spaghetti Western, *Yojimbo, the Bodyguard* (1961), where our first glimpse of the dirtiest town in nineteenth-century Japan features a dog trotting down the main street with a dismembered human hand in its mouth.

31. We quote Gilles Deleuze, *Cinema 1: The Movement-Image*, trans. Hugh Tomlinson and Barbara Habberjam (Minneapolis: University of Minnesota Press, 1986), p. 206, and draw on Meaghan Morris's discussion of the action film in "Tooth and Claw: Tales of Survival and *Crocodile Dundee*," in *The Pirate's Fiancée: Feminism, Reading, Postmodernism* (London: Verso, 1988), pp. 241–69.

32. Laura Mulvey, "Changes: Thoughts on Myth, Narrative, and Historical Experience," in *Visual and Other Pleasures* (Bloomington: Indiana University Press, 1989), p. 163.

33. The only completed narrative in *Eijanaika* is Itoman's: in the film's last minutes, as Ryōgoku dances, he obtains his vengeance. He murders the Satsuma samurai who, five years before, had used his political power in the Ryukyus to murder Itoman's family. Whereas the samurai thinks only of his "important business," of making history and bringing down the Shogunate, Itoman breaks this man's appointment with destiny and forces him to remember the past. After the massacre of the *eijanaika* dancers, Itoman sets sail for his homeland. Iné, who survives the shootings, bids him farewell and muses that perhaps she will visit the Ryukyus one day: the unlikelihood of her ever realizing that wish underscores the problematic of advance and arrival in the film.

34. Stam, *Subversive Pleasures*, p. 119.

35. Wilson, *Patriots and Redeemers*, p. 96.

Chapter Five
Hiroshima Mon Amour

1. See, for example, the following essays: "Cultural Criticism and Political Theory: Hayden White's Rhetorics of History," *Political Theory* 16, no. 4 (1988): 636–46; "Narrative as Enclosure: The Contextual Histories of H. Stuart Hughes," *Journal of the History of Ideas* 51, no. 3 (1990): 505–15; review essay on Richard Rorty's *Contingency, Irony, and Solidarity, History and Theory* 29, no. 3 (1990): 329–57; and "Foucault on Discourse and History," in *The Philosophy of Discourse*, ed. Chip Sills and George H. Jensen (Portsmouth, N.H.: Heinemann, 1991).

2. Parts of this project have been published as the following: "Remembering Forgetting: Maladies de la Mémoire in Nineteenth-Century France," *Representations* 26 (1989): 49–68; "Dying of the Past: Medical Studies of Nostalgia in Nine-

teenth-Century France," *History and Memory* 3, no. 1 (1991): 5–29; and "The Time of Nostalgia," *Time and Society* 1, no. 1 (1992): 271–86.

3. Robert Benayoun, *Alain Resnais, arpenteur de l'imaginaire: De Hiroshima à Mélo* (Paris: Stock, 1980), p. 52.

4. Ibid.

5. Marguerite Duras, *Hiroshima Mon Amour* (Paris: Gallimard, 1960), p. 28. Unless otherwise indicated, translations are my own. Henceforth, references to the screenplay will be given in the text.

> De même que dans l'amour cette illusion existe, cette illusion de pouvoir ne jamais oublier, de même j'ai eu l'illusion devant Hiroshima que jamais je n'oublierai.

6. B. A. van der Kolk and Onno van der Hart, "The Intrusive Past: The Flexibility of Memory and the Engraving of Trauma," *American Imago* 48, no. 4 (1991): 447.

7. Cathy Caruth, "Introduction," *American Imago* 48, no. 1 (1991): 3.

8. Sharon Willis, *Marguerite Duras: Writing on the Body* (Urbana: University of Illinois Press, 1987), pp. 33–62, 24. Willis's interesting reading of the screenplay depends heavily on Lacan's notion that the "real appears under the form of trauma"(p. 39). Although such a notion has the virtue of dramatizing everything one concentrates on as *always already traumatic*, it makes distinguishing trauma from other forms of experience (or from experience, properly so called) impossible. Since *Hiroshima Mon Amour* is crucially concerned with the connections between trauma and experience and their connections with memory and forgetting, Lacan's formulation is particularly unfortunate. If the real is always already traumatic, one cannot question how particular traumas exist in painful tension with other elements of one's reality or memory of the real.

9. ELLE: Pourquoi parler de lui plutôt que d'autres?

LUI: Pourquoi pas?

ELLE: Non. Pourquoi?

LUI: A cause de Nevers, je peux seulement commencer à te connaître. Et, entre les milliers et les milliers de choses de ta vie, je choisis Nevers.

ELLE: Comme autre chose?

LUI: Oui.

> *Est-ce qu'on voit qu'il ment? On s'en doute. Elle, elle devient presque violente, et, cherchant elle-même ce qu'elle pourrait dire (moment un peu fou).*

ELLE: Non. Ce n'est pas un hasard. (*Un temps.*) C'est toi qui dois me dire pourquoi. (pp. 80–81)

10. Van der Kolk and van der Hart, "The Intrusive Past," p. 448. On the "cure" produced through mourning (but not available in Duras) see Carol Hofmann, *Forgetting and Marguerite Duras* (Nitwot: University Press of Colorado, 1991), pp. 86–100.

11. In this regard see Sanford Scribner Ames, "Edging the Shadow: Duras from Hiroshima to Beaubourg," in *Remains to Be Seen: Essays on Marguerite Duras*, ed. Sanford Scribner Ames (New York: Peter Lang, 1988), p. 17.

12. Tu n'étais pas tout à fait mort.

J'ai raconté notre histoire.

Je t'ai trompé ce soir avec cet inconnu.

J'ai raconté notre histoire.

Elle était, vois-tu, racontable.

Quatorze ans que je n'avais pas retrouvé . . . le goût
d'un amour impossible.

Depuis Nevers.

Regarde comme je t'oublie . . .

—Regarde comme je t'ai oublié.

Regarde-moi.

13. Stephen Heath, *Questions of Cinema* (Bloomington: Indiana University Press, 1981), p. 123.

14. Ibid., p. 122.

15. Carl E. Schorske, "History and the Study of Culture," *New Literary History* 21, no. 2 (1990): 408. Reprinted in Michael S. Roth and Ralph Cohen, eds., *History and . . .* (Charlottesville: University of Virginia Press, forthcoming).

16. Robert Dawidoff, "History . . . but," *New Literary History* 21, no. 2 (1990): 395–406. Reprinted in Roth and Cohen, eds., *History and . . .*

17. Claude Lanzmann, "Hier is kein Warum," in *Au sujet de Shoah: le film de Claude Lanzmann* (Paris: Belin, 1990), p. 279.

18. Hans Kellner, "Beautifying the Nightmare: The Aesthetics of Post-Modern History," *Strategies* 4, no. 5 (1991): 292–93.

Chapter Six
Memories of Underdevelopment

1. Among the awards garnered by *Memories* was its selection as the best Third World film made during 1968–78, according to a poll published by James Monaco, "What's the Score? The Best of the Decade," *Take One* 6, no. 8 (July, 1978). It was also picked as one of the ten best films shown in the U.S. during 1973 by the *New York Times*.

2. Edmundo Desnoes originally published the novel *Memorias del subdesarrollo* in 1962. It has been reprinted several times since. An English version appeared under the title of *Inconsolable Memories* in 1968.

3. Desnoes has stated: "I do not share the indigation of so many writers who feel betrayed by the awkward director. I do not deny the betrayal: I enjoyed it. . . . He objectivized a world that was shapeless in my mind and still abstract in the book. He added social density to the subjective elements of a diary." "Se llamaba Sergio," *Cine cubano* 45–46, (August–October 1967): 27.

4. Gutiérrez Alea, "*Memorias del subdesarrollo:* Notas de trabajo," ibid., pp. 22.

5. *Dialéctica del espectador* (Havana: Unión, 1982), p. 70. This valuable work has been translated into English by Julia Lesage as "The Viewer's Dialectic," in *Jump/Cut: A Review of Contemporary Cinema* 29–30 (1984–85): 18–21, 48–53.

6. Georg Lukács, *The Historical Novel* (Harmondsworth: Penguin, 1969), pp. 32–38.

7. Alea, "Notas de trabajo," p. 23.

8. Arthur Cooper described Sergio as the "ultimate outsider" in his review in *Newsweek* (17 April 1972); cited in Julianne Burton, "*Memories of Underdevelopment* in the Land of Overdevelopment," *Cineaste* 8, no. 1 (1977): 16.

9. "The image of reality offered in *Memories* is multifaceted, like an object contemplated from various points of view." Alea, *Dialéctica*, p. 65.

10. "If the beginning of the film leaves us with a disconsolate impression, it is evidently because the protagonist . . . projects his own spirit over the reality which surrounds him and we see it through his eyes." Ibid., p. 67.

11. The concept of the "mindscreen" is Bruce Kawin's, who provides an interesting introduction to this type of film in *Mindscreen: Bergman, Godard, and First-Person Film* (Princeton: Princeton University Press, 1978).

12. Gregory Bateson, *Mind and Nature* (New York: E. P. Dutton, 1979), p. 35.

13. Both Gutiérrez Alea and Corrieri have been greatly influenced by Bertolt Brecht. See Alea, *Dialéctica*, especially the chapters "Identificación y distanciamiento, Aristóteles y Brecht" and "Enajenación y desenajenación, Eisenstein y Brecht." On Corrieri, see Laurette Séjourné's interview with him in *Teatro Escambray: una experiencia* (Havana, 1977), and my essay in *The International Dictionary of Films and Filmmakers*, vol. 3: *Actors/Actresses* (Chicago: St. James/Macmillan, 1986), pp. 152–53.

14. Julianne Burton, "'Individual Fulfillment and Collective Achievement': An Interview with Tomás Gutiérrez Alea," *Cineaste* 8, no. 1 (1977): 9.

15. On the reception of *Memories* in the U.S., see Burton, "*Memories of Underdevelopment* in the Land of Overdevelopment."

16. Gutiérrez Alea, "Notas de trabajo."

17. These photos appear in Carlton Beals, *The Crime of Cuba* (Philadelphia: J. B. Lippincott, 1933).

18. Hugh Thomas, certainly never a friend of the Cuban revolution, stated: "The extent and horror of the Batista era became apparent only after it ended. Bodies and skeletons, torture chambers and tortures, were discovered and photographed in the press." See *Cuba: The Pursuit of Freedom* (New York: Harper and Row, 1971), p. 1073. Obviously it was apparent to some Cubans long before, and some of the photographs and footage that appear in this sequence may have been taken before Batista's fall.

19. I am here paraphrasing Lukacs, *The Historical Novel*, p. 39.

20. It is worth observing that Desnoes emigrated from Cuba to the United States during the 1970s.

21. K. S. Karol, *Guerrillas in Power* (London: Thames and Hudson, 1971), p. 427.

22. Guevara's most explicit statement on the "New Man" can be found in "Socialism and Man in Cuba," many times reprinted. It can be found in *Che: Selected Works of Ernesto Guevara*, ed. Rolando E. Bonachea and Nelson P. Valdés (Cambridge, Mass.: MIT Press, 1969), pp. 155–69.

Chapter Seven
The Moderns

1. *The Forger's Art*, ed. Denis Dutton (Berkeley and Los Angeles: University of California Press, 1983), p. vii.
2. Ibid., p. 205.
3. Ibid., p. 184.
4. See Anne-Marie Stein, *Three Picassos before Breakfast* (New York: Hawthorne Books, 1973).

Chapter Eight
Radio Bikini

1. The United States acquired Bikini and the other Marshall Islands, which had been under Japanese mandate from the League of Nations, at the end of World War II as a United Nations Trust Territory. The use of these newly acquired territories, which had no effective voice in U.S. policymaking, at the very least stretched the limits of the permissible under trust territory protocols.
2. On the military's considerations behind the tests see Gregg Herken, *The Winning Weapon: The Atomic Bomb in the Cold War, 1945–1950* (New York: Knopf, 1980), pp. 224–26.
3. These elements of nuclear mythmaking, particularly the language of universalization and duty, closely resemble Roland Barthes' analysis of myth as "depoliticized speech." (See Roland Barthes, *Mythologies* [New York: Hill and Wang, 1972], esp. pp. 142–45.) Although Barthes is writing of what he terms "bourgeois myth," the traits he describes seem applicable to forms of discourse other than the bourgeois.
4. The Able bomb exploded in shallow water, two miles off target; some naval officers suspected the air force, which dropped the instrument, of sabotaging the test. See Herken, *The Winning Weapon*, p. 225.
5. Considerable scientific data on the lethal effects of radioactivity had been accumulated since 1930. Colonel Stafford Warren, a University of California at Los Angeles Medical School professor, who was in charge of media safety at Crossroads, deplored the lack of precautions, in particular the "hairy-chested attitudes" that allowed men to sleep on deck in nothing but shorts and be exposed to radioactive spray. General Leslie Groves, head of the wartime Manhattan Project, feared lawsuits from the sailors who were exposed. Warren's recommendation that radiation risks be publicly acknowledged was buried—part of a pattern of concealing the peril by both the military and the Atomic Energy Commission. See Howard Ball, *Justice Downwind: America's Atomic Testing Program in the 1950s* (New York: Oxford University Press, 1986), p. 204; and the *New York Times*, 25 May 1983.
6. Bradley too criticized the shroud of secrecy about Crossroads' radiation danger. His book, published two years after the tests, became a bestseller and contributed importantly to public understanding of the issue. See David Bradley, *No Place to Hide* (Boston: Little, Brown, 1948). See also Paul Boyer, *By the*

Bomb's Early Light: American Thought and Culture at the Dawn of the Atomic Age (New York: Pantheon, 1985); and Spencer R. Weart, *Nuclear Fear: A History of Images* (Cambridge, Mass.: Harvard University Press, 1988).

Chapter Nine
Repentance

1. William Shakespeare, Sonnet 66 (a poem that is, as we shall see, central to *Repentance*), in *The Complete Works of Shakespeare*, Cambridge edition text, ed. William Aldis Wright (New York: Doubleday, 1936), p. 1412.

2. For an excellent examination of this critical issue see R. W. Davies, *Soviet History in the Gorbachev Revolution* (Bloomington: Indiana University Press, 1989).

3. Alexander Batchan and Victor Dyomin, "Mad Russian," *Film Comment* 23, no. 3 (May–June 1987): 51. This is an interview with Viktor Demin, a prominent Soviet film critic.

4. For an interesting report on these reactions, see Andrei Bitov, "The Courage of an Artist," in Michael Brashinsky and Andrew S. Horton, eds., *The Russians Are Coming: Russian Critics on the End of Soviet Cinema, 1984–1990* (Cambridge: Cambridge University Press, forthcoming); originally published in *Moscow News*, 15 February 1987. Other examples of the early Soviet response to the film are collected in *The USSR Today: Perspectives from the Soviet Press*, 7th ed., ed. Robert Ehlers et al. (Columbus, Ohio: Current Digest of the Soviet Press, 1988), pp. 168–70.

5. Batchan and Dyomin, "Mad Russian," p. 51; and Igor Aleinkov, "Between the Circus and the Zoo," in Brashinsky and Horton, *The Russians Are Coming*; originally published in *Sine-fantom* 7–8 (1987).

6. As good examples of the former, see Josephine Woll, "Soviet Cinema: A Day of Repentance," *Dissent* 35, no. 2 (Spring 1988): 167–69; Peter G. Christensen, "Tengiz Abuladze's *Repentance*: Despair in the Age of *Perestroika*," *Soviet and East-European Drama, Theatre, and Film* 8, nos. 2–3 (December 1988): 64–72; and L. G. Ionin's review in *Sotsiologicheskie issledovanie* 3 (1987): 62–72 (discussed in Davies, *Soviet History*, pp. 91–92). For a look at *Repentance* in the context of Abuladze's oeuvre, see Julie Christensen, "Tengiz Abuladze's *Repentance* and the Georgian Nationalist Cause," *Slavic Review* 50, no. 1 (Spring 1991): 163–75. The other two films in Abuladze's trilogy are *The Prayer* (1967, Vedreba [Georgian]/Molba [Russian]) and *The Tree of Desire* (1975, Natvris xe [Georgian]/Drevo zhelanie [Russian]).

7. That is, apart from my own brief review in the *American Historical Review* 95, no. 4 (October 1990): 1133–36.

8. Davies, *Soviet History*, p. 183.

9. Aleinikov, "Between the Zoo and the Circus."

10. And, of course, it is not specifically Soviet—witness the uproar over Oliver Stone's *JFK*, which led to an unprecedentedly quick response in the *American Historical Review*; see the forum on *JFK*, with articles by Marcus Raskin, Michael Rogin, and Robert A. Rosenstone, *AHR* 97, no. 2 (April 1992): 487–511. For an example from the USSR, see Youngblood, "'History' on Film: The Historical

Melodrama in Early Soviet Cinema," *Historical Journal of Film, Radio, and Television* 11, no. 2 (June 1991): 173–84.

11. Aleinikov, "Between the Zoo and the Circus," finds this detail especially offensive.

12. Abuladze is not, of course, the only director to utilize surrealistic devices in historical films. It is interesting to note that other exemplars of this approach, notably Hungarian director Miklós Jancsó and Czechoslovak director Jan Němbc, were working, like Abuladze, in states where art was "tongue-tied by authority," and a direct approach to controversial material was automatically doomed to failure.

13. Bitov, "Courage of an Artist."

14. Ibid.

15. As will become clear, I am using this term very loosely, in a functional rather than a theoretical sense.

16. I am indebted to Maureen Turim's provocative book *Flashbacks in Film: Memory and History* (New York: Routledge, 1989) for my understanding of the flashback in *Repentance* (although she does not discuss this film).

17. Julie Christensen, "Tengiz Abuladze's *Repentance*," p. 166.

18. Although Guliko Aravidze will be discussed only in passing in this essay, her presence in the film is so dominant that a feminist reading of the work would surely yield fascinating results.

19. Certainly, it is the same actress (Zeinab Botsvadze), but whether Abuladze intends her to be playing the same character is not so certain.

20. Janet Maslin, in her *New York Times* review of the film (4 December 1987), remarks quite inexplicably that actor Avtandil Makharadze "would resemble Stalin even without the costumes and hair-cut he has been given here." He in no way resembles Stalin physically, nor did Abuladze intend him to.

21. "Bukharin's Last Plea," in Robert V. Daniels, ed., *A Documentary History of Communism*, vol. 1: *Communism in Russia* (Hanover, N.H.: University Press of New England, 1984), pp. 271–72.

22. Again, see as an example Bukharin's final speech to the court, ibid., and what was apparently his last plea, dated the day he was shot, 13 March 1938: "I do not say—and I am not able to say—that I can expiate my guilt; the crimes I committed are so monstrous, so enormous, that I cannot atone for my guilt" ("A Grim Record," *New York Times*, 15 June 1992, A11). Finally, the Russian word *pokaianie*, used as the Russian title for this film, means "confession" as well as "repentance" or "atonement."

23. Avtandil Makharadze's depiction of Abel Aravidze is excellent, but his portrayal of Varlam is a genuine tour de force.

24. Cannon Group/Media Home Entertainment's identification of the film as being in "Russian with English subtitles" notwithstanding, the dialogue is in Georgian, with the exceptions noted.

25. Shakespeare, Sonnet 66, in *The Complete Works*, p. 1412.

26. See Woll, "Soviet Cinema," p. 168.

27. See the numerous examples in what is arguably the greatest memoir of the Terror, Eugenia Ginzburg's *Journey into the Whirlwind*, trans. Paul Stevenson and Max Hayward (New York: Harcourt, Brace, Jovanovich, 1967)—or in

Evgenii Tsimbal's fascinating docudrama *Defense Counsel Sedov* (Zashchitnik Sedov, 1989).

28. Varlam claims this is an aphorism from Confucius, but Josephine Woll suggests (in a letter to the author, 29 June 1992) that Abuladze is probably also making an anachronistic reference to Bulat Okudzhava's well-known song "The Black Cat" (Chernyi kot), in which the cat represents Stalin.

29. Julie Christensen notes that in Georgian, Aravidze means "no man" or "every man" ("Tengiz Abuladze's *Repentance*," p. 166).

30. *Repentance*'s Abel is not the innocent victim of Genesis—or is Abuladze commenting on that parable, too?

31. This scene reminds me very much of Marlon Brando's anguished soliloquy over his wife's coffin in *Last Tango in Paris*.

32. Andzhaparidze also provides another Chiaureli connection. Chiaureli's wife, she played in several of his films, including the notorious tribute to Stalin, *The Fall of Berlin* (Padenie Berlina).

33. Abuladze died on 10 March 1994 at the age of ten years.

34. Quoted by Stephen F. Cohen in *Rethinking the Soviet Experience: Politics and History since 1917* (New York: Oxford University Press, 1985), p. vii.

Chapter Ten
Hitler: A Film from Germany

1. Saul Friedländer, *Reflections of Nazism: An Essay on Kitsch and Death* (New York: Harper and Row, 1984); Susan Sontag, "Syberberg's Hitler," in *Under the Sign of Saturn* (New York: Farrar, Straus, Giroux, 1980), pp. 158, 163; Anton Kaes, *Deutschlandbilder: Die Wiederkehr der Geschichte als Film* (Munich: edition text + kritik, 1987), chap. 5; trans. as *From "Hitler" to "Heimat": The Return of History as Film* (Cambridge, Mass.: Harvard University Press, 1989), and "Holocaust and the End of History: Postmodern Historiography in Cinema," in *Probing the Limits of Representation: Nazism and the "Final Solution"*, ed. Saul Friedländer (Cambridge, Mass.: Harvard University Press, 1992); Eric Santer, *Stranded Objects: Mourning, Memory, and Film in Postwar Germany* (Ithaca, N.Y.: Cornell University Press, 1990), chap. 4; Thomas Elsaesser, "Myth as the Phantasmagoria of History: H. J. Syberberg, Cinema and Representation," *New German Critique* 24–25 (Fall–Winter 1981–82): 108–54, and *New German Cinema: A History* (New Brunswick, N.J.: Rutgers University Press, 1989), 264–67.

2. See Hans-Jürgen Syberberg, *Vom Unglück und Glück der Kunst in Deutschland nach dem letzten Kriege* (Munich: Matthes and Seitz, 1990). Syberberg has responded to criticisms of his book by insisting that he is not anti-Semitic and that he has been misunderstood. See John Rockwell, "An Elusive German Director Reemerges in Edinburgh," *New York Times*, 2 September 1992, B1, B4.

3. Sontag, "Syberberg's Hitler," p. 150; Kaes, "Holocaust and the End of History"; Elsaesser, "Myth as the Phantasmagoria of History," p. 139; and Vincent Canby, "Free-Form Meditation," *New York Times*, 13 January 1980.

4. See for example the interview with Syberberg, "Hans Jürgen Syberberg: *Our Hitler* as Visual Politics," *Performing Arts Journal* 12, no. 3 (1980): 50–58.

5. Hayden White, "AHR Forum: Historiography and Historiophoty," *American Historical Review* 93, no. 5 (December 1988): 1193.

6. I take the term from Raymond Williams, *Marxism and Literature* (Oxford: Oxford University Press, 1977), chap. 9.

7. Kaes, "Holocaust and the End of History," p. 216, calls the cosmic model "dubious."

8. Canby, "Free-Form Meditation," mentions the Universal Pictures motif.

9. Sontag, "Syberberg's Hitler," p. 161.

10. Ibid., pp. 155–56.

11. Hans-Jürgen Syberberg, *Hitler: A Film from Germany*, trans. Joachim Neugroschel (New York: Farrar, Strauss, Giroux, 1982), p. 41. Hereafter, parenthetical page references in the text refer to this film script.

12. Hans Kellner, *Language and Historical Representation: Getting the Story Crooked* (Madison: University of Wisconsin Press, 1989), p. vii.

13. David Carr, *Time, Narrative, and History* (Bloomington: Indiana University Press, 1986), p. 168.

14. Canby, "Free-Form Meditation"; Sontag, "Syberberg's Hitler," p. 146. The girl is played by Syberberg's nine-year-old daughter.

15. For a good overview, see Ian Kershaw, *The Nazi Dictatorship: Problems and Perspectives of Interpretation* (London: Edward Arnold, 1985).

16. Kaes, "Holocaust and the End of History," p. 212.

17. See Richard Sennett, *The Fall of Public Man: On the Social Psychology of Capitalism* (New York: Vintage Books, 1974).

18. See Kershaw, *The Nazi Dictatorship*, chap. 4.

19. On the "look" of the Nazi dictatorship, see Peter Reichel, *Der Schöne Schein des Dritten Reiches: Faszination und Gewalt des Faschismus* (Munich: Carl Hanser Verlag, 1991).

20. See the introductory comments in Kaes, "Holocaust and the End of History," p. 208.

21. See the discussion in Greil Marcus, *Lipstick Traces: A Secret History of the Twentieth Century* (Cambridge, Mass.: Harvard University Press, 1989), pp. 14–15. Marcus mistakenly places Belsen in the former East Germany, assuming that Rotten's desire to visit the "new Belsen" meant he literally had to get through the Berlin Wall to see it. Instead, it seems that the merging of these images had to do with Rotten's need to "get through" the recent history of contemporary Europe before making it to the core of the "misery" represented by the extermination camps. In any case, Marcus makes a useful observation about the song's ruthless parodying of a commercialized desire to "see some history," a desire that in England in this period found one particularly bizarre expression in "alternative" vacations in Nazi-like concentration camps. I might add that a song such as "Holidays in the Sun" points to the critical-historical and heuristic possibilities of commercial culture, a feature that is overlooked in arguments about "pop fascism," to use Alvin H. Rosenfeld's term in *Imagining Hitler* (Bloomington: Indiana University Press, 1985), p. 104.

22. "The 'worklike' supplements empirical reality by adding to and subtracting from it." See Dominick LaCapra, "Rethinking Intellectual History and Read-

ing Texts," in *Rethinking Intellectual History: Texts, Contexts, Language* (Ithaca, N.Y.: Cornell University Press, 1983), p. 30.

23. The phrase comes from Alan Megill's discussion of the link between Neitzsche's and Heidegger's aestheticism in *Prophets of Extremity: Nietzsche, Heidegger, Foucault, Derrida* (Berkeley and Los Angeles: University of California Press, 1985), p. 141.

24. Marcus, *Lipstick Traces*, p. 23.

25. For a concise discussion, see Max Weber, "The Sociology of Charismatic Authority," in *From Max Weber: Essays in Sociology*, trans. H. H. Gerth and C. Wright Mills (New York: Oxford University Press, 1958), chap. 9.

26. As Kaes points out in "Holocaust and the End of History," p. 209, this is precisely the aspect of the film that so many German intellectuals criticized.

27. Williams, *Marxism and Literature*, p. 131. For the origins, development, and problems of the concept in Williams's work, see Alan O'Connor, *Raymond Williams: Writing, Culture, Politics* (Oxford: Basil Blackwell, 1989), pp. 83–85.

28. See Santner, *Stranded Objects*, chap. 4.

Chapter Eleven
From the Pole to the Equator

1. For representative pieces by Rosenstone and Toplin, see the "AHR Forum" in *American Historical Review* 93 (1988): 1173–1227. Rosenstone further elaborates his ideas in "What You Think about When You Think about Writing a Book on History and Film," *Public Culture* 3 (1990): 64. Also, see Natalie Zemon Davis, "'Any Resemblance to Persons Living or Dead': Film and the Challenge of Authenticity," *Yale Review* 76 (Summer 1987): 457–82.

2. Robert A. Rosenstone, "Revisioning History: Contemporary Filmmakers and the Construction of the Past," *Comparative Studies in Society and History* 32 (1990): 822–37.

3. Comerio may also have purchased documentary footage from other filmmakers, as was common practice at the time. I am indebted to Charles Musser for suggesting this possibility.

4. Charles Musser, *Before the Nickelodeon* (Berkeley and Los Angeles: University of California Press, 1991) and *The Emergence of Cinema* (New York: Scribner's, 1990).

5. Daniel Sipe, "The Future of Oral History and Moving Images," *Oral History Review* 19, nos. 1–2 (Spring–Fall 1991): 75–87.

6. Benjamin Goldberg, *The Mirror and Man* (Charlottesville: University of Virginia Press, 1985).

7. Beaumont Hall, ed., *Photography: Essays and Images* (New York: Museum of Modern Art, 1980), pp. 53–54.

8. Hayden White, *The Content of the Form* (Baltimore, Md.: Johns Hopkins University Press, 1987).

9. Hayden White, "Historiography and Historiophoty," *American Historical Review* 93 (1988): 1193–99.

10. I am drawing on Kaja Silverman's *The Subject of Semiotics* (New York: Oxford University Press, 1983), pp. 14–25.

11. John Berger, *Ways of Seeing* (London: Penguin, 1972), p. 7.

12. Hall, *Photography*, p. 60.

13. Walter Benjamin, *Illuminations: Essays and Reflections* (New York: Schocken Books, 1969), p. 238.

14. Silverman, *The Subject of Semiotics*, pp. 50–53.

Chapter Twelve
Walker and Mississippi Burning

1. Otis L. Graham, Jr., "Premature Reports: The 'End of History,'" *OAH Newsletter* 18 (May 1990): 3, 23; James Atlas, "What Is Fukuyama Saying?" *New York Times Magazine*, 22 October 1989, pp. 38–42; Alan Ryan, "Professor Hegel Goes to Washington," *New York Review of Books*, 26 March 1992, pp. 7–13; and Peter Fritzsche, "Francis Fukuyama, *The End of History and the Last Man*," *American Historical Review* 97 (June 1992): 817–19. See also Francis Fukuyama, *The End of History and the Last Man* (New York: Free Press, 1991).

2. Fredric Jameson, "Postmodernism, or, the Cultural Logic of Late Capitalism" *New Left Review* 146 (July–August 1984): 64; reprinted in *Postmodernism, or, the Cultural Logic of Late Capitalism* (Durham, N.C.: Duke University Press, 1991). See also Jameson, "Reification and Utopia in Mass Culture," *Social Text* 1 (Winter 1979): 130–48; "Postmodernism and Consumer Society," in Hal Foster, ed., *The Anti-Aesthetic: Essays on Postmodern Culture* (Port Townsend, Wash.: Bay Press, 1983), pp. 111–25; "Progress vs. Utopia; or, Can We Imagine the Future?" in Brian Willis, ed., *Art after Modernism: Rethinking Representation* (New York: New Museum of Contemporary Art, 1984), pp. 239–52; and "Nostalgia for the Present," *South Atlantic Quarterly* 88, no. 2 (Spring 1989): 517–37. See also Michael Walsh, "Postmodernism Has an Intellectual History," *Quarterly Review of Film and Video* 12, nos. 1–2 (1990): 147–61.

3. Jameson, "Postmodernism and Consumer Society," p. 125.

4. Jameson, "Postmodernism, or, the Cultural Logic of Late Capitalism," pp. 77–78; David Harvey, *The Condition of Postmodernity: An Inquiry into the Origins of Cultural Change* (Cambridge: Basil Blackwell, 1989), part 2, p. 273.

5. See Robert A. Rosenstone, "History in Images/History in Words: Reflections on the Possibility of Really Putting History onto Film," *American Historical Review* 93 (December 1988): 1173–85. For critical theorists on historical film, see Vivian Sobchack, "'Surge and Splendor': A Phenomenology of the Hollywood Historical Epic," *Representations* 29 (Winter 1990): 24–49; and Janet Staiger, "Securing the Fictional Narrative as a Tale of the Historical Real," *South Atlantic Quarterly* 88 (Spring 1989): 393–412.

6. See "AHR Forum: The Old History and the New," *American Historical Review* 94 (June 1989): 654–98. Essays read at the AHA annual meeting in December 1987 include Theodore S. Hammerow, "The Bureaucratization of History"; Gertrude Himmelfarb, "Some Reflections on the New History"; Lawrence W. Levine, "The Unpredictable Past: Reflections on Recent American Historiography"; Joan W. Scott, "History in Crisis? The Others' Side of the Story"; and John E. Toews, "Perspectives on 'The Old History and the New': A Comment."

7. On the *Annales* school, see Lynn Hunt, "French History in the Last Twenty

Years: The Rise and Fall of the *Annales* Paradigm," *Journal of Contemporary History* 21 (April 1986): 209–24; and Hunt, *The New Cultural History* (Berkeley and Los Angeles: University of California Press, 1989), pp. 1–22. See also Georg G. Iggers's introduction, "The Transformation of Historical Studies in Historical Perspective," to Georg G. Iggers and Harold T. Parker, eds., *International Handbook of Historical Studies: Contemporary Research and Theory* (Westport, Conn.: Greenwood Press, 1979), pp. 1–14. On Braudel's concept of structure, see Samuel Kinser, "*Annaliste* Paradigm? The Geohistorical Structuralism of Fernand Braudel," *American Historical Review* 86 (February–December 1981): 63–105. On the *Annales* school critique of narrative history, see Hayden White, "Narrative in Contemporary Historical Theory," in *The Content of Form: Narrative Discourse and Historical Representation* (Baltimore, Md.: Johns Hopkins University Press, 1987), pp. 31–32.

8. Fernand Braudel, "Time, History, and the Social Sciences," trans. Siam France, in Fritz Stern, ed., *The Varieties of History* (New York: Vintage Books, 1973), pp. 424–25. Originally published as "Histoire et sciences sociales: La Longue durée," *Annales* 13 (1958): 725–53.

9. Kinser, "*Annaliste* Paradigm?" p. 99.

10. Rudy Wurlitzer, *Walker* (New York: Harper and Row, 1987), p. 41.

11. Charles Jencks, *Post-Modernism: The New Classicism in Art and Architecture* (New York: Rizzoli, 1987), pp. 20–21.

12. For a brief account of Walker's filibusters, see Karl Berman, *Under the Big Stick: Nicaragua and the United States since 1948* (Boston: South End Press, 1986), pp. 51–102. A standard account is William O. Scroggs' aptly titled *Filibusters and Financiers: The Story of William Walker and His Associates* (New York: Russell and Russell, 1916). Walker wrote an account of his adventures in third person, *The War in Nicaragua* (Mobile, Ala.: Goetzel, 1860).

13. A Broadway musical entitled *Nicaragua, or, General Walker's Victories* that opened in New York in 1856 included a character named Ivory Black, "a superior nigger." See Karl Berman, *Under the Big Stick*, p. 76.

14. She was actually Helen Martin. See Scroggs, *Filibusters and Financiers*, p. 14.

15. Andreas Huyssen, "Mapping the Postmodern," *New German Critique* 33 (1984): 37–38, reprinted in *After the Great Divide: Modernism, Mass Culture, Postmodernism* (Bloomington: Indiana University Press, 1986), pp. 178–221; Brook Thomas, "The New Historicism and Other Old-fashioned Topics," in H. Aram Veeser, ed., *The New Historicism* (New York: Routledge, 1989), pp. 182–203; T. J. Jackson Lears, *No Place of Grace: Antimodernism and the Transformation of American Culture, 1880–1920* (New York: Pantheon, 1981), p. xix; Marshall Berman, *All That Is Solid Melts Into Air: The Experience of Modernity* (New York: Simon and Schuster, 1982), pp. 33–34; and Linda Hutcheon, *A Poetics of Postmodernism: History, Theory, Fiction* (New York: Routledge, 1988), p. 5. See also Thomas, *The New Historicism and Other Old-Fashioned Topics* (Princeton: Princeton University Press, 1991).

16. Hutcheon, *A Poetics of Postmodernism*, p. 5; Quoted in Iggers, "The Transformation of Historical Studies," p. 9. On Marxism and the *Annales* school,

see Hunt, "French History in the Last Twenty Years" and *The New Cultural History*.

17. See, for example, Natalie Zemon Davis, *The Return of Martin Guerre* (Cambridge, Mass.: Harvard University Press, 1983), which was made into a film. See also Staiger, "Securing the Fictional Narrative."

18. David Ansen, "A Yankee Devil's Manifest Destiny: History as a Bad Joke," *Newsweek*, 7 December 1987; "Walker," *Variety*, 2 December 1987; untitled review, *Wall Street Journal*, 3 December 1987; Michael Wilmington, "'Walker' Dramatizes Bizarre Historical Exploit Gone Awry," *Los Angeles Times*, 4 December 1987; in *Walker* clipping file, Margaret Herrick Library, Academy of Motion Picture Arts and Sciences, Los Angeles, Calif.

19. Richard Schickel, "Bananas Republic," *Time*, 7 December 1987; David Sterrit, "'Walker': History as Tragedy . . . and Farce," *Christian Science Monitor*, 7 January 1988; "Stanley Kauffman on Film," *New Republic*, 28 December 1987; Vincent Canby, "Film: 'Walker,' Starring Ed Harris," *New York Times*, 4 December 1987; "'Walker' Is an Amusing Hit in Nicaragua," *Los Angeles Times*, 5 March 1988, in *Walker* clipping file, Margaret Herrick Library, Academy of Motion Picture Arts and Sciences.

20. Quoted in Patrick Goldstein, "Hollywood Invades Nicaragua," *Los Angeles Times Calendar*, 19 April 1987, p. 17; Wayne King, "Fact vs. Fiction," *New York Times*, Arts and Leisure section, 4 December 1988, p. 20. According to *Variety*, *Straight to Hell* and *Walker* "convinced Hollywood [that Cox] . . . couldn't be trusted; as a renegade the director has been making films in Mexico." See "Missing Persons," *Variety*, 8 June 1992, p. 83.

21. Richard Corliss, "Fire This Time," *Time*, 9 January 1989, p. 58.

22. Also cited as an example of blatant racism is the fact that James Cheney, the black civil rights worker, was driving, rather than sitting in the back seat as shown in the film. See Seth Cagin and Philip Dray, *We Are Not Afraid: The Story of Goodman, Schwerner, and Cheney and the Civil Rights Campaign for Mississippi* (New York: Macmillan, 1988).

23. "Orion Giving 'Mississippi' Straight Promo Push, Avoids Controversy," *Variety*, 18–24 January 1989, p. 13. According to *Variety*'s "Weekend Box Office Report," a weekly feature of the trade journal, the film remained on the charts from the time that it was released in December until June 1989. Released in video format in July, the film ranked no. 12 among the top fifty video rentals in 1989. See "Top Video Rentals 1989," *Variety*, 24 January 1990. The film even spawned a television docudrama called *Murder in Mississippi* that was aired on CBS in February 1990 and received an Emmy nomination for best comedy-drama special.

24. "Mississippi Burning," *Variety*, 30 November 1988, p. 12; Pauline Kael, review of *Mississippi Burning*, *New Yorker*, 26 December 1988, p. 74; letters, *Nation*, 13 February 1989, p. 182.

25. *Time*'s own Richard Schickel had written earlier that the film's "power finally sweeps away one's resistance to the film's major improbabilities." See "The Fire in the South," *Time*, 5 December 1988, p. 90; Vincent Canby, "Alien Visions of America," *New York Times*, Arts and Leisure section, 18 December

1988, p. 14; and Canby, "Taking Risks to Illuminate a Painful Time in America," ibid., 8 January 1989, p. 13.

26. Robert Brent Toplin, "*Mississippi Burning* Scorches Historians," *Perspectives* (April 1989): 20; Sundiata K. Cha-Jua, "*Mississippi Burning*: The Burning of Black Self-Activity," *Radical History Review* 45 (1989): 132–35; Cha-Jua argues that depiction of Klansman as rednecks (more than half the men eventually indicted held white-collar positions) fails to show that racism transcends class and that repressing black activism in favor of FBI heroics precludes an exploration of the economic base of racial injustice; Thomas Doherty, "*Mississippi Burning*," *Cineaste* 17 (1989): 48; editorial, ibid., p. 2; "Weekend Box Office Report," *Variety*, 7–13 June 1989, p. 8; "Who Benefits from the Academy Awards Promo Campaigns?" *Variety*, 22–28 March 1989, p. 5; "Top Fifty Video Titles," *Variety*, 20–26 September 1989, p. 43. *Rain Man*, starring Dustin Hoffman and Tom Cruise, and *Twins*, starring Arnold Schwarzenegger and Danny DeVito, had earned $160 and $110 million, respectively, at the time *Mississippi Burning* disappeared from *Variety*'s charts.

27. Fritzsche, "Francis Fukuyama," p. 817.

28. Peter Novick, *That Noble Dream: The "Objectivity Question" and the American Historical Profession* (Cambridge: Cambridge University Press, 1988), pp. 1–2; Lawrence Stone, "Resisting the New," *New York Review of Books*, 17 December 1987, pp. 59–62.

29. See my "Ethnicity, Class, and Gender in Film: DeMille's *The Cheat*," in Lester Friedman, ed., *Unspeakable Images: Ethnicity and the American Cinema* (Urbana: University of Illinois Press, 1991), pp. 112–39.

30. Ansen, "A Yankee Devil's Manifest Destiny," p. 73.

Chapter Thirteen
Walker

1. Louis Mink, *Historical Understanding* (Ithaca, N.Y.: Cornell University Press, 1987), p. 34.

2. In the United States, *Walker* is distributed in 35 mm. by Universal and has been released on video by MCA Home Video.

3. The basic works from the period are William Walker, *The War in Nicaragua* (New York: Goetzel, 1860; facsimile ed., Tucson: University of Arizona Press, 1985); and William V. Wells, *Walker's Expedition to Nicaragua* (New York: Stringer and Townsend, 1856). Book-length accounts of Walker in English include James J. Roche, *The Story of the Filibusters* (London: Unwin, 1891); William O. Scroggs, *Filibusters and Financiers: The Story of William Walker and His Associates* (New York: Russell and Russell, 1916); Lawrence Greene, *The Filibuster: The Career of William Walker* (Indianapolis: Bobbs-Merrill, 1937); Albert Z. Carr, *The World and William Walker* (New York: Harper and Row, 1963); Noel B. Gerson, *Sad Swashbuckler: The Life of William Walker* (New York: Thomas Nelson, 1976); and Frederick Rosengarten, *Freebooters Must Die* (Wayne, Pa.: Haverford, 1976). Chapters on Walker include E. Alexander Powell, "The King of the Filibusters," in Powell's *Gentlemen Rovers* (New York: Scribner's, 1913); Abdullah Achmed, "William Walker," in *Dreamers of Empire*

(New York: Stokes, 1929); and chapters in David I. Folkman's *The Nicaragua Route* (Salt Lake City: University of Utah, 1972) and Robert E. May's *The Southern Dream of a Caribbean Empire, 1854–1861* (Baton Rouge: Louisiana State University, 1973). Spanish-language sources on Walker are rich and include Lorenzo Montufar y Rivera Maestre, *Walker en Centro America* (Guatemala: Tipografia "La Union," 1887), 2 vols.; Alejandro Hurtado Chamorro, *Willliam Walker: Ideales y propositos* (Granada: Centro America, 1965); and Enrique Guier, *William Walker* (San Jose, Costa Rica: Tipografia Lehmann, 1971).

4. Powell, *Gentlemen Rovers*, p. ix.

5. Scroggs, *Filibusters and Financiers*, p. 396.

6. Greene, *The Filibuster*, p. 117.

7. "Like Writing History with Lightning," *Contention* 2 (Spring 1993): 191–204.

8. Ibid.

List of Contributors

NICHOLAS B. DIRKS is Professor of History and Anthropology and Director of the Center for South and Southeast Asian Studies at the University of Michigan. His book, *The Hollow Crown: Ethnohistory of an Indian Kingdom* (Cambridge, 1987) was recently reprinted in a new edition (Ann Arbor, 1993). He is the editor of *Colonialism and Culture* (1992) and, with Geoff Eley and Sherry B. Ortner, of *Culture/Power/History: A Reader in Contemporary Social Theory* (Princeton, 1993). He is currently working on a variety of projects in colonial constructions of India, postcolonial politics in India, and film theory.

GEOFF ELEY is Professor of History at the University of Michigan. The author of *Reshaping the German Right: Radical Nationalism and Political Change after Bismarck* (New Haven, 1980; reprint, 1991), *The Peculiarities of German History: Bourgeois Society and Politics in Nineteenth-Century Germany* (Oxford, 1984, with David Blackbourn), *From Unification to Nazism: Reinterpreting the German Past* (Boston, 1986), and *Wilhelminismus, Nationalismus, Faschismus: Zur historischen Kontinuitat in Deutschland* (Münster, 1991), he has published widely in German history and on general questions of historiography. He is co-editor of *Culture/Power/History: A Reader in Contemporary Social Theory* (Princeton, 1993) with Nicholas B. Dirks and Sherry B. Ortner and is currently finishing a general book on the European left in the nineteenth and twentieth centuries.

SUMIKO HIGASHI teaches history, film, and women's studies at SUNY Brockport. She has published essays on film theory and criticism in various anthologies and journals and has rewritten film history in *Cecil B. DeMille and American Culture: The Silent Era* (Berkeley and Los Angeles, 1994) to show how cultural history and cultural studies intersect. Currently she is writing about orientalism and early cinema in the context of turn-of-the-century American politics.

MIN SOO KANG is a doctoral candidate in Modern European History at the University of California, Los Angeles. He has published an essay, "De la Sagasse Inaboutie du Barbare," in *Alter Histoire*, ed. Daniel S. Milo and Alain Boureau (Paris, 1991), and has written film reviews for the *American Historical Review*. He is currently writing a dissertation on the automaton in the Western imagination.

THOMAS KEIRSTEAD teaches Japanese history at SUNY Buffalo and is the author of *The Geography of Power in Medieval Japan* (Princeton, 1992). His current work investigates the formation of the Japanese nation-state in late nineteenth- and early twentieth-century historiography.

CLAYTON R. KOPPES is Professor of History at Oberlin College, where he teaches courses in contemporary American history and film history. His recent publications include "Women, Workers, and African-Americans in World War II Movies: Hollywood and the Politics of Representation," in *The American Home Front in World War II*, ed. Kenneth O'Brien and Lynn Parsons (Westport, Conn., forthcoming); "Legislatures and the Media," in *Encyclopedia of the American Legislative System*, ed. Joel Silbey (New York, 1994); and, with Gregory D. Black, *Hollywood Goes to War: How Politics, Profits, and Propaganda Shaped World War II Movies* (New York, 1987). He is writing a book on film censorship in the United States.

RUDY KOSHAR is Associate Professor of History at the University of Wisconsin–Madison and was recently a Jean Monnet Fellow at the European University Institute in Florence, Italy. He is the author of *Social Life, Local Politics, and Nazism: Marburg, 1880–1935* (Chapel Hill, N.C, 1986) and the editor of *Splintered Classes: Politics and the Lower Middle Classes in Interwar Europe* (New York, 1990). His current project is a study of "national memory" and historic architecture in twentieth-century Germany.

DEIDRE LYNCH teaches feminist cultural studies and British literature in the English Department of SUNY Buffalo. She is the co-editor of the anthology *Cultural Institutions of the Novel* (Durham, N.C., forthcoming). In her most recent work she has begun to explore cultural nationalisms, the invention of tradition, and the invention of femininities.

JOHN MRAZ is a Senior Researcher in the Instituto de Ciencias Sociales y Humanidades of the Universidad Autonoma de Puebla (Mexico) and Associate Editor of *Film Historia* (Barcelona). He describes himself as a "photophonic" historian and has focused on various areas of visual and auditory history: studying the representation of the past in cinema and analyzing films as expressions of their contexts, using photographs as a source for social and cultural histories, and directing videotape documentaries.

ROBERT A. ROSENSTONE is Professor of History at the California Institute of Technology and editor of the Film Review section of the *American Historical Review*. Author of *Crusade of the Left: The Lincoln Battalion in the Spanish Civil War* (New York, 1969), *Romantic Revolutionary: A Biography of John Reed* (New York, 1975), and *Mirror in the Shrine: American Encounters with Meiji Japan* (Cambridge, Mass., 1988), he served as writer for the documentary *The Good Fight* and historical consultant for *Reds*. He is currently working on a screen version of *Mirror in the Shrine* and writing a book on history and film.

MICHAEL S. ROTH is the Hartley Burr Alexander Professor of Humanities at Scripps College and the Director of European Studies at the Claremont Graduate School. He is the author of *Psycho-Analysis as History: Negation and Freedom in Freud* (Ithaca, N.Y., 1987) and *Knowing and History: Appropriations of Hegel in Twentieth Century France* (Ithaca, N.Y., 1988), the editor of *Rediscovering History: Culture, Politics, and the Psyche* (Palo Alto, Calif., 1994), and the co-editor, with Ralph Cohen, of *History And . . .* (Charlottesville, Va., forthcoming). He is series editor for Twayne's *Studies in Intellectual and Cultural History*.

DANIEL SIPE is Associate Professor of History at Moore College of Art and Design in Philadelphia. He was executive producer of the documentary *Small Happiness* (1985), which won a Peabody Award; co-producer of the series *One Village in China* (1987), which was broadcast on PBS and the BBC; and creator and producer of *Tigertown* (1986). His more recent media work includes the television program "Beyond 1492" (1992) and the performance piece "Nature Preserve" (1993). At present he is developing a CD-ROM program for doing multimedia representations of history.

PIERRE SORLIN is Professor of Sociology of Cinema at the Sorbonne. He is the author of *European Cinemas, European Societies* (London, 1990), *Esthetiques de l'audovisuel* (Paris, 1992), and *Mass Media* (London, 1994) and of documentaries and historical films. He is currently completing a television movie, *The Dreyfus Affair*, to be released in October and is working on a book about Italian national cinema.

DENISE J. YOUNGBLOOD teaches Russian and East European History at the University of Vermont. A specialist in Russian popular culture and cultural politics, she has written extensively on Russo-Soviet cinema, including *Soviet Cinema in the Silent Era, 1918–1935* (Ann Arbor, 1985; reprint, Austin, Tex., 1991) and *Movies for the Masses: Popular Cinema and Soviet Society in the 1920s*. She is currently writing a book about the commercialization of culture in late imperial Russia.

Film Credits

Distant Voices, Still Lives. Directed by Terence Davies. 1985/87. Color. 85 mins. English. Film distributed by New Yorker Films. Video distributed by Live Entertainment.

Eijanaika. Directed by Shōhei Imamura. 1981. Color. 151 mins. Japanese with English subtitles. Film and video distributed by Kino International.

From the Pole to the Equator. Produced and directed by Yervant Gianikian and Angela Ricci Lucchi. 1986. Color. 96 mins. Film distributed by the Museum of Modern Art. Video not available.

Hiroshima Mon Amour. Directed by Alain Resnais. 1959. Black and white. 91 mins. French with English subtitles. Film distributed by New Yorker Films. Video distributed by Discount Video.

Hitler: A Film from Germany. Written and directed by Hans-Jürgen Syberberg. 1977. Color. 6 hours, 45 mins. German with English subtitles. Film and video distributed by West Glen Films.

The Home and the World. Directed by Satyajit Ray. 1984. Color. 130 mins. Bengali with English subtitles. Film distributed by European Classics Release. Video distributed by Nelson Home Video.

Memories of Underdevelopment. Directed by Tomás Gutiérrez Alea. 1968. Black and white. 110 mins. Spanish with English subtitles. Film and video distributed by New Yorker Films.

Mississippi Burning. Directed by Alan Parker. 1988. Color. 127 mins. Film and video distributed by Orion.

The Moderns. Directed by Alan Rudolph. 1988. Color. 126 mins. Film distributed by New Yorker Films. Video distributed by Columbia/Tri-Star.

The Night of the Shooting Stars. Directed by Paolo and Vittorio Taviani. 1983. Color. 106 mins. Italian with English subtitles. Film and video distributed by Metro-Goldwyn-Mayer/United Artists.

Radio Bikini. Directed by Robert Stone. 1987. Color. 56 mins. Film distributed by New Dimension Films. Video distributed by Pacific Arts Video.

Repentance. Directed by Tengiz Abuladze. 1986. Color. 151 mins. Georgian with English subtitles. Film distributed by the Cannon Group. Video distributed by Media Home Entertainment.

Walker. Directed by Alex Cox. 1987. Color. 95 mins. Film distributed by Universal. Video distributed by MCA Distributing.

Index

PRINCETON STUDIES IN CULTURE/POWER/HISTORY